*Architecture and Body*

**Editors:**
Scott Marble
David Smiley
Marwan Al-Sayed
Sean Flynn

Dan Lobitz
Amy Miller
Gene Villalobos
Russ Drinker
Judy O'Buck Gordon
Daniel Lawler
Michael Tribe

**Copy Editor:**
Melissa Pierson

**Design Consultant:**
Thomas Cox

*Architecture and Body* is a special project of *Precis*, The Columbia Architectural Journal.

The editors would like to extend special thanks to Kenneth Frampton for his continuous support and belief in this project.

Thanks to:
Amy Anderson, Anderson/Schwartz Architects, Diana Barco, Bruce Cutler, Charles Davey, Vivian Ditisheim, Giuliano Fiorenzoli, David Hinkle, Garrett Kalleberg, Michelle Kaplan, David Ling, E-Ping Nie Medalia, John Nichols, Alexandra Papageorgiou, Tom Reiss, Richard Schaffer, Cathy Scullion, Pi Smith, Bernard Tschumi, Scott Weston, Solveig Williams

First published in the United States of America in 1988 by Rizzoli International Publications, Inc.  597 Fifth Avenue, New York, NY  10017.

ISBN  0-8478-0947-1
LC    88-62205

*Architecture and Body* was designed by the editors with the assistance of  Thomas Cox. Editing, design, composition, and layout were done on Apple Computer Corporation's MacIntosh computers and printers using Microsoft Word, Aldus Pagemaker and the Adobe Type Library. Repros were made on a Linotronic 300  by The Postscript Design Studio, a division of Stat Store, Inc., New York, N.Y.
Printed in Japan.

# ARCHITECTURE AND BODY

NEW YORK

**Introduction**

The return of the body has been noted in many fields of social praxis: Subtractive anthropology 'segregates' man from the animalic environment; the abstractness of the goals of economic production and of everyday modern life induces people to seek refuge in the concreteness of the therapeutically treated body and in surrounding themselves with the concreteness of things with "personal" details; gestalt theories postulate the relational unity of *Umwelt* and self; medicine tends to reduce the body to mere partial functions; there is an increase in the incidence of iatro-genic, socio-genic, and pyscho-genic diseases; the repression of death leads to the accumulation of infinite capital.[1]

To encourage the re-valuation of the body by the discipline of architecture, we have attempted to open a speculative and critical discussion focused on the body—on the other of the body and on the bodies of others. We believe that an emphasis on the value of the body is essential to the production of a rich and empowering architecture. As students we came to recognize that critical discussion of the body is tangential to the major concerns of architectural education. As cultural producers we cannot dismiss the issue of the body as being of merely academic or historical interest; in fact, the body is in a position of crisis, a status that highly conditions our engagement with the world and which must be challenged.

The body has always maintained an elusive, if not ambiguous, relationship to the built environment, despite a long history of presumed naturalness accorded this relationship throughout Western culture—buildings as the image of man. This transparent identification elides the problematic nature of material relations, in which architecture plays a significant role, and ignores an even longer and continuing history of cultural enclaves and specific movements that have have been particularly resistant to official culture. As the repressed histories of marginalized lives and cultures continue to unfold and make themselves known the irreducible presence of the body poses itself as a challenge to abstraction and to the manipulation of desires.

Originally modernism attempted, through the respatialization of desire, to free the body and consciousness from the limits of history and material relations. However, as architectural modernism became institutionalized, its capacity for economic rationalization was exploited for the purpose of domination. Notwithstanding recent attempts to "humanize" buildings, whether through contextualism, typology, or historicism, the body remains at best marginalized in the built environment; at worst, it is the focus of concerted manipulation or outright brutalization. We have only to visit the recent housing and office development at Battery Park City to be reminded that public space remains vacuous despite all attempts to dress it up—once again in the emperor's new clothes. These and other post-modern stratagems fail because they simply draw a mask over the economic and political realities which shape our lives and built environment. The center of this reality is an economy whose direct material consequences are dictated by an economic and administrative rationality: cheapness, disposability, and the ubiquitous "flexibility." This rationality is why families live in cars in this country and in cardboard houses in poorer places. Complicity with the status quo only exacerbates an already critical situation delaying the possibility of enfranchising the irritable body. A passage by the Italian architect Giancarlo de Carlo is even more valid today than it was in 1968:

> ...We have the right to ask why housing should be as cheap as possible and not, for example, rather expensive; why, instead of making every effort to reduce it to minimum levels of surface, of thickness, of materials, we should not try to make it spacious, protected, isolated, comfortable, well equipped, rich in opportunities for privacy, communication, exchange, personal creativity. No one, in fact, can be satisfied by an answer which appeals to the scarcity of available resources, when we all know how much is spent on wars, on the construction of missiles and antiballistic systems, on moon projects, on research for the defoliation of forests inhabited by partisans and for the paralysation of the demonstrators emerging from the ghettos, on hidden persuasion, on the invention of artificial needs, etc.[2]

It is toward engendering the enfranchisement of the body that we, among others, propose its fundamental re-valuation. We are not promoting a "touchy-feely" essentialism, nor are we endorsing an ahistorical (re)turn to the self. Neither is it our intention to reject the importance of theory, or to reject the valuable tools of our discipline's methodologies of design and problem-solving. In support of our project, this collection of essays, works, and events registers a profound unease with the plethora of abstract and alienating theories and methods being offered both in the academy and in the profession as remedies to the failures of architectural modernism, as well as with with architecture's questionable flirtations with other discourses (linguistic theory, semiology, post-structuralism, musical harmony, etc.). The problem with these approaches is that they remain analytical and abstract with respect to the specifics of the discipline of architecture, which should gyrate around the material

The body has the power of concrete presence, and [yet] its absence can be its power: Because it is elusive, because it always exists only at the margins of the disciplines, because it oscillates between seemingly allowing itself to be reified and commodified on

relations of the life-practices that engage it. Inevitably flirtations with such discourses have led either to architecture's over intellectualization or, conversely, its total aestheticization.

"More than the other senses, the eye objectifies and masters. It sets at a distance, and maintains that distance. In our culture, the predominance of the look over smell, taste, touch, hearing, has brought about an impoverishment of bodily relations....The moment the look dominates, the body loses its materiality." [3]

On one level this statement by Luce Irigaray can be understood as the problem of phenomenological impoverishment. It is important to examine the body and the experience of space, invoking the need to engage all of the senses and not only the visual. It is important to consider, for example, the significance of materials and methods of construction and how they interact with the body. These are concepts which are available in the discourse of architecture, and their history and value are clear. Nonetheless they are susceptible to being used as isolated, prescriptive methodologies. What is all too often missing from these approaches is a politically specific dimension that would rescue them from their quarantined status. This is what Irigaray is ultimately talking about: the relationship between bodies and discourses, the discourses of power which control and direct our bodies and minds. Architecture is one of these institutionalized discourses, and one which is particularly resistant to a critical discussion in terms of its (political) effect on the body.

This has led us to look for essays and work that might reinforce the body and cultivate our ability to resist the discourses of power that repress it. We hope to identify work that demands that we see and feel and confront the means by which people are controlled. We hope to identify work that synthesizes an enjoyment of the body's capacities and a respect for its limits. We hope to show how specific cultures, and culturally specific lives, use the

the one side, and in ekstasis rejecting the powers formed by civilization on the other, because of this elusiveness, it will always remain the opening through which resistance to repression and exploitation can erupt into the [physical] forms that are designed to restrain such resistance. [4]

presence of body as the means of achieving a fully lived life. We hope to encourage activities that enrich the relationships of individuals and create from this a genuine body of the social.

The questions that remain with us concern the degree to which architecture, from its privileged position as a material practice, can expose and resist methods of control and domination? To what extent can it affirm and heighten the nonreducible experiences of life? To this end, we are interested in the political deployment of the body, the political control of the body, and, finally, the connection between the intimate body and the social body, that is to say, "bodily relations."

Sean Flynn
Marwan Al-Sayed
David Smiley
Scott Marble
Dan Lobitz

Left: Aldo van Eyck, Playground in Amsterdam. 1952.
Previous page: Demonstration: Mothers of the Disappeared, Plaza de Mayo, Buenos Aires, Argentina. 1982.

1. John Knesl, "The Art of Space, the Participation of Art." Unpublished manuscript.
2. Giancarlo de Carlo, as quoted in Kenneth Frampton, *Modern Architecture: A Critical History,* New York: Oxford University Press, 1980, p. 278.
3. Luce Irigaray, as quoted in Craig Owens, "Feminism and Postmodernism" in Hal Foster, ed., *The Anti-Aesthetic,* Port Townsend: Bay Press, p. 198.
4. John Knesl, *ibid.*

## Preface

## Student Work
## at Columbia:
## A Discussion with
## Kenneth Frampton

**Editors:**    In selecting projects, the editors did not seek resolution per se but "traces" of the systems constructed by students to move toward resolution, an open system of "design research" that did not preclude other answers. Do you find evidence of these "traces"? Do you think this is a valid criterion for judging the work?

**Frampton:**    I think this depends on what we mean by the term "design research." If we mean some kind of semi-autonomous evocation or combination of elements or volumes to make particular figures or rhythms—let us say a sort of surrealist automatic writing—then I suppose one could say that there are traces of such in the work assembled here.  On the other hand, these projects also remind one of the effort made by Ladovsky in the Vhkutemas to develop a completely "other" language of architecture and to try to evolve an architecture that would be more related to geometrical progression than to additive formal systems.

This question evokes the whole tradition of the avant-garde and raises the issue as to how we may relate ourselves to that tradition in the late twentieth century.  This problem is as much an issue in general practice as in student work.  If we look back at the avant-garde of the twentieth century—we can say that it attained its apogee between the two wars—there was a kind of energy and hope and a utopianism which is difficult to sustain today with comparable conviction.  Nevertheless the strong anti-modernist reaction of the last decade, which is loosely referred to by but differentiable from the term postmodern, is perhaps fading now and losing its grip on public opinion.  This swing in taste is evident in the work assembled here.

**Editors:**    Our insistence on process implies a questioning of the nature of building—its formal organization, volume, and materiality—as reflecting an attitude toward meaning and experience.  Process also implies a questioning of the implicit cultural position of program; the conceptualization of the hierarchies that regulate the possession of space.

**Frampton:**    There is a tendency here perhaps to emphasize process so much as to suggest that there is no final product. I am skeptical about this, although one should not fetishize the finality of the product—clearly one should always allow for further process.  This is so obvious as to be banal but nonetheless I think process and product can not really be pried apart.

This becomes evident when one looks at the *Oeuvre Complète* of Le Corbusier where one finds that the plans, sections, and elevations do not quite correspond.  This is explained by the fact that they are from different stages of the design.  One may readily notice this schism in one's own work; that there is sometimes this "generational" separation at the moment of committing the design onto paper.  Sometimes this may arrive out of error, or out of exhaustion, when one inadvertently forgets about this or that element, but it can also arise out of a transformation. When working on one section of a project, one suddenly sees this or that possibility and fails to note the consequences of this change in the design.  Inside schools of architecture the "product" invariably refers to the drawing per se whereas in practice, of course, the product is the built work itself. Even this last is not entirely stable, for the work is further transformed when it is occupied so that in a sense transformation never ends.

Alvaro Siza's comment that "Architects don't invent anything, they transform reality" is very pertinent here. While it may seem restrictive, I believe, on the contrary, that it is mature and open-ended. He is "hyper-aware" of the process of transformation; of the fact that the architect intervening in society is first and foremost involved in an act of transformation. What's convincing about this idea is its active quality and the way that it distances itself from idealism, from the notion that there is finally some ideal object, and that the artistic/poetic statement depends upon its "perfect" state. This is the fetishized object that has to be photographed then and there before the people and the furniture are in. Siza is completely antithetical to this notion, which is paradoxical given that his work is so fragile; it has an attenuated delicacy that virtually anticipates its own destruction.

Obviously, as you suggest, hierarchy is inseparable from meaning, and in detailing a work one unavoidably has to confront the issue of hierarchy and the question of the relative importance of the different components. Furthermore, one has to reveal the difference between meaning thought of in a linguistic sense as a decoding of signs which are collectively understood in an unambiguous way, and meaning thought of as the experience of the physical environment which conveys its content in a more multivalent way not just through intellection but also through the senses. Hierarchy has to be embodied in a work so that it is accessible to all the senses and not reduced through the intellect to some schemata which, in the end, is a communicational fiction. This invariably touches on the role played by metaphor in the constitution of architecture.

In the work of Liz Diller and Rick Scofidio one finds an unusually precise use of metaphor. They produce works in which there are often multiple levels of metaphor and meaning; different levels of significance which are, at the same time, kept under strict control. Their metaphors tend to engage both the iconic image and the constructional framing of that image. The two are coupled in such a way that the metaphor operates on several levels at once. I think that this is important in view of other current work produced by very energetic and creative people that tends to be bereft of any precise metaphorical dimension. These works seem to be too abstract. They indulge in a de-constructive proliferation of dynamic pieces without any experiential anchorage.

**Editors:** Do you think that metaphor also brings the work back into intellected experience in order to make a connection, as in poetry, with understanding?

**Frampton:** Perhaps, particularly if the intellectual aspect is not separated from other aspects. The full power of the metaphor derives from the fact that it has a precise initial meaning. The subsequent nuances that might have to do with material, tone, detail, and scale introduce further inflections of the basic meaning or analogy.

This kind of elaborated metaphor can be readily found in the recent work of Siza where, for instance, the fragmentary, even romantic, figurative application of polished stonework serves, despite its disjunctive form, to introduce classical/humanist allusions into his work. At the Omar house stone is used on the walls to give the tone of an upper-class villa. The villa tradition is invoked and simultaneously questioned by virtue of the fact that the stone is not idealized; it is fractured and broken. While it evokes status it is handled in such a way as to prevent it being fetishized. It immediately implies other anti-establishment values; above all, as in Aalto, it evokes the capriciousness of nature and the erosions of time. It also suggests competing values, of a poetic, historical, and class nature; it expresses a conflict that can never be settled, in which the meaning constantly oscillates between one reading and another.

**Editors:** Could you comment on the increased use of metaphor in recent student work? This increase is especially apparent when one compares current Columbia work to that of a few years ago, when most student projects were more blatantly formal or typological in nature.

**Frampton:** The first-year work that has been recently produced under Steven Holl's leadership is full of energy. Much of this derives, perhaps, from a strong intuitive feeling for metaphorical form. The student has not been compelled to ask "What is the reason for this volume or the rationale for this mass-form?" The exuberant, plastic, narrative approach of Holl has the advantage of generating a lot of energy but it may also have the disadvantage of not engaging certain basics early enough in the three-year curriculum. While Steven is always attempting to address "tectonic" issues this aspect often seems to be absent from the student work. In the end the approach is more formal than constructional.

**Editors:** How does this label "student work" affect the reception of the projects? By avoiding the structure of deci-

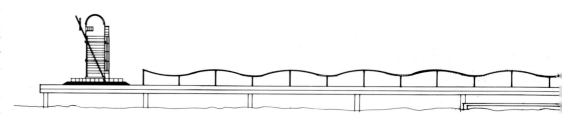

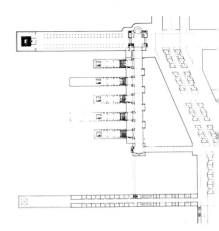

**Ferry Terminal**
**Hudson River at 57th Street**
**Susan Payne**
**Second Year, Spring, 1985**
**Critic: Lauretta Vinciarelli**

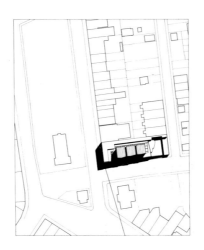

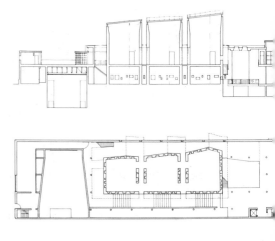

**Museum of Natural History**
**Staten Island**
**Knut Hansen**
**Third Year, Spring, 1986**
**Critic: Steven Holl**

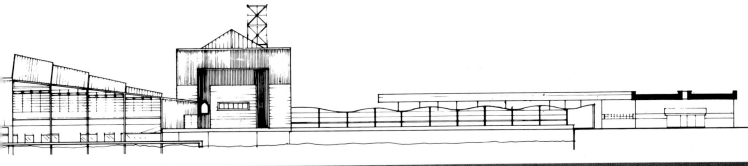

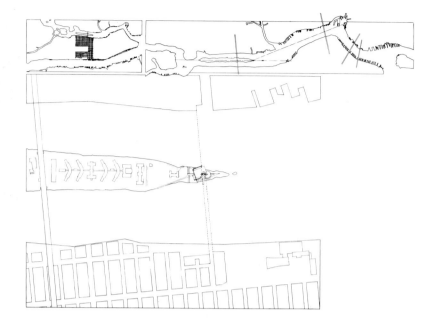

sion making based upon economic and legalistic consequence are they relegated to temporarily acceptable experiments excluded from "legitimate" professional practice?

**Frampton:** You use the term legitimate and it might be interesting to talk about different forms of legitimation both inside and outside the academy; for example, the ways in which museums legitimize certain forms of practice. Since most student work is never going to be realized, it is excluded from practice. One of the problems with student work is that there is always a false pressure to make drawings which are interesting in and of themselves; particularly since the resurgence of interest in architectural draw-

**Job Retraining Center**
**Roosevelt Island**
**Michael Tribe**
**Third Year, Spring, 1986**
**Critic: Paola Iacucci**

**Clinton Waterfront**
**Development**
**Jennifer Schab, Dan**
**Shannon, and Brian McLaren**
**Building Design, Fall, 1985**
**Critic: Lauretta Vinciarelli**

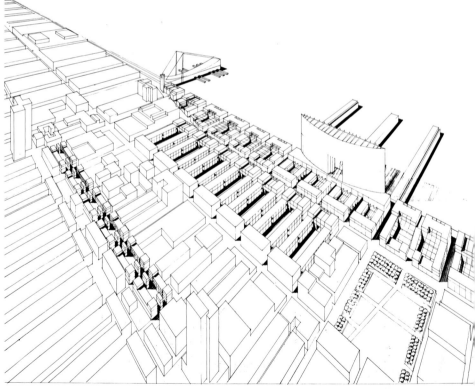

PERSPECTIVE VIEW

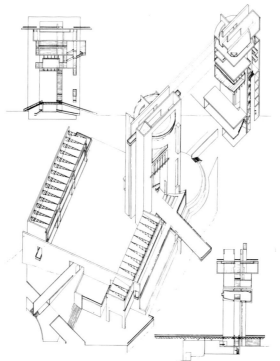

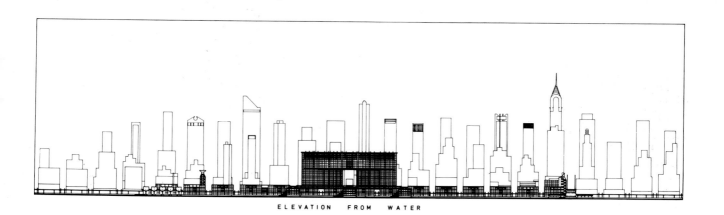

ELEVATION FROM WATER

ing since the late seventies.

You could say that the pressure on students, and even on graduates, to be interesting on paper is something of a cultural problem. It discourages one from penetrating into the latent power of laconic form and thought. I think one feels this when one looks at the work of someone like sculptor Donald Judd, who has a completely different background but is close to architecture. One is amazed by the tectonic and plastic power he achieves with such minimal elements. This is something we are not very good at inside architecture schools, and we're not very good at it in terms of our general discourse outside either. In the forthcoming exhibition at the Museum of Modern Art featuring

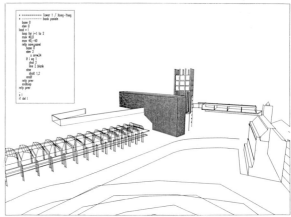

**Textile Research and Development Facility Paterson, New Jersey Amy Miller Third Year, Spring, 1986 Critic: Steven Holl**

**Medical Conference Center Roosevelt Island Arthur Chabon Third Year, Spring, 1986 Critic: Jose Oubrerie**

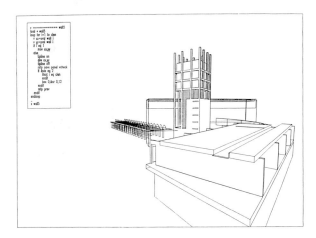

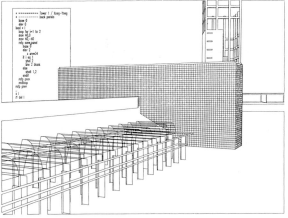

Bernard Tschumi, Peter Eisenman, Frank Gehry, Zaha Hadid, Daniel Liebeskind and Coop Himmelblau two things can be generally expected: first, it will be promodern as opposed to antimodern, and second, it will not be laconic in any way. These works will, however, meet your criteria of being "temporarily acceptable experiments excluded from legitimate professional practice."

I am reminded again of Siza, whose urban design work I recently saw in Naples, amid a series of projects by different architects that were all elaborately rendered and highly colored. In contrast to these works, Siza's project was graphically minimal. Everyone wondered what his intent was and questioned the rele-

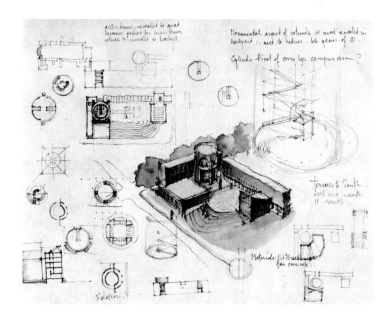

**Cornell University School of Agriculture**
**Ithaca, New York**
**Ron Milewicz**
**Third Year, Fall, 1985**
**Critic: Dan Rowan**

**Energy Think Tank**
**Roosevelt Island**
**Denise DeCoster**
**Third Year, Spring 1986**
**Critic: Jose Oubrerie**

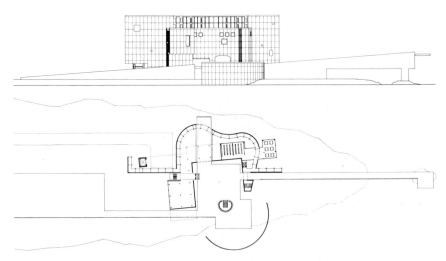

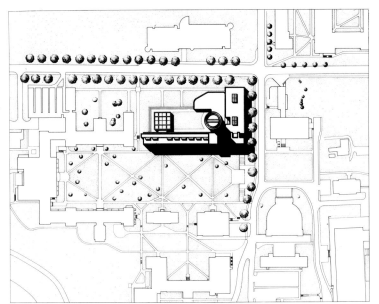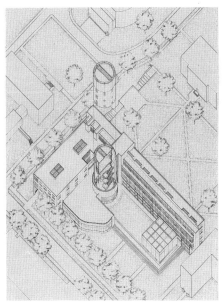

vance of the work. Even critics as sensitive as Cesare de Serta maintained that there was nothing there. Given an existing site where the highway cut the urban fabric off from the sea, Siza made one or two inflections in a sculptural manner which were meant to link the extended fabric back to the sea in a more decisive way without actually demolishing the road. Otherwise there was nothing to see. Siza's drawings invariably suggest a subtle transformation and that is all: in this instance the restoration and reparation of the existing fabric, together with a modest extension and a subtle inflection. In general, one finds that there is relatively little difference between his presentation drawings and his working drawings; they are equally

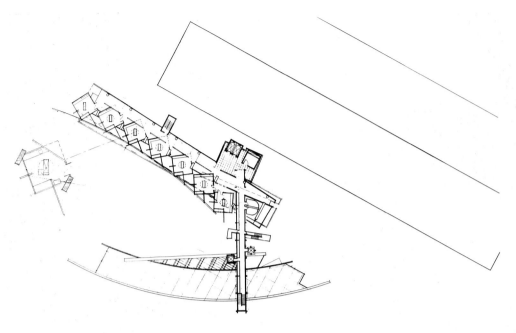

City Morgue
25th St. at the Hudson River
Sean Flynn
Third Year, Spring, 1986
Critic: Paola Iacucci

Biological Research Center
Berkshires, Massachusetts
Gilly Youner
First Year, Spring, 1985
Critic: Jim Tice

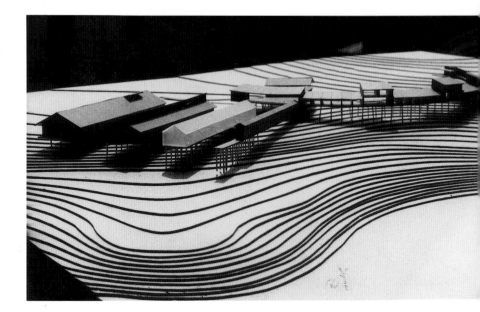

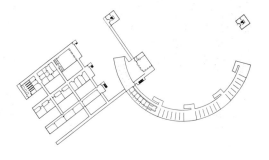

laconic. They seem to flow into each other in a way which challenges the fetish of the presentation drawing. The beauty of his drawings seems to derive from the fact that they "speak" of the process itself. One has a powerful sense of craft that runs through the work; into its economy and sensibility. If one compares this to the division of labor in big corporate offices one can see how the technique of drawing alone reveals the level of thought. Consciously or otherwise the implicit values behind the work are revealed through the drawing.

The other person I would cite in this connection is Johannes Duiker, a much neglected figure of the prewar avant-garde. His Cineac Cinema in Amsterdam is astonish-

**Cube House**
**Ingrid Hustvedt**
**First Year, Fall, 1984**
**Critic: Amy Anderson**

**Double Perimeter Housing**
**Lower East Side**
**Knut Hansen and Scott Marble**
**Second Year, Fall, 1984**
**Critics: Marta Gutman and**
**Richard Plunz**

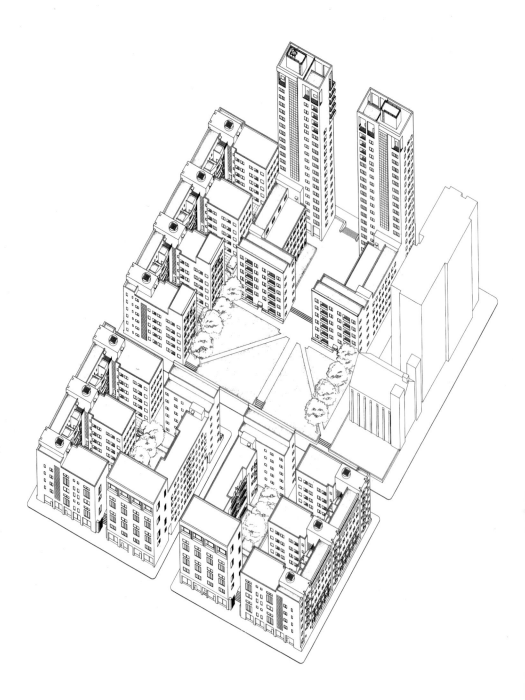

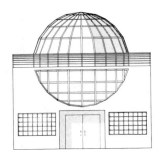
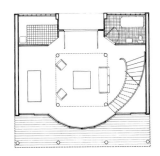
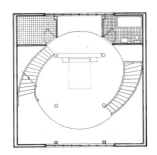

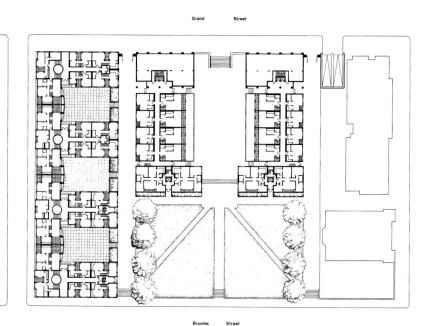

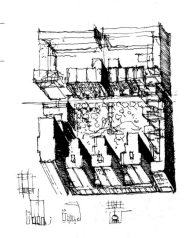

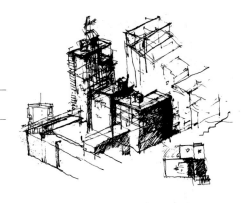

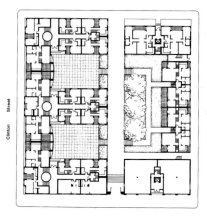
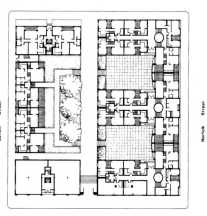

Grand    Street

Clinton    Street

Suffolk    Street

Norfolk    Street

Broome    Street

Delancey    Street

ing in photographs but if you look at the drawings in the documentation, you will find working drawings which are absolutely laconic. Max Protetch is never going to sell a Duiker drawing in his gallery.

When reflecting on the relationship between the academy and the workplace perhaps we also ought to bear in mind the old, now remote, tradition of apprenticeship. At one time architects were not educated inside the university or in schools of architecture. They were trained as apprentices inside craft houses closely connected to production. This is one of the reasons why schools of architecture sit awkwardly inside universities. Despite the frame and influence of the liberal university there remains this obdurate

"Il Murate:" The Prison
converted to a Museum
Florence, Italy
David Smiley
Third Year, Spring, 1986
Critic: Richard Plunz

Seminary
Lower East Side
Gene Villalobos
Third Year, Spring, 1986
Critic: Tod Williams

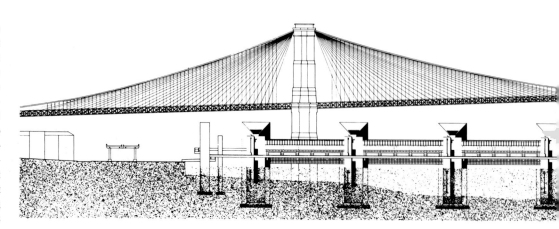

connection of the discipline to craft culture. The humanist university is a product of the Renaissance, with its roots in the fundamental division between liberal arts and mechanical arts. This profound split hardly allows the two classes of discourse to sit comfortably together. The university is not about craft in that sense. One has to face the fact that the most important thing the university has to give us is the capacity to actually evaluate what things "are" in an ontological or socio-historical sense. The weakness of the apprenticeship system is that one tends to lack the capacity to make more profound judgments about the differences between things.

**Editors:** The clarity and self-understanding of these proj-

**Pedestrian Bridge**
**East River**
**Scott Marble**
**Second Year, Spring, 1985**
**Critic: Giuliano Fiorenzoli**

**Urban Marketplace**
**Lower East Side**
**Marwan Al-Sayed**
**Third Year, Spring, 1986**
**Critic: Tod Williams**

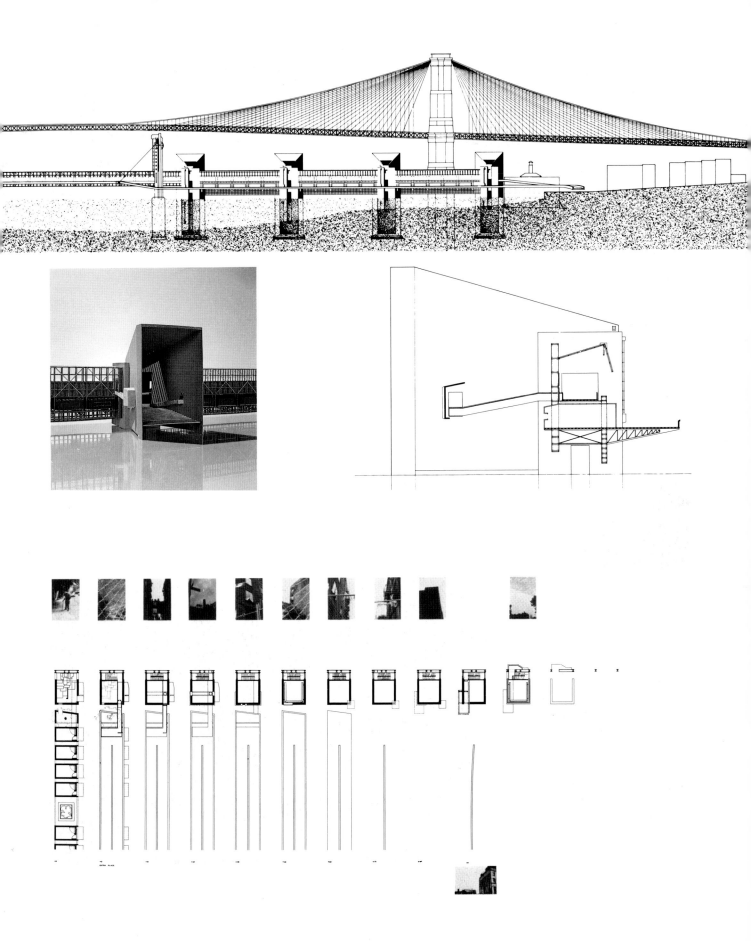

ects—what might be called their authenticity—should not be unique to the academic environment. Is it possible or relevant to view these projects outside the security of the academy? Can their pursuit be understood as a method of self-understanding, an exploration of the self through the process of design? Finally, does the university have a role in encouraging or acknowledging this potential?

**Frampton:** The emphasis on the self in this question is misleading since it is not dialectically formulated; it's not formulated as the self in relation to the collective "other." These projects are not real in the sense that they do not arise from any "real" interaction with society. In a recent talk at Columbia Yehuda Safran

**Laser Research and Performance Center**
**Paterson, New Jersey**
**Marwan Al-Sayed**
**Third Year, Fall, 1985**
**Critic: Steven Holl**

**Center for Invention and the Production of Prototypes**
**Paterson, New Jersey**
**Dan Lobitz**
**Third Year, Fall, 1985**
**Critic: Steven Holl**

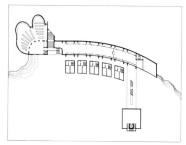

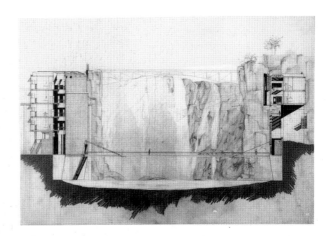

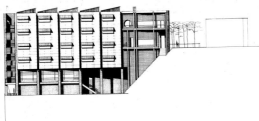

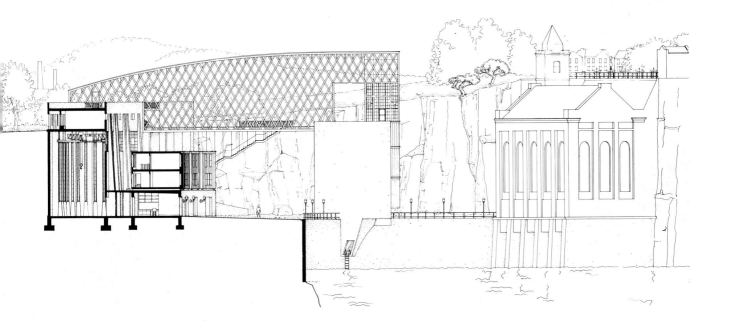

spoke of Adolf Loos and of the difference between the inner time of the subject and collective time. I think that this distinction hints at a more dialogical approach to the understanding of the self. The question as to the role of the university in encouraging or acknowledging this potential also brings up the academy again. Should there be an imposition of method, of ideology, or of a mode of beholding? I think that if the institution is really effective it must inevitably do just that. Enlightened and powerful teachers understandably indoctrinate students with their point of view. At the same time, the precise way in which people convey what they have to give to the student remains a fascinating, intractable, and unex-

**Pilot Plant for Inventors**
**Paterson, New Jersey**
**Susan Payne**
**Third Year, Fall, 1985**
**Critic: Steven Holl**

**Pilot Plant for Inventors**
**Paterson, New Jersey**
**Ralph Cunningham**
**Third Year, Fall, 1985**
**Critic: Steven Holl**

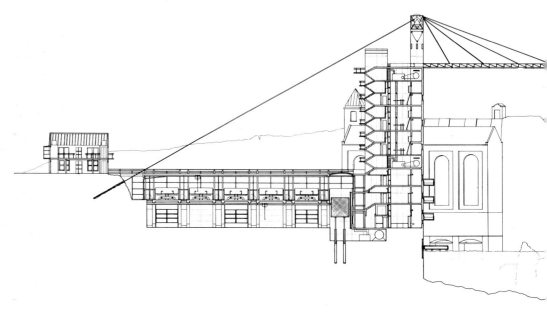

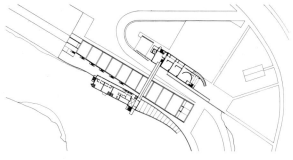

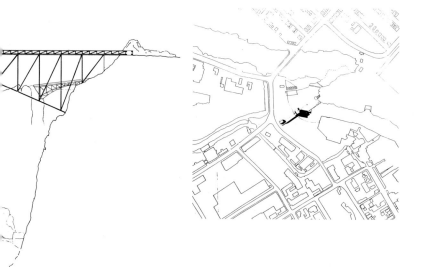

amined question.

The attitude I have taken, versus the distanced application of certain criteria in public reviews, is that being a drawing board critic is to be involved in the act of co-design. I can't understand studio teaching in which the studio tutor doesn't assume a degree of responsibility for the project. This attitude does, of course, begin to evoke the apprenticeship system. In any event I don't think it is possible for a tutor to dissociate him or herself from a student's work. We have to face the fact that the tutor has been present or absent and has inevitably played a role in the project. If the teacher is a co-designer, then the discussion must be in terms of the "self" and the "other," and the project comes

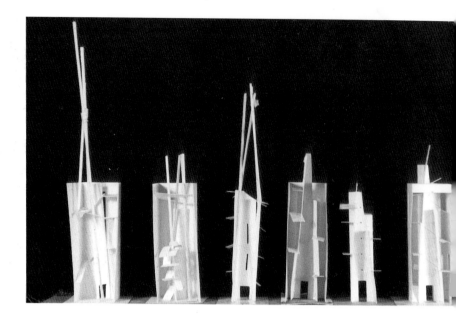

**Diamond District Midblock Arcade**
**47th Street, NYC**
**Heidi Arad**
**Third Year, Spring, 1986**
**Critic: Klaus Herdeg**

**Museum of Movement**
**Staten Island**
**Wally Miller**
**Third Year, Spring, 1986**
**Critic: Steven Holl**

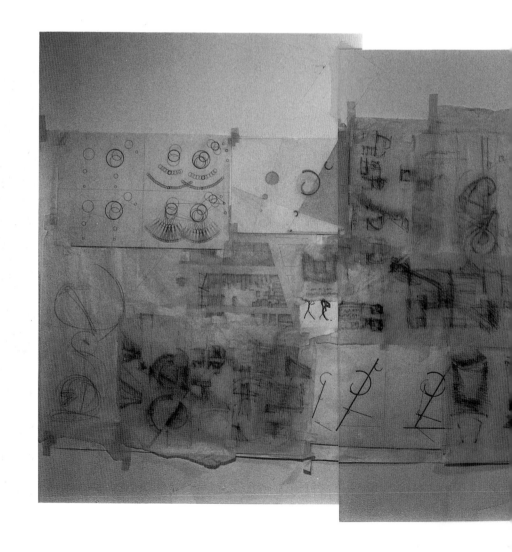

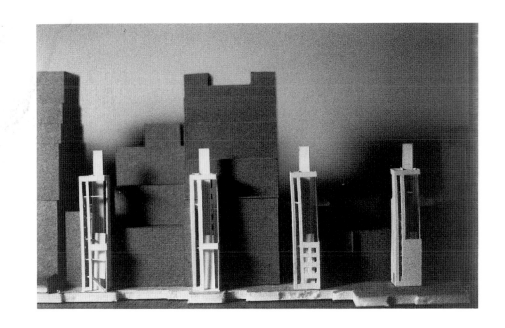

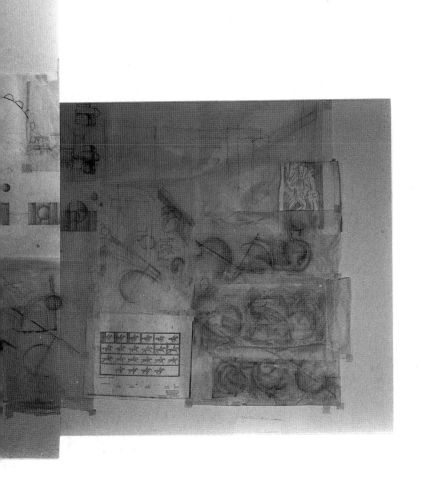

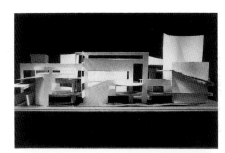

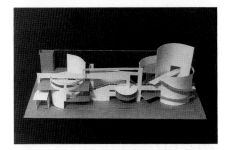

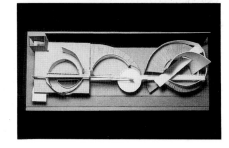

into being through this interaction. In professional practice, of course, the dialogue between "self" and the "other" involves many different "others"; co-workers, clients, contractors, specialists, etc., and is continually changing.

**Editors:** To what extent can a school formulate a sequence of problems that allows the student to test the experiences, emotions, and expressions of the self against the differing identities that form the institutions of the collective?

**Frampton:** One thing that does arise vis-à-vis this question of institution and body is the question of the individual body in relation to social bodies. It seems important pedagogically and in terms of trying to talk about the subject to

**Medical Research Center
Roosevelt Island
Dan Lawler
Third Year, Spring, 1986
Critic: Jose Oubrerie**

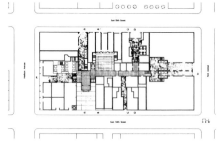

**Trade Union Headquarters
54th/55th Street, NYC
Nancy Soloman
Third Year, Spring, 1986
Critic: Graham Shane**

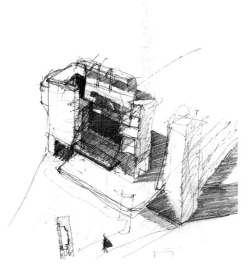

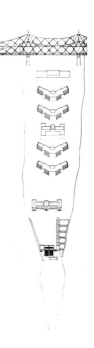

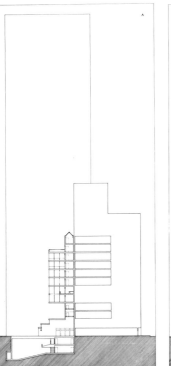

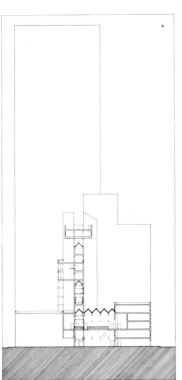

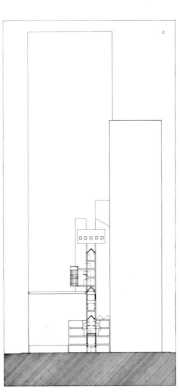

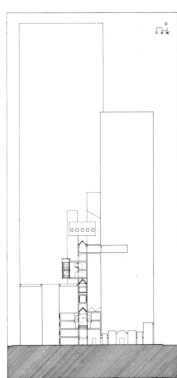

have some institutional material to work with in order to have a volumetric or a topographic sequence within which the body is "placed." If you strip the problem of that institutional point of focus there is a tendency for the sequence to become vague and without boundary and thus, the "placement" of the body becomes equally vague.

One of the problems of assigning studio programs like research laboratories is that these buildings tend to be programless from either a civic or a hedonistic standpoint. A laboratory is essentially a processal instrument and not a "space of public appearance" or a "paradise garden"; it is hard for the student to arrive at what the work is at an institutional level and so they must

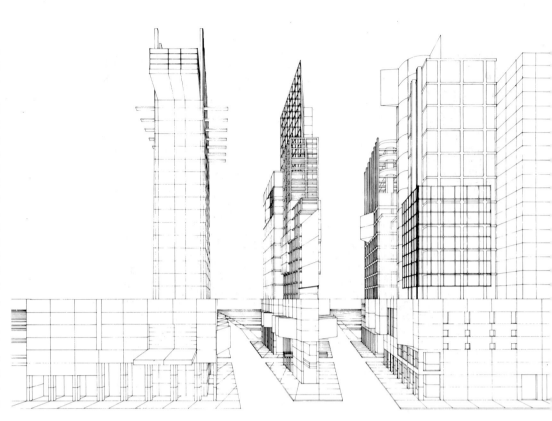

**Times Square Redevelopment**
**Peter Shinoda and**
**Bryce Sanders**
**Third Year, Spring, 1985**
**Critics: Steven Holl, Kenneth**
**Frampton**

**Clinton Waterfront**
**Development**
**Jonathan Jaffe and**
**Elizabeth Thomson**
**Building Design Studio**
**Fall, 1985**
**Critic: Lauretta Vinciarelli**

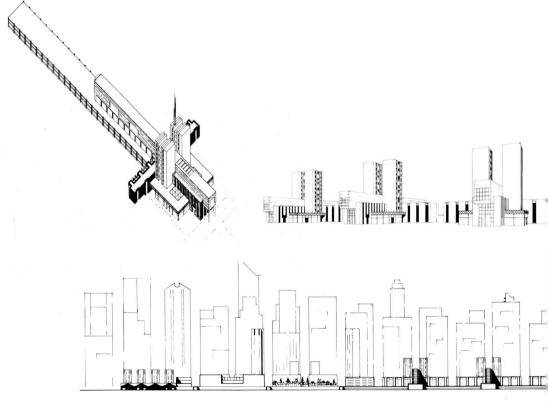

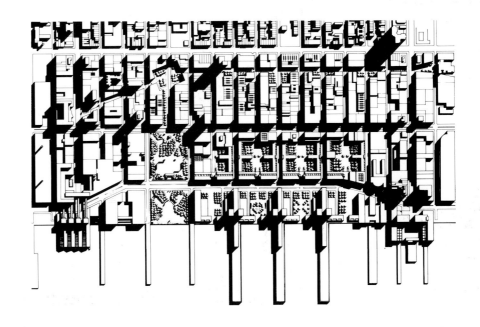

work solely off the site. The gratuitousness that sometimes results can perhaps be obviated by utilizing "instrumental" types, such as banks or museums which have specific programs, and are, in any event, very prevalent in late capitalist society. The problem then is to identify the space of public appearance and/or the hedonistic aspect within the given program or even to invent such an element. One may argue that Norman Foster's Willis Faber Building is just such a type, wherein the "coldness" of the instrument is compensated for by the public aspect of the central escalator hall and dining room and the hedonistic dimension latent in the swimming pool and roof garden. Of course one cannot avoid the

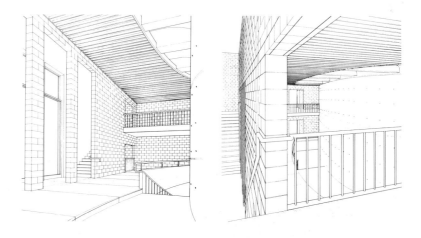

**The National Theater**
**West 42nd Street, NYC**
**Knut Hansen**
**Second Year, Spring, 1985**
**Critic: Peter Gluck**

**Communications Center**
**Long Island City**
**Richard Martinez**
**Second Year, Spring, 1986**
**Critic: Neil Denari**

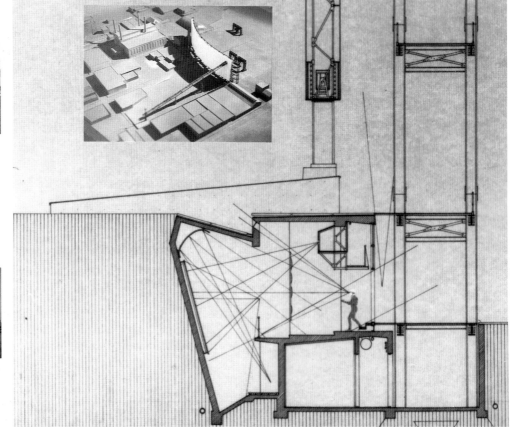

negative panoptic dimension in all this, but nonetheless I feel such components are inherently civic and political and help to create the institution from the point of view of its impact on the body—both the sensuous body and the body politic.

Columbia has been criticized for being somewhat petrified about this question of type and for attempting to predicate all problems on a typological base. This typological approach may have been exaggerated in the curriculum and certainly I have played a part in this but, on the other hand, if you don't select an institutional form or type with a rigorous pedagogical intention,as I have said, students are left with nothing to work with. The keystone of the

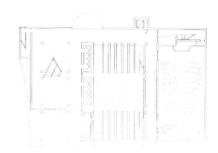

**Public Library**
**East Broadway and Rutgers**
**Street, NYC**
**Anne Steichen**
**First Year, Spring, 1985**
**Critic: Amy Anderson**

**Museum of Natural History**
**Staten Island**
**Russ Drinker**
**Third Year, Spring, 1986**
**Critic: Steve Holl**

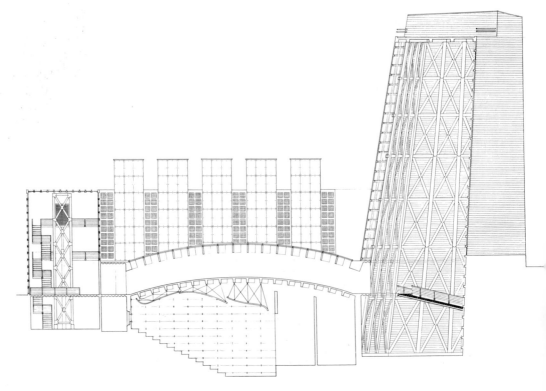

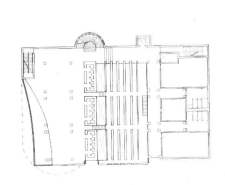

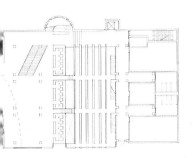

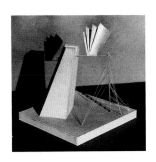

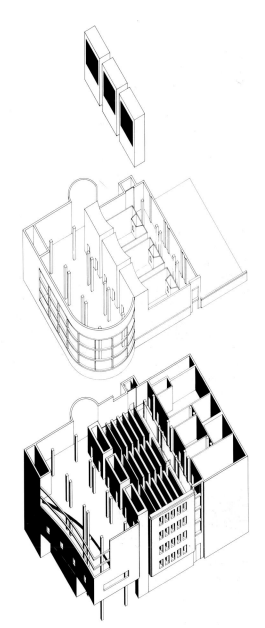

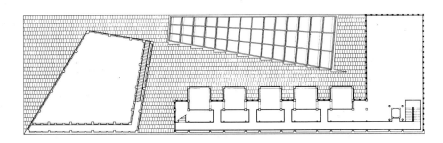

typological approach at Columbia is obviously the housing studio in that it has the capacity to raise both architectural and urbanistic dimensions. Moreover, in New York one is able to mediate between the real and the poetic and between the social and the political. On the occasions when I have taught in the housing studio, I have always given a perimeter block because it is possible to treat this type from the double aspect of the "real" outer New York context and of the "ideal" inner condition postulated by the project. The perimeter block can be employed as a critique not only of the socio-economic apparatus but also of the state of architectural practice. With this type one may pass from a consideration

**Primitive Art Museum**
**Houston Street, NYC**
**Bruce White**
**First Year, Fall, 1985**
**Critic: Amy Anderson**

**Museum of Natural History**
**Staten Island**
**Bruce Cutler**
**Third Year, Spring, 1986**
**Critic: Steve Holl**

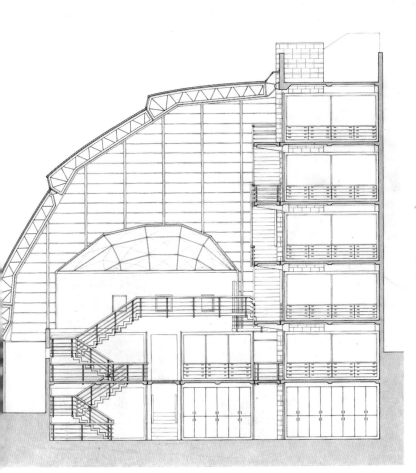
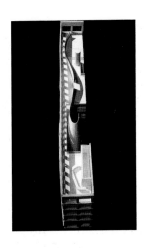

of the "body" within the dwelling unit to a consideration of the collective "body" within the space of the courtyard or garden. With such a project one can also question the nature of a family apartment, the different kinds of families that exist today, and the relation of women to the unit and of all the members of the family within the unit. This allows one to question how children are to be nurtured, what kinds of social and sensual life may or may not be framed and, more generally, to what extent space can be made more "political" through design.

**Redent Type Housing**
**Roosevelt Island**
**Sean Flynn and Melanie Cahn**
**Second Year, Fall, 1985**
**Critics: Mary McLeod and**
**Roy Strickland**

**Cube House**
**Allison Mears**
**First Year, Fall, 1985**
**Critic: Amy Anderson**

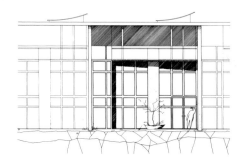

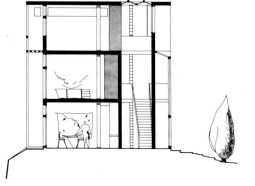

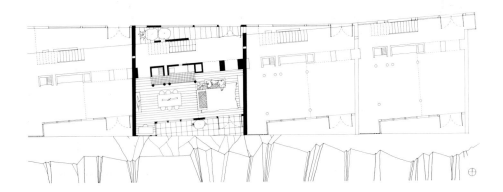

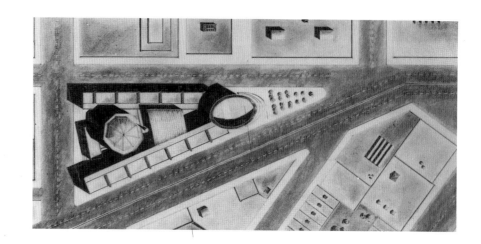

New York Film Institute
Brooklyn
Judy Gordon
Second Year, Spring, 1985
Critic: Diana Agrest

Writers' Institute
West Village, NYC
Jennifer Schab
Building Design Studio,
Spring 1986
Critic: Anthony Ames

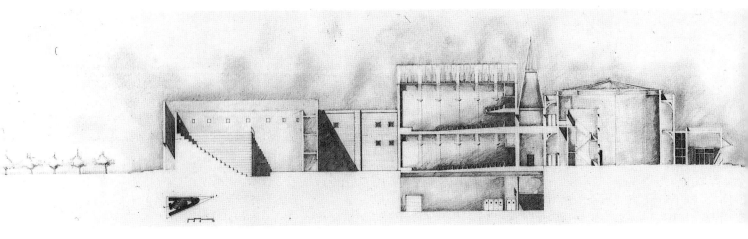

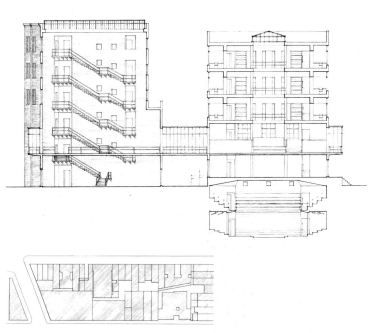

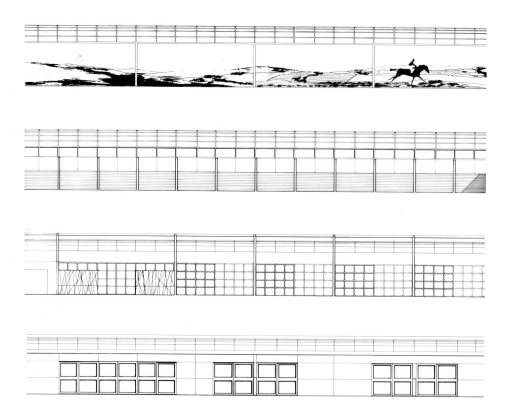

**Equestrian Farm**
**New York State**
**Scott Weston**
**Second Year, Spring, 1986**
**Critic: Robert Kahn**

**An Urban Structure**
**NYC**
**Melanie Cahn**
**Third Year, Spring, 1986**
**Critic: Paolo Iacucci**

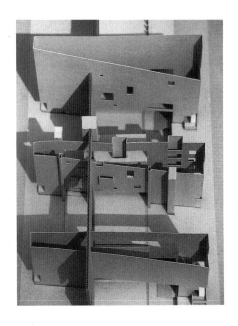

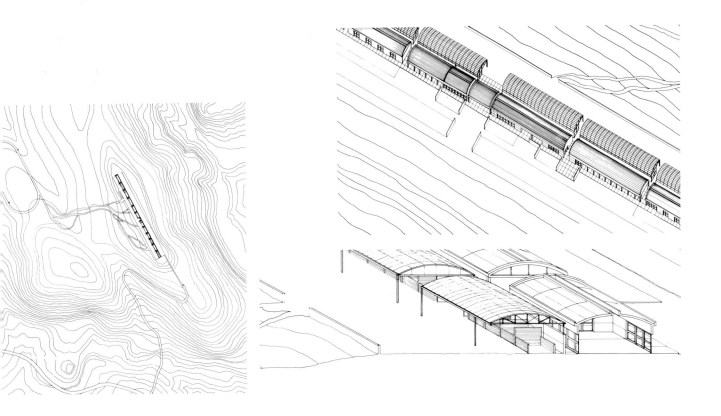

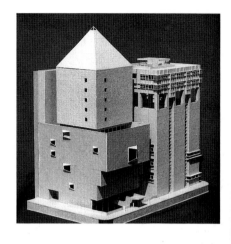

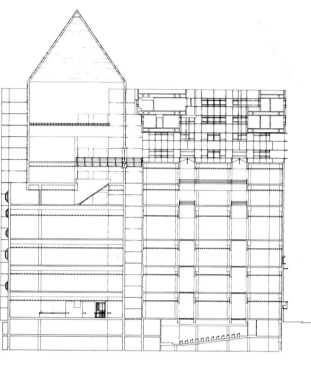

**Addition to the Whitney
Museum
NYC
Michael Harrington
Second Year, Spring, 1985
Critic: Richard Plunz**

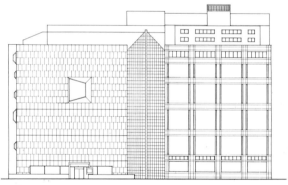

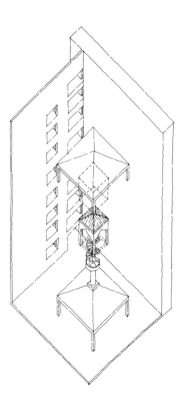

**Addition to the Whitney
Museum
NYC
Tom Nugent
Second Year, Spring, 1985
Critic: Richard Plunz**

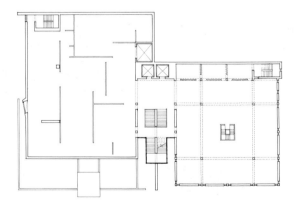

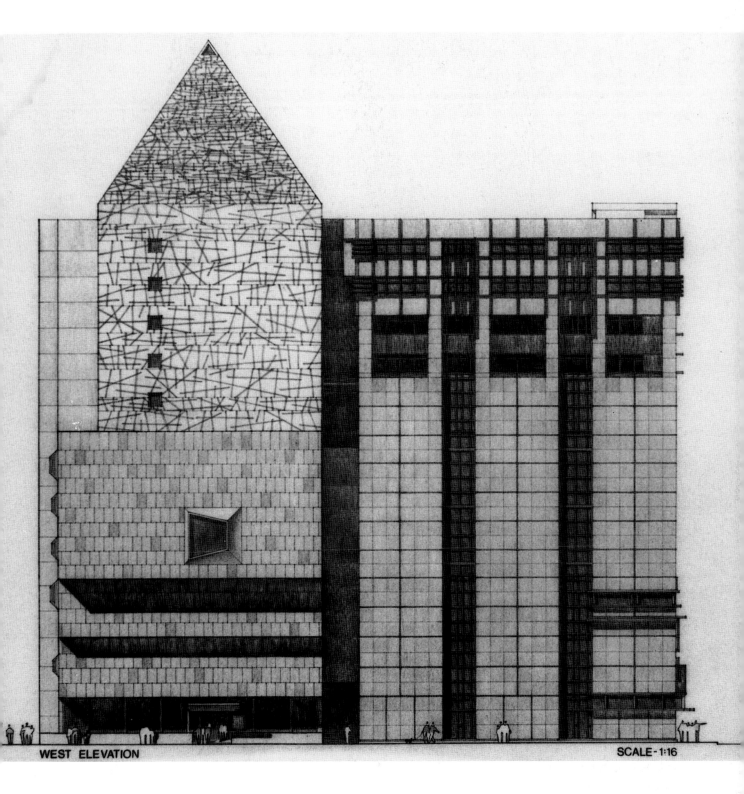

WEST ELEVATION                                    SCALE - 1:16

MY FIRST IMPRESSIONS OF THE TOWN WERE
VAGUE AND CONFUSED...

Fred Thompson was born in Canada and received a B. Arch. in 1958 and an M. Arch. in 1969 from the University of Toronto. He has worked as an architect in Italy, Sweden, Japan, and Finland. He has published and lectured extensively on Japanese culture, urbanism, and architecture and is currently Professor of Architecture at the University of Waterloo. His publications include: *Res 13: Anthropology and Aesthetics* (Cambridge: Harvard University Press), *and FUDO: An Introduction*, (co-editor), in which his article: "Ritual Renewal of Space in Kakunodate & Shiraiwa" appears.

John Knesl was born in Vienna, Austria, in 1944. He has worked as an architect and urban planner in Vienna and the U.K. He has taught architectural design and theory in Austria, and in the U. S. at Pratt Institute, Rensselaer Polytechnical Institute, and Parsons School of Design. His articles have appeared in *Environment and Planning, Ekistics*, and *The Pratt Journal*. He is currently the Director of Urban Design for the New York City Department of Transportation.

Jill Waterman was born in Marblehead, Massachusetts, in 1958. She received a B.F.A. in printmaking from Massachusetts College of Art in 1981, and did graduate work at the University of Paris I from 1982-85. Her photographs have been exhibited at the Fondation des Etats-Unis in Paris and in numerous group shows. Her work has been published in *Passion, Fragmentaires, Sphinx,* and *Frank*.

Born in Nantes, France, in 1932, José Oubrerie worked in the atelier of Le Corbusier from 1958 to1965, where he was project architect of the still incomplete Firminy Church. He has taught architecture at U.P.A.U. 8 Paris, Milan Polytechnic, U.I.A. Venice, the Cooper Union, and Columbia University. He is currently Director of the College of Architecture at the University of Kentucky. Oubrerie's building for the French Cultural Center in Damascus, Syria, received a Medal of Architecture in 1985 from the French Academy of Architecture.

Rogelio Salmona was born in 1929. He received an architecture degree from the Universidad de los Andes, in Bogota, and then worked in the atelier of Le Corbusier from 1945 to 1957. In the same period he did graduate work in social studies at the Sorbonne. Salmona established his own office in 1958 in Bogota where he currently lives and practices. He received the Premio Nacional de Arquitectura in 1975 and 1986, and his work is widely published in Latin America.

Born in Bogota , Colombia, in 1948, Silvia Arango studied architecture at the Universidad de los Andes, Bogota, urban design at Oxford Polytechnic, and semiology at the Ecole Pratique des Hautes Etudes. She received a doctorate from the Institut d' Urbanisme, Paris XII, in 1979. Arango teaches theory and history of architecture at the Universidad Nacional de Colombia. She has written extensively on the history of architecture in Colombia and contemporary architecture in Latin America.

Born in Japan, Kunio Kudo received a Doctor of Engineering from the Tokyo Institute of Technology in 1970 and an M. Arch in Urban Design from Harvard University in 1978. He worked with Louis I. Kahn from 1970-1971. Kudo has taught at Parsons School of Design and is currently Adjunct Assistant Proffessor of Architecture at Columbia University. He has published numerous articles and books in Japan, including three books on Louis Kahn.

Walter Pichler was born in Deutschnofen, South Tirol, in 1936. He graduated from the Academy of Applied Arts in Vienna in 1955. His drawings and sculpture have been exhibited throughout the world, including at the Venice Biennale in 1982. Pichler received the Great Austrian State Prize for Visual Art in 1985. He lives and works in St. Martin in south-east Austria.

Beatriz Colomina was born in Madrid, Spain. She studied at the Escuela Tecnica Superior de Arquitectura in Barcelona and received a professional degree in 1976. She taught in Barcelona from 1976-80 and then moved to New York in 1981. She has taught at Princeton University and is currently an Associate Professor of Architecture at Columbia University. Articles by Colomina have been published in *9H* and *Assemblage* and she is guest editor of the second issue of *Revisions; Architecture: Production and Re-production*.

Sverre Fehn was born in 1924 in Kongsberg, Norway. He received a State Architectural Diploma from the Architectural School of Oslo in 1949. He worked in the office of Jean Prouvé from 1953-1954. Fehn opened his own office in Oslo in 1953. He is Professor of Architecture at the Architectural School of Oslo, and has taught at the Cooper Union and Yale University. His work has been exhibited in Europe, Brazil, and the U.S. and published in *Sverre Fehn: The Thought of Construction*.

Peggy Deamer was born in San Francisco, in 1950. She received a B.A. in philosophy from Oberlin College in 1972, a B. Arch. from the Cooper Union in 1977, an M. A. in architecture from Princeton University in 1973 and a PhD. from Princeton in 1988. She has taught at the Cooper Union, the University of Kentucky, Carleton University, and is currently Adjunct Assistant Professor of Architecture at Columbia University. Deamer's work has been published in *Assemblage, Lotus International, Ritual: The Princeton Journal*, and in the show and catalog *Detail: The Special Task*.

Lars Lerup was born in Sweden. He received his civil engineering diploma from the Helsingborg Higher Technical College in 1960, A B. Arch. from the University of California in 1968, and an M. Arch. from Harvard University in 1970. He is Professor of Architecture at the University of California at Berkeley and Executive Director of the Institute for Environmental Action. Lerup has published numerous articles and is the author of *Building the Unfinished: Architecture and Human Action* and *Planned Assaults: Nofamily House, Love/House, Texas Zero.*

Kenneth Frampton was born in Woking, Surrey, in 1930. He received a Trop. Diploma from the Architectural Association School in London, and practiced architecture in the U.K. and in Israel before coming to the United States to teach full-time. He has taught at Princeton University, the Cooper Union, the Royal College of Art, and currently is Chairman of the School of Architecture at Columbia University. Frampton's essays have been published widely and he is the author of several books on architecture, including *Modern Architecture: A Critical History.*

Dimitrios Pikionis (1887-1968) was born in Piraeus, Greece. He received a civil engineering degree from the Technical University, Athens, in 1908. From 1909-12 he studied painting and sculpture in Munich, and in Paris under I. Simon. At the same time he studied architectural composition under G. Chifflot. Returning to Greece Pikionis began a career as an architect, and became a Professor of Architecture at the Technical University in 1925. In 1966 he was appointed lifetime member of the Academy of Athens in the chair of architecture.

Giuliano Fiorenzoli was born in Florence, Italy, in 1943. He received a degree in fine arts at the Academy of Fine Arts in 1963 and an M. Arch. from the University of Florence in 1969. In 1972 he received an M. A. in Architecture and Urban Studies from M.I.T. He has taught architectural design at Temple University, and Columbia University. He is currently a Professor of Architecture at Pratt Institute, and lives and practices in New York. His designs have been published in the U.S. and Italy.

Tadao Ando was born in Osaka, Japan, in 1941. Beginning in 1962 he taught himself architecture through extensive travel in Europe, Africa, and North America. Prior to these studies he was an amateur boxer. Ando opened his own office in Osaka in 1969. In 1979 he received the Annual Prize of the Architectural Institute of Japan for his Row House Sumiyoshi. In 1985 he received the Alvar Aalto Medal. Publications devoted to his work include *Tadao Ando: Buildings and Projects* and most recently, *GA Architect no 8, Tadao Ando.*

Alvaro Siza was born in Oporto, Portugal, in 1933. He studied architecture at the Oporto School of Fine Arts where he graduated from the School of Architecture in 1965. Siza returned to the school in 1976 as Assistant Professor of Construction. His work has been widely published in Europe. In 1982 the Portuguese section of the International Association of Art Critics awarded him their annual prize for architecture. He currently lives and practices in Oporto.

ARCHITECTURE AND LAUGHTER

John Knesl

Only when the ideas of salvation, of the One, of linear time with origin and end, only when these nightmarish burdens have been shaken off, will the strongest affirmation of becoming, of life, become at once possible and necessary:

*Therefore the laughter that resounds far afield, laughter that is the shuddering of the universe, the breaking up of space in its seriousness and the divine humour as such. …In dying of laughter [the gods] make laughter into the godhead itself, into the "highest manifestation of the godly" in which they absorb themselves when they disappear in order to thereby arise anew. …Laughing as bacchic manifestation of the true and laughing as the laughter of the unending error that continuously lets one thing pass into the other. And thus everything returns to the absolute ambivalence of the sign that alone is valid, the sign that searches for equivalents because it wants to be made known, and when it has found them it loses itself in them, when it loses itself in them it believes to have found itself.* —Maurice Blanchot[1]

What is this sign if not the sign that like a seal affirms the ultimate affirmation, an affirmation that would go far beyond the sign that Aldo Rossi's realism has pursued?

Quite out of tune with the currently prevailing spirits I will say that we need a really new beginning very badly. And to fly in the face of contemporary (false) modesty and convenient relativism, I will even say that I am offering something like a ground for a renewed architectural discipline—although, as we will see, this ground is not easy to walk. Work for this new beginning was done by Marx—with the materiality of the body of man and the implied natural multiplicity of human individuals; by Freud—with the unconsciousness of the will and the power of the sign. Nevertheless what they had uncovered got buried in old-style metaphysical elaboration. More work was done by such people as Bataille and Foucault. However, the biggest step was taken by Nietzsche, in whose shadow we still stand today. How could it be that ever since Herakleitos we have repressed the challenge and risk of becoming and have gone instead for representational systems designed to erect, classify, and re-represent hierarchical stabilities and redundancies in order to allay the fright of facing Chaos? How could we have been prisoners so long of the kind of dialectics that invents the idea and the ideal in rancorous opposition to life? A dialectics that has (almost) triumphed over life by judging it in the supernatural light of the highest concept that would subordinate everything to itself, that would contain everything in itself: the culmination of classical humanism in Hegel.

Let us face it courageously and serenely: all is beginning, becoming, and returning; nothing endures unless it is reaffirmed again and again. The only way to affirm the unity of this universe is to affirm all multiplicity and plurality. This is so because a unity affirmed as such, as represented by a representative architecture, is the affirmation of a unity secretly imposed on multiplicity. Such unity rots and thus betrays fear of the risk of becoming. With this sentence all classicist architecture (but also its "organicist" and "functionalist" sisters) is revealed as an expression of anxiety, negativity, and fear.

Affirmation is the first and the last discipline. We all are its disciples, first because it is all beginning and enduring, last, because at the end, after the wills and forces have turned "reactive," it initiates a new becoming. Affirmation is not easy. Affirmation is the awakening and returning of the will of each potential being to come into life, to become power. This affirmation is radical and will be, as such, critical in a new way. It is not

1. Maurice Blanchot, "The Laughter of the Gods," in *Languages of the Body*, P. Klossowski, G. Bataille, et al. Berlin: Merve Verlag, 1979 German pp. 67-81.
2. Marcel Mauss, "The Techniques of the Body," *Journal de Psychologic*, v. 34, No. 3-4,1936.
3. Michel Foucault, *Discipline and Punish: The Birth of the Prison*, translated by Alan Sheridan. New York: Vintage Books, 1979.
4. Herbert Marcuse, *An Essay on Liberation*. Boston: Beacon Press, 1969. Also: *Eros and Civilisation*. Boston: Beacon Press, 1955.

based on any principles other than itself as the affirmation of life in this universe as it may come. This does not mean at all simply accepting things but using every chance to seduce dormant will into coming into life.

Affirmation requires strength and cunning and, therefore, must be learned. Today's "culture" affirms a mode of living that ultimately is governed by reactive values. Unease is prevalent and "traditional" values are desperately shored up. A true sense of what affirmation means for the discipline of living and for architecture requires that one has faced the abyss—be this as a cumulative result of having lived or be it as a result of having experienced risk of death—and has decided not to hide this sight behind the great signs of immortality. This makes the discipline of affirmation notoriously unpalatable to academicism and busy professionalism alike and unattractive to those who would rather float along, and be floated, smoothly. In an essay such as this one I can only hope to point to the abyss as it has been seen so vividly by some of the critical, suffering, yet so joyful spirits of our time.

The title notwithstanding, this essay will not be funny. In fact I must try to take you to the depths of despair because it is only from there that one can summmon up the strength to laugh the laughter of the gods. To speak to the theme of the body a detour through some critical views must be taken because the very body itself is at stake.

## 1. The Body

Our interest in the body is generated by a highly ambivalent configuration of forces. On one hand we react to the techniques that have been refined to tame, to exploit, and to "develop" the body. Mauss was one of the first to identify such techniques;[2] more recently it has been Foucault who has conducted historical research into the microtechniques of power.[3] The body is being tuned as an instrument of production as well as of cultivated consumption. As the techniques instrumentalize the body more

and more deeply we seem to lose the fullness of experience, of touching the real. On the other hand, the refined sensibilities produced by tuning the body have developed a longing for ever new, more subtle, and stronger feelings and values. Both the very success and also, paradoxically, the failure of the body techniques spur the development of yet new techniques. Whether these will inevitably lead to the disappearance of the body we know into the loneliness of direct neural stimulation remains to be seen.

Hegel formulates the classical position as it has been re-elaborated from Vitruvius to Alberti up into modernity: The body is the only natural expression of the spirit; the building is an image of this body or actually an artificial body which represents the idea/type of the human body. However, the dilemma of all classicist idealisms remains that neither art nor even the word are ultimately pure enough to reach the heights of the idea, of a purely formal logic and world order that makes itself through a history that is merely its instrument.

For Marx the body is primarily the natural producer, of needs and of powers, and the body is social insofar as man is naturally a member of a species.

Freud dared to descend to where the life force, the drive, metamorphoses in eternal becoming between Eros and Thanatos. His discovery,

5.  J. Baudrillard, "From the Ceremonial to the Cloned Body: The Eruption of the Obscene," in: *The Return of the Body*, Editors: D. Kamper and C. Wulf. Frankfurt: Suhrkamp Verlag, 1982 (German). First the body had been the theater (of cruelty), the arena of metamorphoses, the scene on which the gods appeared, pure signs of power and desire, dance and masks which did not represent anything. Then it became mere metaphor of the

however, of the limitless convertibility of signs in the unconscious (known intuitively to the arts before) was used to adjust desire to a culture which he presumed to be inherently repressive. Becoming was split, Eros and Thanatos were made to oppose one another: Eros was linked to the ego, to desire; it became the builder of ever greater unity. Thanatos was linked to the perversity of polymorphous libidinality, to the partial drives, to the id, to destruction, chaos and disunity. Oedipus was to teach us forever how to control the wild id, the body, through the ego.

Seeking to understand the motivation of the working classes, the Frankfurt School developed a critique that put Freud to work inside an enlightened Marxism. Marcuse argued for the recuperation of leisure from consumption, for a liberated sensibility to engage in nonrepressive sublimated art which would hold before us images of greater peace and reconciliation with nature and history. He rejected the sinister Thanatos of Freud and opted for a philosophy based on the affirmation of life.[4]

For Merleau-Ponty, the body is a structure of relationships and therefore not ever separable from the world. They are intertwined and thus the body can make sense long before "we" know it. His interrogations of the "seeing" going on between object/world and the body show us how intensively body and world are open to one another, how they must affirm one another. However, there is unnecessary mysticism in Merleau's "flesh," the category that grounds both body and world.

Julia Kristeva follows Freud: the body is the drives which reject the object and thereby found the Husserlian thesis of the object/outside and the subject/inside. Desire is bound in the object, cannot be fully released in discharge, and is vented by poetic practice that destroys the old object (which has never been "real" but always the sign/structure).

For Foucault the body is the ultimate object/subject of power. Since the modern form of power grows from knowledge and knowledge grows from power, power seeks knowledge. Modern power is the power exercised by the physician and the cyberneticist/regulator who "correct" and grow bodies as living useful materials.

Jean-Francois Lyotard approaches the body through Freud's thoughts on the nonverbalized object, the "figure." The figure looks directly into the unconscious, releasing (or redirecting, barring, reconfiguring) there the hallucinatory gratification of desires which were originally formed in union with the mother. The figural is close to the unlimited motility of the unconscious primary process which respects neither semantics nor syntax, time, causality, or contradiction. Thinking like Benjamin and Brecht he defines the function of critical art to make impossible the hallucinatory gratification of unconscious desire through the image on the movie screen by deconstructing [sic] the narrative and the levels of organization that organize the figure into a unity-object.

Deleuze sets free both body and mind from the violently synthesizing dialectic into which they had been bound. The body becomes the field of multiplicity and plurality of intensities, of "desiring machines" no longer subjected to an Oedipal arche-machine, no longer subject to causality models but obeying its own laws of "machinic consistency." The sign, the forms, are therefore now free-floating abstract machines that can be "found" by intensities that are seeking to become. These signs are, in principle, nonsignifying (not or not yet part of the signification systems that bind all forms and their corresponding energies into oppositional structures) and "diagrammatic" in the manner in which they can become the conductors of energies of agencement (actions without a Freudian subject) by virtue of their own formal qualities alone.

Jean Baudrillard warns those who expect the body to lead a new revolution that the body, at least the

truth that belonged to a subject, the body of Christianized desire, split in itself. And now we have the cloned body, body without an unconscious, body that is a "rhizome, a metastasis"(p.361 op. cit.), the final and total artifact produced by genetic engineering. Are we on the way to the physchotropic body, "a body modelled from inside—without the detours via the perspectival space of representation, of the mirror and of discourse. A silent, mental, molecular (no longer specular) body, a directly metabolized body, without any mediation of action or glance, immanent body, without Otherness, without putting in scene, without transcendence...Tactile body

body of the wild life that accepts the challenge of the universe, is about to disappear. The body is being made over into an obscene body (since one has no more distance from it), an obese body (because constantly fed with nourishments, exercises, impressions, etc.), a body turned into a system constantly observed, reclassified, instrumentalized, and regulated.

This "feel" has been captured inimitably in Baudrillard's observations on the obesity of the body and of architecture as the transpolitical form and mode of disappearance. The hypertrophy of body and of architecture expresses "the hyper-dimensionality of a sociality at once saturated and empty

without glances or images (except for endogenous hallucination), but hallucination belongs to the tactile universe, as already McLuhan realized"(p. 359, op. cit.)…"After the body had been the place of metamorphoses and joys, it became a place of drives, interdictions, and lusts, and has now finally become a place of network technology and fascination." (p. 362, op. cit.)…"Perhaps the molecular dispotifs of Deleuze and the intensity

in which the scene of the social as well as that of the body has lost itself. This obesity is evidence of the system, of its empty bloatedness. Paradoxically, it reflects, yes, it is a mode of disappearance. It is the nihilistic expression of it: The body has no more meaning. The scene of the body—the secret rule that limits a body, that gives it its room to play, its extension, its gestural and morphological limits—has disappeared."[5]

Only Nietzsche felt something so powerful and mysterious at work in the body that he was prompted to say that we do not know what a body is capable of, that we must suspect that it is the body, its "taste," that is responsible for all those lofty achievements of the spirit. The body gives us the noblest—i.e., the most distinctive—sensitivity which is necessary for affirmative will to awaken and to become creative power, and it is the body which then carries the noblest power.

## 2. Simulation

The current interest in the body is part of the search for new or refurbished referentials (God, the individual, the family, the state). Referentials must be represented—although never too fully—so that they can support the reigning significaton systems. The weakening of the refer-  entials begins with the Enlightenment: loss of the origin that had always guaranteed reality, an origin that had in turn been re-presented by the referentials.

Henri Lefebvre had pointed to this loss as well as to the rise of "publicity" and to the "talk" that cover over, overcode, and smother the real under the clouds of signifiers signifying one another interminably. Lefebvre had seen us living in the signs and thus anticipated Baudrillard's "hyper-reality" that is produced and re-produced by endless instant simulations.[6] Lefebvre proposes new referentials on which to build a new "social project": desire (the sexual revolution), the festival (the marking and making of special times, i.e., experiences to build the collective), the urban (as the making of special spaces for the utmost concentration of means, ideas, and people). The socialist ideology aside, these "referentials" do refer to critical themes: desire, power, the lived time and the space and place in which experience and life take place.[7]

It is of crucial importance that one distinguish between two kinds of representation, or rather, of the sign. Originally, the sign is the repetition of an intensity felt by a life force, an intensity re-evoked by the thought-form in order to make a certain life return.[8] This is a most fundamental tenet: what life desires most is to return.

fields of Lyotard,…are only 'revolutionary,' 'hot,' anticipations of the disposability of the body which is completely subject to the soft postmodern technologies of sensory expansion and of molecular regulation." (p. 358, op. cit.) Yet he concludes with the assertion that appearance is indestructible and "that it is impossible to operationalize the world or the body right down to their smallest peripeties…The obscenity, the desert of transparence,is growing. And with it grows our being fascinated by it." (p. 359, op. cit.)

All depends on the quality of the life force which seeks to reaffirm itself in this way. Representation can be made to castrate the threatening experience of the abyss of life and death and of the return. It can seek to capture the force of the real inside the structure behind a form, to incorporate (literally) the flows of energy into signifying systems. It can be made to establish, stabilize, and sanctify systems of meaning, i.e., of powers and forces that are geared to secure the (quiet) predominance of the mediocre, of the merely reactive and negative; it can be made to toy with the ultimate risk of being alive by turning itself into safely contemplatable romantic kitsch at various levels of sophistication.

However, representation can also force us to face and to affirm the deepest fears and desires slumbering in our lives. In this latter form, representation is hostile to systems of stable meanings and forms since the risk of existence has to be mastered ever anew in a diverging multiplicity of differences. Only such differences can do justice to the multiplicity of fates opening up in the universe. The current debate and the continuing attractiveness or even infatuation with classicism has to be brought back to this fundamental distinction with respect to representation. Truly classical architecture enables us to face the abyss; classicist architecture merely refers to that experience, defusing and redirecting it by building it and its energetic charge into a representational signifying system in which the safe, the mediocre, and the average hold sway—in which, in Nietzsche's words, evil, *ressentiment*, and bad conscience are the ruling ideas. Truly classical architecture can therefore really haunt us, can even be nostalgic, if only it strives to bring back to us the lust and the power to face the abyss.[9] It does not simply represent an image of the abyss made small enough to be viewed without risk. It does not represent anything but itself as the direct expression of the joy and tragedy of life in this universe. This sign merely conducts, as does a diagram or a map, the energies that answer to it and to which it answers.[10]

The development of the media has allowed the sign and the nature of the powers whom it serves and who serve it to reach a new level. Baudrillard sees the crisis of representation and of the referentials as symptoms of the agony of the real brought on by a capitalist system that no longer revolves around production or profit but which is based on the control of reality through the sign values and codes which it produces and reproduces. Once power maintained itself by silencing the real through the signs it imposed on it. Now power searches out the real, immediately assigns signs to it, classifies it, and simulates it in all the sign media available. Reality is covered over by simulacra. Power needs to take over the real in this way in order to be "legible" and "legitimate." This continuous re-production and recodifying of reality produces a kind of hyper-reality, a reality that brings us everything too close, too magnified, too "real," a reality that moves in on us and smothers us with an unending assault of simulacra. "Anticipation, deterrence, preventive transfiguration, etc. …the model acts as a sphere of absorbtion of the real."[11]

Beneath the formal interest much current architecture indeed smothers "us" and the "other" and the "things" as it creeps and expands all over the real and life, as it reduplicates and coats life. It makes us and the things inaudible and invisible between its forms exactly by ostensibly seeking to read our wishes from our lips and putting them before us so that we may consume them and ourselves in "seeing" rather than be challenged by them.

Seen against these thoughts, Rossi's "refusal," his "empty signs," gain a deeper meaning. His "realism" seeks to reach through the simulacra to reaffirm the real as the locally and historically formed practices of living and of building as part of living. The starkness of his type-forms is the force that is meant to refuse to relinquish this life, and its desire, to the grip of the system. One that seeks to overcode, control, and thus possess this life by generating, through simulations, the architectural hyper-real. Nevertheless we have as yet no adequate critique of the relation between his forms and this life, nor of what happens as this architecture turns away from the pleroma of current reality, nor of the particular working method that generates his spatial types.[12]

Our current preoccupation with history must also be traced back to this agony of the real. A history, a meaning for "us" in the universe, is what contextualism seeks and exploits so naively, as it warms up the "man" of humanism as the new/old center. Real history would be the history of affirmations, of becoming and of returning. Nostalgic contextualist architecture simulates, both the past and the present, with a certain quality of cold perfection. We see this quality of simulative hyper-reality in front of which we lose all words and feelings, in the works of Cesar Pelli, but also of such avant-gardists as O. M. Ungers and Henri Ciriani.

Whether the plural and multiple intensities of Deleuze could not

6.  Henri Lefebvre, *Everyday Life in the Modern World.* New York: Harper & Row, 1971.
7.  Foucault has shown how, in the Enlightenment, representation comes into its own as free-floating internally coherent systems of a discourse, all the meaning of which derived from the concept of "man" as the center. Today representation is no longer centered, it becomes the play of pure similitude; as in Magritte's work where

succeed in establishing an entirely different structuration of local affirmations that would reestablish meaning in a way not so distant from Baudrillard's ideas of "symbolic exchange," of the challenging symbol, remains to be seen.

### 3. Architecture and the Body

Truly classical architecture is a symbol that holds out a threatening but also life-giving challenge, presents a deadly risk and secret. Such "symbols" cannot be made serviceable as signs that organize and are organized into systematic edifices (Heidegger says that the classical temple does not represent anything else).[13] Rather, these symbols offer themselves to life for an interpetation of this life by itself. In this sense it also is a symbol of the greatest power, the power to affirm itself and to return. However, this power of the work of art and of architecture is taken into service soon enough by the signification systems through which the established, the smallish, social powers rule. At this point the wholeness, grace, daring, balance, and the unselfconscious unity of a self-affirming power is transformed into the unity of the harmonizing subordination of the parts to a "whole." This system models life on the organism and the latter as nothing more than a self-preserving unit. In truly classical architecture the quality of unity is a by-product of the strength of an affirmation lived and expressed at the risk of death. Epigonal classicist architecture can only aspire to sweetened images of that shattering unity.

Classical architecture makes the body dance and sing. Rather than speak it makes the body celebrate the fatefulness of being alive. In the discourse of such a "gay science," frenetically to try to capture truth inside the fences of words is not the goal; the intention is to edify.[14] What is first the expression of the enigma of becoming, of life, to seduce the will into new life becomes quickly conscripted to serve in the mills of the signifying machines. Then the wild symbols of architecture become linguified, subjected to the double articulation that structures verbal language. Its syntactic richness is tamed by the establishment of canonic types, of a formal spatial typology, and its semantic and pragmatic richness is controlled by a typology of architectural "character" (including such characters as "convenience" and "firmness"). Architecture is made into an academicized re-presentation of a systematized world order. Small wonder then that architecture should be considered nothing more than a "primitive" version of the book of truth that expresses what the mind, the mirror of nature for Plato as well as the mirror of the body, has seen or should see.

Ledoux and Lequeu continue this trend to the talkative. Premature post-modernists, they demonstrate how architectural form implodes, how it loses all meaning, once this linguification is driven far enough to lead to deconstructive results. From then on architecture is to tell and retell the story, the total story—of society, of history, of "man," of modern man, of post-modern man, etc…. In telling the story in ever more "correct" detail, with more truth, more realistically, like a TV report, it begins no longer just to represent but also to simulate reality.

the painted object does not resemble a model or the original, or an ideal type, but simply shimmers in and plays with relations of similitude.

8.  P. Klossowski, "Nietzsche's Experience of the Eternal Return," in *The New Nietzsche*, edited by D. B. Alison. New York: Dell Books, 1977.
9.  Manfredo Tafuri and Georges Teyssenot, "Classical Melancholies," in *Classicism is not a Style*, edited by Dimitri Porphyrios. London: Architectural Design, 1982.
10. Felix Guattari, *Molecular Revolution*. New York: Penguin Books, 1984. Also: Gilles Deluze and Guattari, *On the Line*. New York: Semiotext(e), Columbia University

The book actually killed only that older classical architecture that confronts us with the mystery and the challenge of the symbol. Hugo notwithstanding, the book has created modern architecture whose mission is to drive ever farther the overcoding of the real and of the imaginary. This architecture presumes to enhance but actually somehow emasculates the vitality of life. Like Midas it touches life and turns it into signs of life. In this respect, heroic modernism was ambivalent: it sought to free the body, to free life, but too often it was unable to see how its own values tended to go along with or directly support the "development" of the body into a more efficient machine for the production of goods, and later also the consumption and production of pleasure. Above all, architecture learned to manipulate the body, to steer it as to what life to make of itself. Modernism was about both functionalism and the liberation of creativity dormant in (material) nature, but most of all it was about developing signifying systems to encode and help enforce the new organization of social and individual life. The potential for the misuse of liberated energies is inherent in a certain scientificism present, for instance, in Purism setting out to find a "natural" and therefore universal language that would unequivocally link forms and sensations to elementary units of meaning. And does not today Lyotard seem close to this position when he says that the affinity of the body and of the "figure" results from the fact that both have been written on the same code?

The beginning of the post-modern era, with its discussion of the autonomy of architecture, has shown how ambivalent a discipline it is. While this discourse helped to shake off the yoke of cyberneticist social engineering and of a cruder or subtler instrumentalism, it has also helped to remove architecture to its own, the "cultural" realm, to lock it into its own discourse and truths, to circle forever between references to the accumulating "body" of (dead) works.

But how far could the autonomy of architecture go? First, Baudrillard's sobering assessment: since

"the matrix of the city is no longer that of the realization of a force (the labor force), but that of the realization of a difference (the operation of the sign)"[15] architecture and urbanism function as the "operational semiology, the political instrument of that operationalization of the city by means of signs."[16] "Architecture as a mass medium leaves the people collectively without an opportunity to answer."[17] Architecture can only recycle, provide for "participation" and animation, and simulate the existence of free and wild spaces in the city.

While the first phase of Hausmannian modernization achieved "the signalization and domestication of unoccupied and wild spaces by signs,"[18] the current second phase of design follows this reticulation of the urban jungles with an architecture that strives to "anticipate beforehand that free space lost forever and to simulate the free space for children, of the free paths, of the lost time, of the long way round, of the urban imagination and of the revolt. For all this one will invent *dispositifs* [arrangements, filters], structures which will make this acceptable, one will invent sign-traps, simulacra: once again green space, culture institutions, yes even street theaters and city walls."[19] This city is about absolute security, a security impressed upon everybody by dissuasion: "This space of dissuasion, articulated via the ideology of visibility, of transparence, of polyvalence, of consensus, and of contact, and sanctioned by blackmail into security, today is seemingly the space of all societal relations."[20] In the Centre Pompidou everything wants to be animation but succeeds in only becoming ever accelerating recycling.

Everything is being reproduced and simulated and the very reproduction which Walter Benjamin expected to make art political now destroys the political, the social, and the real. Only an architecture struck by affirmation can shake off simulation and erect Baudrillard's symbol, the challenge of life to life. Here it is appropriate to say that Venturi's enterprise was, at least initially, mainly about the affirmation of a mode of living and not about the simulation of this mode. This affirmation always had an ironic twist that rendered it unusable to simulation but which also weakened the force of its affirmation and removed it to the field of cultured discourse "about."

Press, 1983.

11.  Jean Baudrillard, *In the Shadow of the Silent Majorities.* New York: Semiotext(e), Columbia University Press,1983, p. 84.

12.  John Knesl, "Riposte," unpublished manuscript. Troy: Rensselaer Polytechnic Institute, 1978.

What is the relation of simulation and representation? Simulation pretends to possess power and reality which it sucks out of life; it is the extreme of a representation performed by weak, mean, and reactive powers. Truly classical "mimesis," however, invents a challenge to interpret life and to valuate it, whereas imitation at the stage of simulation begins to fabricate "a real" in the image of the noncreative powers and obliterates the difference between itself and the real. Polemically Deleuze has posed the map as the nonsignifying sign in opposition to the representative image, to the tracing that sees in the object only what it wants to see.  The "map" in the sense in which Deleuze uses it,[21] the "symbol" as used by Baudrillard, as well as the "figure" as used by Lyotard,[22] do not represent anything as part of a signifying system but open up ways of becoming power, of seeing oneself against the sign, of forming a self with the form-energy of the sign, of building imagining machines of, and for, libidinal energies.

A building such as the Ishii house by Ando does not represent the family, the individual, etc. through any of the conventional signs for these entities on any of the levels of figural form that Lyotard distinguishes:  the image, the Gestalt, the structure.  It merely seeks to affirm in presenting itself, and it represents conventional meanings only inasmuch as they are needed to ask fundamental questions.

Here is the critical point about the question of representation.  So many today are hoping that architecture will again recover deeper meaning through representation (which they understand as the systematic structuration of [established] signification systems).[23]  The sign is necessary only because simple affirmation is not enough for life to unfold itself fully.  The second affirmation, of the affirmation itself, is what creates the sign.[24]  It is the second wave of affirmation that "overtraces" the first, that wills the first life to return.  This willed return of the intensity of life created in the first affirmation is the sign.  It is the second affirmation which gives the sign a meaning, a now potentially re-presentative meaning.  In Baudrillard's "symbol," the meaning comes out of the second affirmation itself rather than out of pre-existing signification systems and codes.  This affirmation is so formidable that it shatters any code ever anew, requiring and constituting that direct answer that Baudrillard sees in "symbolic exchange" and which cannot be given while hiding within the framework of the existing codes.  Representation is liberative and creative if it is a by-product of an affirmation that risks everything again and again.

Architecture has always been the representation of what was felt to be the most real.  As God died "man" took his place.  Today the real is taken prisoner by simulation which is threatening to overcode also the presumed last *refugia* of the real, the body and the place.  The architecture that felt itself inspired by the body has most often had a fatal leaning to the organicist image of the body—a kind of functionalized, desacralized, and pedestrianized classicism.  The resemblance (and not the free relations of similitude) between architectural and bodily forms so often found in "organic" architecture is disconcerting, obscene, and theatrical.  "Organic" architecture tends either to join in the instrumentalization and cyberneticization of the living, of life—present in Scharoun's work—or it seeks to hypnotize us with images of an intact, powerful body.  Graves's "abstract representation" constitutes a naturalistic re-classicism that abstracts the imagery of the body enough to let us play the game of recognition in reconstructing the soothing idea of "man" (Humana building, Louisville).  The building as an eroticizing representation of the body or of body parts leaves an aftertaste of the obscene (I. Makovec, B. Goff), and so does the bulding as an autopsy of life producing but a carcass opened up in search of the metaphysical, the "real" (IBA housing, Berlin: R. Abraham).  This latter work reaffirms the idea of classicism:  The monumentalized

13.    Martin Heidegger, "The Origin of the Work of Art," in *Basic Writings*.  New York; Harper & Row, 1977.
14.    Richard Rorty, *Philosophy and the Mirror of Nature*.  Princeton: Princeton University Press, 1979.
15.    Jean Baudrillard, *Kool Killer or the Revolt of the Signs*.  Berlin: Merve Verlag, 1978, p. 20.  (German)
16.    *Ibid*, p. 19.

body, in displaying itself as dead and pure form, ambivalently reaffirms both the ultimate victory of death and the survival of the spiritual form, and—vestigially—the return of life to view itself again and again against the image of the living body represented in stone.

Ungers' "theme" charms the body through representative allusions.  The figures he produces are exactly those "form-figures" that Lyotard wants to deconstruct because they absorb the creative energies of unconscious fantasy.  Was the earlier Ungers more powerful in his unabashed combinatorial, cyberneticizing rage?  Similarly, in Eisenman's work, the body and all thinking other than the geometric are to be paralyzed, making all libidinal energy flow into the visual organ so that this energy may build up and expend itself in the transformations

of geometric objects. As Eisenman's work betrays, there is still an author hiding behind the direction and the rules imposed on these transformations. Further, this kind of "open series" of transformations surreptitiously constitutes a filmic narrative that attracts and absorbs unconscious fantasy so that it will repeat itself forever in its Freudian cages.

Is Venturi the king of simulation who would speed the coming implosion of the simulacra? He showed architecture the nightmare of its obsession with conceiving itself as the symbolic representation of unity. Modern architecture as a modern art should reflect the ambiguities and contradictions of modern life, as they had been reflected in the literary arts first: The transposition from rhetorics into spatial form of the figure of irony, in particular, seemed to enable him to both affirm and deny so-called popular culture

17. *Ibid*, p. 33.
18. *Ibid*, p. 34.
19. *Ibid*, p. 34.
20. *Ibid*, p. 62.

and life-style, to keep a distance from his subjects and objects that would prevent his work from becoming simulation. In the later works, however, irony has flattened out, the signs that once represented popular culture have become mere emblems, have come closer to the nonsignifying signs of graffiti. The affirmation of the speculator's rationality represented by the box, the "applique" and decor, seems to have lost the subtle power to distinguish between what is to be truly affirmed and what is merely ironically represented. A certain almost laconic positivism now merely elegantly restates the flatness of our current "popular" culture made of simulations.[25]

The "flatness" of the emblematic quality in ornament and also in three-dimensional spatial structure[26] is the same as the flatness of the media like the presentation of architecture in the journals. The image puts the architecture into scene, leaves no depth of the unexpected, unexplored, mysterious, threatening, or challenging—all is exposed there in this hyper-reality. All interpretations are premade for this architecture overcoded by the verbal narratives that lead us through the images. We must learn from Deleuze: to think divergently, to think in energetic differences between the verbal discourse and the mute expression of the symbolic and of the more or less representative retracings of the spatial object. Thinking them as differences will let both emerge as new powers, powers that exist as difference, a difference that is interpreted, evaluated, given form and life, a difference that alone can illuminate them both.

## 4. Still, the Body

Despite its fallibility the body has gained in potentially critical importance because the death of God

has, in Nietzsche's words, freed it to "interpret" and to "evaluate" life through life. Drives, instincts, and desires could now potentially occupy a new and higher level by affirming themselves as life. The body undertakes the first affirmation; the second is performed by mind/language/form, by art. For as long as the body was a slave in the hands of a god, the first affirmation itself was weakened by the negative spirit of this slave, burdened by the inventions of bad conscience, negative morality, and life-negating ascesis. By "the body" we ought to refer to the intensities it feels and pursues which find their first expression in intensive living, in acting; through expressing intensive energies in nonsignifying or trans-signifying forms that simply reaffirm the lived and yet to be lived. This newly freed body must not again be subjected to a patronizing and disciplining code, even if well meaning and tolerant. Most body-oriented therapies impose on the body an ideology of the compulsory pursuit of exactly those kinds of happiness that are conducive to maintaining and extending the controls established by the reigning codes.[27]

Why is the body of potentially critical importance for a renewed discipline of architecture? As

21.  Deleuze and Guattari, *On the Line.* New York: Semiotext(e), Columbia University Press, 1983.
22.  Jean-Francois Lyotard, "The Connivances of Desire with the Figural," in *Driftworks.* New York: Semiotext(e), Columbia University Press,1984.
23.  Charles Jencks, *Abstract Representation.* London: Architectural Design.
24.  P. Klossowski, *The New Nietzsche.* op. cit.

Lyotard, in the footsteps of Freud, argues, it is the "figure," the bodily, that has direct access to the unconscious, to desire, to fantasy, to the body itself. It is an access that bypasses the filter of the verbal preconscious. The figural connects directly with the body and that is with life, with the first source and object of affirmation. The figure reaches the unconscious, the "representation" (Freud's *Vorstellung*) of life closest to life in a more direct, speechless, terrifying, commanding, and potentially fascinating way than the already more distanced art of poetry.

It would be wrong to say that the body is critical simply because it is what senses and what "does," because it is what smells the low and the high motive, because it places us in the here and now, in the concrete, in the "real" that we have lost under all the simulations. The body must not replace god. Simulation lets us "have" reality without having to risk or to "work," or I should rather say, "play," through the resistances and the lead-ons of the real.

This resistance underlies, whether consciously or not, the concept of "critical regionalism" advanced by Kenneth Frampton.[28] The exhortation to emphasize the tactile senses is in need of finer critical distinctions. It is fine that the tactile does require risking contact and does lack the distance necessary for voyeuristic visual consumption that turns everything into sign value. The tactile may even somewhat counteract the obscenity of the visual scene that has been set up to simulate the real as it assaults us with its obscene details flying into our eyes. Yet the tactile could become the next dimension to be conquered by simulation, close to hallucination as it always has been. What is ultimately critical for regaining the real is not the mechanical resistance and inertia of reality but the real being affirmation without reservation.

A radically new morality can develop only on the basis of such affirmation: the acceptance of otherness as challenge, as an opportunity to create more difference, i.e., more life, more nuances of values and forms. It is with this affirmation in mind that work such as Schumacher's ought to be read. For him, language reflects only what the biology of the body has already prestructured for us: we face the world as separated beings because of the way our bodies' perception is built. Yet there is no real separation of body and world, self and other; they are always together and "are" only when they are together.[29] Seen in Nietzschean terms, the body affirms life, its life in its difference from the world. The danger here, as always, is to see such argumentation as a more sophisticated version of interpeting the body as a organismic cybernetic feed-back system, or alternatively to sanctify the "flesh" in which body and world seem bound up within one another.[30]

Who affirms? It is the Nietzschean will that affirms. This will can be interpreted as the tensional

difference between the idea/form and the real/concrete. The body is what affirms the universe; it can do this in *ressentiment*, or it can do this as the spectacle hungry body of the mass. However this is not full affirmation, not the affirmation of the dice throw. The "real" affirmation must affirm the wildest plurality and multiplicity, the wildest becoming. Only through affirming this multiplicity can it affirm the real unity, the unity that exists by virtue of the most radical multiplicity and divergence.

The critical difference lies in the quality of the affirmation. Real affirmation has the quality of the tragic which, according to Nietzsche, is not sad but is joyful. This joy, this serenity, of facing the challenge requires and produces a body of "great health." Life is all interpretation (by forces) and evaluation (by wills). Both of these are affirmations. Affirmation is radical and can do without the dialectical idea of reconciliation with nature, with God, with fate. "Differential affirmation against dialectical negation, against all nihilism."[31] We have to find, for every force and will, the special thing by which it is so fully affirmed that only what is truly strong about it is able to sustain our affirmation of it, and of ourselves—a Nietzschean morality. Such affirmation in architecture will reestablish the most real/concrete and the most imaginary, not as an opposition to be sublated by praxis, but rather as a continuing difference, made ever stronger by affirmation, between the real and the ideal. In this way, not by grabbing for it, must the real be regained from the simulations that reduplicate it even before we can encounter it.

In this light, place and region become important not as stylistic refugia but as special forms for the reaffirmation of the affirmation. Place is not allowed to become the instrument of a totalizing dialectic, be it "merely" a cultural-stylistic one, or one of politics, or one of economics. Place is to concretize a divergent kind of dialectic that makes multiplicity become and unfold, that affirms it so much that only what is most vital will be able to be

25. See R. Venturi's Khulafa Street project.
26. Klaus Herdeg, *The Decorated Diagram*. Cambridge: MIT Press, 1983.
27. Kamper and Wulf, editors, *The Return of the Body*, op. cit.
28. Kenneth Frampton, "Towards a Critical Regionalism: Six Points for an Architecture of Resistance," in Hal

reaffirmed and to become the "good" repetition, or better, return. It is this return that brings about a historical typology of spatial forms. Again, only the finest nuances in the affirmations will determine whether we will have to speak of a bad regionalism or of a healthy regionalism—which in this light turns out to be a form of a critical and creative realism.

Nothing less will do than to create again the kind of space that presents a "challenge," that is, a "symbol." We need an architecture that opens up ever new ways to the real and to the imaginary. This essay argues that only affirmation will be able to cut through the simulations and the codes that support the simulations. Such affirmation needs to be learned, built and rebuilt in the face of despair. Such affirmation is fed by laughter and it manifests itself as a special kind of laughter.

## 5. Finally, the Laughter of the Gods

Laughter is the outbreak that takes place when one truly faces the absence of a predesigned sense to life. More than relief it is a tonic that prepares us to impose a sense. One must distinguish Bakhtin's laughter from the laughter of Nietzsche. The former provides liberation from oppression by direct force, and by the meanings which it enforces, which are then unmasked by laughter as overbearing and silly insofar as they pretend to a greatness they cannot have. The latter is the laughter in which the gods died when the one god declared himself to be only One. This laughter builds the courage and energy to move toward the overman; it is the cry of total affirmation come what may. Unlike a merely mental affirmation this one is lived in the spasms of laughter by the body and makes the mind lofty. This laughter makes us, in a certain sense, defenseless, because it creates a new, freer "us" involved in an interaction without any reserve with the big "other," the universe.

In architecture such laughter becomes the quality of a boundless serenity, a serenity that affirms all, but affirms so strongly that it becomes at once affirmative and critical. This active serenity of the creator and doer could not be farther from contemplative letting-the-world-be, from the melancholy of all neoclassicisms, and from the melancholy felt by the cloned body.

This serenity appears in Nietzsche's life and work as the "great health" of the will, reached only after having shed the burdens of all made-up sense and morality. Serenity is the stage for the Dionysian affirmation of life come as it may, of a true and boundless "realism." The real is nothing but the struggle of wills and forces, not bloody battles to "have" power as a spoil to be owned and shown off, but the winning out of a superior will that must be freely acknowledged by the "obeying" will. This is why the real can only be touched in the play of resistance, as *Gegenstand*, and why it is missed whenever it is erected into the positivity of the concept.

The real is the struggle between form-giving wills, i.e., "selves" that make other wills obey. Wills are the subjects who interpret and evaluate the world. Will is what the life force becomes at higher stages of develop-

Foster, editor, *The Anti-Aesthetic*. Port Townsend: Bay Press, 1983.
29.  John Shumacher, "On Human Posture," unpublished manuscript. Troy: Rensselaer Polytechnic Institute, 1986.
30.  Merleau-Ponty, *The Visible and the Invisible*. Evanston: Northwestern University Press, 1968.
31.  Gilles Deleuze, *Nietzsche and Philosophy*, New York: Columbia University Press, 1968, p. 17.

ment, and will thus is somehow seated in the body, although it clearly requires the mind, the realm of forms, to "see" a direction, to see a form it wants to become. Such a realism could therefore also be described as an idealism that is based on the material body as closest to the ground of life, on the self-affirmation of life that is expressed in the laughter of the gods. The answer to the disappearance of the real is not in warming up old values. It is the will that seeks and makes its reality.

Now it becomes clearer why, for Nietzsche, the body is ultimately the arbiter and the source. It senses and feels according to the values it brings forth and by which it is drawn. More importantly, it affirms life as the recurrence of becoming; it is Dionysos. The ambivalence of the drives which through their metamorphoses create new life by annihilation of other life is evidence of how the body itself affirms recurrence as the mode of becoming and being of the universe.

It is the body that first feels difference as it arises in the erotic relationships between the body of the mother and the body of the child. The difference between the depression in the cheek and the cusp of the

mother's finger is played out by the bodies to a climax of tension to be released as the play of caressing movements reaches a culmination. Lavie's interpretation of this culmination as an extinction of difference—a dialectical sublation—is unwarranted.[32] Rather, the difference between the bodies is simply brought out and brought to life more and more by the actions until it explodes in the laughter of self-recognition.

It is the body that knows in a more intimate and direct way because it feels affinities. Therefore the body knows what a thing is most of all,

32. J. C. Lavie, "Notre Corps ou le Present d'une Illusion," quoted in M. Bernard, *The Human Body and its Social Significance.* Bad Homburg: Limpert, 1980. (German)
33. Deleuze, *Nietzsche and Philosophy.* op. cit., p.4.
34. This definition only appears homologous to the classical ideal of balance and harmony. The classical

i.e., that it is most itself when it is possessed by and possesses those forces and those wills to which it is most affined. What a thing "really" is depends on the spectrum of its relations to the wills that command it. In Kahn's mythology, the form/will of the creator/architect commands the brick to do what the brick already wants to do most by itself: its affinity is to the arch ("All domination amounts to a new interpretation").[33] But it is one thing to elevate the brick arch to the treasury of ideal forms and another to affirm the will of a life force that interprets and evaluates the brick. What is critical is that the brick be enabled to "speak," to find itself and to become a stronger force through its position against imposing form/wills. When we no longer know whether the "thing" dominates or the force which possesses it, then, says Nietzsche, the thing is becoming its essence.[34]

Serenity is a quality of truly classical architecture. Serenity is what charmed and baffled Marx in Greek art, the childhood of humanity. Serenity is the laughter without sound, a laughter that fills the universe. It is the tonus and the tone of fullest affirmation, of self, of active power and affirmative will, of form-giving power, that affirms becoming. Power is not a capital to be possessed and traded but it is unencodable difference that—speaking through the Baudrillardian symbol—poses a challenge and a deadly risk to life and requires an answer that cannot be found through a code. Becoming the greatest power necessitates finding and answering the most profound challenge.

## 6. Affirmation

Serenity is the tonus and the tone which goes with, brings back, and expresses affirmation. To get serenity we must start with affirmation.

Affirmation must have these qualities: It must affirm multiplicity and plurality, and not the One, in order to prevent the covert

imposition of a unity that usurps the vital powers of multiplicity, of primitivist "primordial" gestures. This affirmation of plurality will generate a kind of ever-absent but more "real" unity of difference. Reaffirmation will be dramatization, gesture, and dance, but the affirmative sign will not be representative, it will not conjure up and reinforce the systems of forms, meanings, and forces to which it belongs. It does not pretend to be more "real" than other forms and places, but as a gesture it draws out the will to become real life force. Meaning is within the act of self-creation and this meaning of life for itself is the opposite to the death and enigmatic stare of the meaningless "empty" sign that produces fascination, a circling around in the prison of fantasy wishes. So that it may meet the challenge, affirmation must open up ever new lines, both threatening and inviting, between the sign, the mind, and

conception of harmony forced the part into a hierachically functionalized whole, a whole only in name since it was organized by the force of a unity added that had not grown out of the relations within it. It is the will that seeks and makes reality, the struggle between wills, and it must be a healthy will, one that looks upon life with serenity.

35. Herbert Marcuse, "On the affirmative character of culture," in *Negations*. Boston: Beacon Press, 1977.

the body, the material and the merely lived. In fact, affirmation can be seen as lived tension between body and mind. This affirmation is therefore what is really tragic—it is both deadly and joyful at the same time. Finally, boundless affirmation is also critical by repeating itself and challenging all the wills until the strong qualities in these become willing helpers or maskers. In architecture, the discipline of affirmation must affirm the "program" in the same way. It must not purge it and reduce it to some prominent functions and signs, but it must allow the wills that become stronger with each round of affirmation to emerge into the real.

For this kind of affirmation, a number of critical qualities must be present together so that it would not simply support certain forces and wills without regard to their intrinsic quality and nature. Marcuse was the first to write a critique of such a system—affirmative culture.[35] However, below the surface messages and images he detected in the work of art a much deeper affirmation of the desire for a stronger and wilder life—which he cast as a negation of the status quo. Marcuse had, after all, made reference to Nietzsche wherever he spoke about Eros and Thanatos and the power of art.[36]

Nietzsche recognized that affirmation must be double: the first affirmation is the primary Dionysian affirmation of life by itself, of the universe as becoming, of chance and fate. The second affirmation affirms the first, affirms becoming as the being of the eternal return. The second affirmation is feminine power, anima become affirmative, it is Ariadne, the "fiancee," mirror and reflection.[37] The second affirmation is the act of thinking, of the poet, of the artist. It produces the return as "the being of becoming, the unity of multiplicity, the necessity of chance.... Dionysos developed, reflected, raised to the highest power: these are the aspects of Dionysian willing."[38] The works of art and architecture are gestures that are necessary to inscribe the affirmation by life of life into the return, to make life return.

The nonrepresentative gesture, the symbol, is not merely expression but it is the ruse by which the burdens weighing down the "higher men" are lifted. Dance, laughter, and play are affirmative powers that transmute low into high, that reflect and develop: "Dance affirms becoming and the being of becoming; laughter, roars of laughter, affirm multiplicity and the unity of multiplicity; play affirms chance, and the necessity of chance."[39] Dance relates to living and breathing, laughter relates to thinking, and play relates to actions taken by the overman. Laughter is the affirmation by the spirit spontaneously set off by the dance and play of architecture. The work of the artist-man becomes child play, the games and the virtuosity that Baudrillard sets against the tyranny of the codes, of the representational systems.

Affirmation brings about difference, which is the "will to power" in action. Thus multiple affirmation transmutes the dialectical opposition of thesis and its negation into a kind of multiplicitous and plural interposition, into the figures of a free play and dance of logics, of forms suspended in laughter.

Regionalism, once it is removed to the exile of the land of culture, tends to become simulation itself,

. . . THEN I NOTICED A SMALL PROCESSION OF PRIESTS PURIFYING THE STREETS AND COL- LECTING THE FIRST RICE OF THE SEASON...

25  AUG.

it turns itself into a style for the representation of reality. Such regionalism cannot create the real. The real eludes representation; it just stares or dances, it is what ultimately defeats simulation and metaphoric representation. It is what answers to affirmation by repetition, by affirmative retracing even of simulacra and simulations which are in this way exploded, de-constructed, and made to uncover deeper, buried affirmations. Yes, place is crucial as the situation through which reality can again appear, can become concrete. Place is what requires an "answer" beyond a ready-made code. Only the affirmative discipline can create an architecture that is place and situation, that is multiple singularity, that is the place of the real or of the imaginary, beyond all representation and simulation.

With place understood as the life to be affirmed in the concrete it is possible to deepen the critique of critical regionalism. First, regionalism cannot remain just "cultural," since as Baudrillard has argued, "culture" itself is the means whereby everything is turned into a simulation of itself. Regionalism, then, has to affirm the whole of the complex of life practices in a region, the practices which are the region.[40] Secondly, instead of conceiving regionalism negatively, as resistance, it must be made into wild self-affirmation. Thirdly, if unity were to be affirmed first, as is the rule with any local "style" or "regional school" that imposes itself on form, this unity will kill off multiplicity,

36.   Marcuse, *Eros and Civilization*. Boston: Beacon Press, 1955.
37.   Deleuze, *Nietzsche and Philosophy*, op. cit., p. 189.
38.   *Ibid*, p.189.
39.   *Ibid*, p.189.

or worse, it will generate simulations of plurality. This precept will also reject the idea that regionalism needs a simple body of rules to be followed. Deleuzian multiplicity is the right idea, a multiplicity that arises from the kind of difference that breaks up any system of classification and encoding. Fourthly, the regionalist tenet that the presumed limits of architecture prevent it from close contact with revolutionary practices has to be refuted. This retreat to the spiritual-cultural eliminates the abyss of the challenge to death. Art and architecture must be reinvented both to seduce and to heal, and to strengthen the will to face death as the secret that makes possible life and the return.

## 7. Critical Affirmation as the Discipline of Design

Working within the discipline of affirmation requires corresponding ways of handling the sign. It will not do merely to refer to an "authentic" experience of the place.[41] Rather, one will have to find new ways of speaking, and showing of images, that allow the earth, the sky, life, and

place to shatter the codes that set out to capture it. This means that the mode of discourse will be outspokenly abstract, perhaps rather repetitive, primarily of intensities but not of complete meaning-and-form complexes that reinforce the established signifying systems. Discourse must remain aware that we never hold the real itself in our mouths or eyes. Further, discourse must be pushed beyond the limits imposed by the "normal" significations, it must be excessive in this sense.

For both analytical and design work the key idea is that of *repetition* and *retracing*. Both the spatial qualities in their multiple manifestations and the various life practices will be repeated to recapture memory and to lure dormant wills into discovering ever new meanings and values. Repetition will eventually make only the strongest wills and corresponding forces return. Repetition reaches the point at which the object and quality, in agreeing freely with the will interpreting it, affirm themselves fully in their essence. In this process, signs, representative or not, are to be only "maps" or "diagrams" that are to make recur the intensities of thinking and feeling that once occurred or could occur again. This process has the form of an open series, or of what I have termed elsewhere a critical montage.[42]

In contrast to the normal design process that reduces the manifold to certain factors and motifs, the design process envisaged here initially affirms everything and embraces chance as it comes with the immersion into place and the program. But in repeating this retracing, in this answering to what is found, affirmation becomes critical by developing differences between the forces and the wills that are themselves brought into life.

In the play of signs that is the design work abstraction will be necessary, but not the kind that reduces forms and people, powers and desires, to instruments and functions serving some mean-spirited power (i.e., economicism, mechanism, pedanticism, etc...). Modernism has often mixed such demeaning abstraction with life-

40. Manfredo Tafuri has recently spoken of the "recreation"—the repetition—of a historical context as the principal task of the critic and historian. Manfredo Tafuri, "There is no Criticism, Only History," in *Design Book Review*, n. 9, Spring, 1986.

41. A fetishization of place, of a reality presumed incorruptible, would turn the place into a sign within a sign system. This system has the power to fascinate because it puts the world into the perfect order of an all-encompassing code. Jean Baudrillard, "Fetish and Ideology: The Semiological Reduction," in *For a Critique of the*

creating abstraction. In the latter, certain formal qualties and certain meanings and values, aspects of the things, wills, and forces, are brought out—but they are not isolated and idealized. Instead these signs and things are involved in "designs," that is, in dramas in which they are forced to, seduced to, or simply find the opportunities to unfold what may become their essence.

Poetic language can be "abstract" in this way, as is a whole range of painting from Impressionism to Klee and Pollock; as is the abstraction of qualities of light and of the movement of the body in the villas of Le Corbusier. The point is that certain pictorial materials and texts are to be freed by abstraction from their bondage to signification systems so that they can float freely enough to be recognized by dormant wills for whom they become maps or diagrams that can conduct the flows of their life energies. If these qualities were not traced over enough, underlined so to speak, through the dramatic mise-èn-scene of forces that interact with the things and the spaces, then these qualities might never be "seen." Instead they would remain subdued by whoever the wills and forces of the order of the day may be.

The pictorial materials used and also the texts used will have to be "abstract" enough for these elements to become such diagrams capable of conducting life energies. This montage of signs speaking to the body, speaking to and of the other, and of the multiplicity of spatial aspects, is indispensable, since, as Lyotard has stressed, the figure has a privileged direct access to the unconscious, that is, to the body, to life. The design process would engage them in a series of affirmations that would deconstruct them and would set free "partial," abstract, diagrammatic forms that are capable of conducting desire streams out of the circles of unconscious fantasies. Images and texts must be worked over to buld the kind of affirmative power that is present, for instance, in Klee's drawings. The "diagrammatic" posesses material-formal qualities that can make lived intensity

recur or create a new intensity. Strictly speaking the diagrammatic is nonsignifying and represents nothing other than itself. In this sense, it could be seen as the mirror in which one does not see what one wants to, but within which appears the riddle of a silent sign that requires an answer to be given with one's life.

Difficulties with practicing the design and criticism of affirmation are the result of how we have been trained. There is no absolute starting point for thought, for design. To start where there exists a major investment of desire may speed up the drama of forces and wills playing and fighting it out. The existing codes that overencode the design situation—moral, epistemological, legal, economic, social, political, cultural—must serve as starting points. They will soon fall as the powers that rely on them for their identities are affirmed beyond the limits set for them by the codes and systems. Only affirmation can reveal the true nature of the wills-to-live which are involved, and only affirmation can create stronger wills, i.e., wills that can be "heard" by freely obeying wills. This means, in confirmation of Kahn's approach, that powers

*Political Economy of the Sign.* St. Louis: Telos Press, 1981.

42.  John Knesl, "The New Objectivity of a Critical Late Modernism," in *The Pratt Journal of Architecture*, n. 1, Brooklyn: Pratt School of Architecture, 1985.

43.  We have been conditioned to work toward a synthesis, i.e. an "organic" unity by imposing hierarchies and

that structure the architectural program will be made to go beyond themselves by being affirmed, or rather, from their point of view, overaffirmed. They will multiply into more and more intensive powers which would come into being through this critical montage design process. In contrast to typical analytical critique, such "deconstruction" through affirmation will, however, not leave nothing but rubble, but it will play out the metamorphoses of what turn out to be pretentious or sickly powers and desires, into powers that create a freer and fuller life.

The structuration of the design process is "open" in the best sense of modernism as is the organization of the resulting spaces and practices. The classical model of organicist subordination of the parts to a superior goal can no longer serve as a model or diagram for life as soon as the excess and luxury of spirit has appeared. With Nietzsche, it is the spirit that wants to become flesh, to raise life to become higher power and desire. With Plato the spirit turns against the spontaneity and impermanence of life: Life blames life, secretes a ghostlike spirit, and erects monuments of eternal truth instead. Affirmation as the affirmation of multiplicity, of difference, of life, can never end, never be complete. I have referred to this open series of affirmations as a "critical montage" since montage, an invention of modernism, seems to anticipate some of the characteristics of the affirmative discipline.

Designing with a truly free structure which outflanks hierarchically structured signifying codes and systems does not mean that any wild-looking network goes. One starts with the ordinary, the program, and with radical openings that allow chance to enter. Affirm everything and anything, superimpose the affirmations so that they will change—be this in nuances or in drastic metamorphoses—which then become stronger affirmations seeking corresponding space forms. Not with high principles nor buried in the details does one start, but as Heisenberg once suggested, "somewhere in the middle," or "in the concrete" as Adorno stipulated. The process invalidates the normal codes by affirming identities, desires, and powers beyond their coded values and coded meanings. Affirmation makes possible the miraculous thinking and communicating without code—it is what constitutes direct response between two wills; it is the "answering" of Baudrillard.

Affirmation takes us right to the Achilles heel of architectural practice: Who affirms? The architect must initially affirm through the interpretations and evaluations that come out of his/her own life. Yet design must ultimately rely on affirmation to play out the given and the still hidden interpretations involved in the design, in bringing out the multiplicity of the strongest life forces. The succession of waves of affirmation transforms the spatial forces and the life forms involved and clarifies—almost as a by-product—the character of the forces and powers initially encountered. Whereas conventional analytical method bases itself on pre-existing values and derives a result which then limits creative action, the discipline of affirmation yields an analytical conclusion as a result of an open series of creative acts.

The architect's work, the mise-en-scène of powers, extant or imaginary, real or yet-to-become, is obligated more to the unfolding of the life powers as they are occasioned by the client's program than to the

stable meanings. But affirmation of multiplicity means not only to exclude but also not to include: Design must work toward the bringing out of stronger, more essential differences between multiple affirmations, toward a kind of divergence that ultimately produces the only 'true' unity: one of plurality and multiplicity. Architecture is a language insofar as it is the second affirmation; the affirmation of the affirmation. Language is structuration of differences and differences are the beginning and end of affirmation: one affirms oneself in the difference to an other.

client's direct needs or even powers. The architect works like the dramatist: in inventing forms, s/he takes sides, but s/he takes multiple sides. This is not a problem because the discipline of affirmation does not work with one truth but with many truths—all true for certain powers and life forms. It works with intensities and not with metaphysical truths represented by signifier/signified pairs. The intensities are libidinal charges, drives, "life energies" in short, that seek forms to build themselves into, to release themselves into, forms for them to be seduced back into becoming real again and again.[43]

For Lyotard art (and architecture) are commutable libidinal energy. He proposes that abstract painting is critical art because it represents nothing but the flow of libidinal energy itself. To repeat this flow, art has to deconstruct the normal representation of things because this normal representation is literally "designed" to set in circular motion Freudian fantasy. We need objects that are both deconstructed and whole. We need to deconstruct those aspects that are re-presentations in the service of questionable powers rather than representations and affirmations of themselves only. We need to rebuild them, let them become whole through how we affirm them with our life. This explains why mere conflictuality and fragmentation in architetural objects tends to be pointless and somewhat obscene. Is this the disturbing quality to be found in the work of Daniel Libeskind, for instance?[44]

Pushing the affirmation of all powers and desires that emerge during the design process farther and farther makes this work both creative and critical. Kahn's metaphors are to be taken seriously if with great caution: architectural forms "are," order "is," not because they live in a Platonic treasury of forms but because a strong will to become, to live, is reaffirmed by these forms and this will affirms these forms in turn. It is only in this sense that one must accept Rossi's argument about the victory of the "strong form" over the ravages of time. The autonomy of architecture as regards the creating will must not be confused with an easy realism that simply accepts form types because they have survived without asking whether they may have survived because they were affirmed by reactive forces, weak and ignoble, but numerous. An animism that is all too close to many architects would have us believe that these strong forms are (still) alive. A "strong" building may be repressive or crass, but it also may simply challenge us to become a more intensive life form. A truly strong building poses a challenge that requires

an answer that cannot be formulated in the codes that overdetermine life.

The "challenge" here is in the nature of a question arising between a sign/form and the real/material, the life force. It is a question in which life is risking itself totally, without any cover extended by either a well-

44. Wholeness of the design process and of the work is always in the process itself rather than a quality determined from outside, from the point of view of extraneous principles, and it is not represented in a closure of the resulting synthetic form. Wholeness is in the nature of the series of changes and in the intensity and quality of the differences that are lived and consummated. As modern designers we can only develop our faculties

meaning or a malicious god. This challenge is not at all the both threatening and reassuring promised reconnection with a simple materialist or idealist substance or ground of being. The real power of affirmation lies, of course, in the beings who are the forms of the life force. Therefore, in a sense, power is in what are called powers in the dimensions of praxis—economic, social, political, cultural. But one must immediately warn that these powers cannot be taken at face value—as do the pragmatists, participationists, etc.—nor can they be derived from theoretical constructs concocted on the basis of an ideology, as do the simplistic Marxists, individualists, etc. These powers are forms and masks assumed by life force. The only correct way to deal with them is to develop ways to make these life forces manifest their nature, their intentions, their history. This means to play them through in the experiment of the drama of design, it means speaking "poetically." A building that is simply to serve us, as the populists demand, merely transfers this instrumental attitude back onto ourselves.

Design is a staging of struggles, or better, of life and death dances of powers and desires. These dances between the powers that seek to affirm and that seek to be affirmed produce the Deleuzian "lines of escape." These lines are forms that offer themselves as crystallizations and localizations to life energies that are awakening and seeking affirmation. Once become, the new life forms seek form and expression in order to become again, to repeat the life they are. (They seek the double affirmation that is necessary so that powers may be inscribed into the eternal return.) It must be repeated that the present concept of a "power" reaches deeper than the power an individual or even an institution can "have."

Power is the power to create, and that means to create life. Power must not be identified with its masculine appearance; the mother's power is also an affirmative will. A power is what affirms and what seeks to be affirmed; it is identified in the manner of Foucault as a difference between forces that as such first creates the individual as a constellation of certain powers and desires. The level of self-affirmation to become a true individual above the fluxes of forces would require the Nietzschean overman.

Affirmation raises us above the alternatives posed by Deleuze, Lyotard, and Baudrillard. Can Deleuzian intensity resist the simulation that turns the real into a simulated hyper-real, does it—potentially—restore to the body the symbols that once challenged it? What used to be called "mind," and

*1er Mai* is a continuous double exposure made in Paris on the afternoon of May 1, 1983 by Jill Waterman.

"vision" were symbols that did not simulate but challenged, threatened, seduced, and pleased without explanation, mute signs that condensed all life into themselves, omnivalent signs that had the power to structure thoughts and the powers and desires of the body by yoking them together, signs that required answers *hic et nunc*, under the ultimate risk of body, of life. Can the body become again the scene it once was, can it become the secret, the

of luring, adumbrating, and forming wills, powers, and values so that they may illuminate themselves in their differences between one another and between themselves and the power that looks at them, that lives its life over against them and 'us'. Any other approach would require a return to normative evaluative scales which in turn would have to be founded on metaphysical meanings and values, that is, on God.

risk and challenge that was found in the body by Bataille, by Lyotard with the sphinx? Even where Derrida finds pure difference with the *stylos*, the *phallos* that is the first trace, it is really life that begins to think about itself in reaffirming itself, bringing itself back through the sign (and not some mystical movement of *differance*). Clearly if we will not succeed in awakening the body's, that is, life's, taste for challenge, risk, and the play of metamorphosis and nuance, "we," the subjects, will disappear in the cloned body, overfed with carefully regulated stimulations, wrapped in equally carefully arranged simulations. Why is it that only fascistoid societal structures have been able to awaken the body to challenge and risk? We have arrived at the most difficult point at which Eros and Thanatos—the challenge and ultimate *jouissance*—seem to become indistinguishable. We can only hope to make forms so "strong," so serene, that only the right powers and desires will be able to respond, that body will engage the mind in silent laughter, a laughter that rises from the earth to the sky, and that will make us strong enough for the unencodable challenge and joy required by the return.

Only flashes of such affirmation, I think, exist in the architectural works of today. The discipline of affirmation applied to criticism should bring out these qualities and allow them to initiate and strengthen farther-going work.

As a preview of further work in this direction, here is a brief look at a work by Tadao Ando: Kojimo Housing, Okayama, 1981.

## I. First Series of Affirmations: Retracings and Repetitions

1. A long wall, free-standing, with an attached cross wall bluntly facing the approaching step, divides the paths. One goes back and behind to a ground-floor apartment; another moves off abruptly to the right into the front cube (the owner's house); the third ascends along that wall to the upper back apartment. The wall stands; it stands against the two cubes, and the space between these three is allowed to fill with overspill spaces: the kitchen and dining room of the front house unit.

The wall and the open stair: Affirmation of movement through space, but only to arrive at a point of repose; at a place enclosed by walls and buffered by courts.

2. Two cubes, staggered, strangely linked by the terrace between, forming an outside court created with the help of another free-standing wall.

Affirmation of being contained inside these cubes, so strongly that windows turn into desperate slits or huge gashes and gaping holes, larger than windows, but too much framed to be just skeletal modernist open bays. The force of "opening" affirmed violently as difference over and against the wallness of the cube walls.

 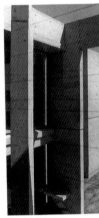

The containment is relieved by the internal courts, walled on one side, with a two-story slit, and open to the shared outside court. Movement from floor to floor through the diagonally placed stair takes one into the light court and back into the covered squares of the cube. This movement juts out into the court; the stair divides the cube into day and night.

The internal courts capture the light and take it to the living rooms.

Light is affirmed a second time through the walls and the square opening at the top of the court. The cubes reaffirmed once again by the cross frame tying them together at the roof level and articulating the interior light courts. No central living room that might pretend to be a center. Instead one small room with a wall to the light court and its own window looking away to the unshielded outside—with all other rooms facing into the light court.

## II. Second Series

1. Affirmation of arriving finally—after the walls, the turns of the body—inside. Inside the cube looking back at an outside that is no more than a framed view. One is not ever to go back to this outside, one is to look back at a representation of outside and thus to feel inside so much more. Attempt to concentrate energies inside the house, face the life lived inside?

2. The inside spaces kept spartan, the materials left to show their brutal materialness, mellowed only by the light that is carefully conducted to caress their roughness. Who caresses? The light, the mind, not the sun?

3. Inside the centered structure of the cube there is no center, except the light courts. Again it is the light that occupies the center.

4. Do the courts, both the internal light courts and the external court concentrate energy inside the life of the house or do they make us contemplating "seers"?

5. What is the nature of the emptiness of these courts, clearly empty of all tokens of nature, of "reality," but this in order to make perceivable the sun, the stone, and glass, or even to make perceivable what is not—the absolute emptiness according to which everything is but a dream dreamt by a soul? Or is it the emptiness that deflates our conventional ideas and memories; one that readies us to see without a code again?

6. Are we still too serious, too studied, too self-conscious here? What is this desire to force concrete walls to do what the paper walls of the traditional house did: to affirm directly and, as a second affirmation, the idea of an infinite and universal space, empty because it is the very ground and condition of all appearances? This emptiness is hereby elevated to a godhead, it is made the creator, it draws our powers into itself, we sink into it.

7. Come out into the inner courtyard and see how the emptiness collapses when you look back at yourself in your rooms. It is the emptiness of the monk's contemplation, not the fullness of an experience so strong in its difference to the one just around the corner or just the other side of a beam of light. The fullness that through its difference becomes a second affirmation, a sign/repetition, a reflection remaining within life rather than moving out into an imaginary ghostland. Turning away to see anew is in keeping with multiple affirmation, walking into the temple is not. The old idea of simplifying askesis versus multiple and plural intensification of experience, thinking, and action through ever more intensively lived differences: the gods of negation versus Dionysos/Nietzsche.

Surely there are times and places for contemplation even in a house, but should all the house be given to it?

8. The isolated house set against nature emerges as the motivating force. Nature is seen, however, already as a sign, already only through images and framed views that are contrived to tell of it. "Such things as light and wind only have meaning when they are introduced inside a house in a form cut off from the outside world. The isolated fragment of light and air suggests the entire natural world."[1] Nature should be an affirmation of life, and would this not mean an affirmation of the other, both the one who shares the house as well as the one who remains outside?

9. Should, then, the house not affirm chance as it ravages the modern Japanese suburb? That is, should it not turn chance into desired, repeated fate? These houses dream themselves into the country, they do not know how to affirm the city.

10. Ando's work cumulatively lets these themes recur: the court as captured outside, domesticated, framed to tell about an outside/nature; the wall around the house; the frame as presence of living space inside the hole cut out of the world. The development of his work has moved from a more literal use of these form types to working up greater tensions between them. More affirmation, performed by Ando himself, has tended to break open the cube, to allow the court to become more "real" rather than an image to look out at. Still more affirmation would bring down the types and turn the limited play of a structure into an unlimited play—at least for a moment, the vital moment.[2] Then Ando could "forget" (in the Nietzschean sense) his desire for the unity of a formal composition. Did not the masters build imperfections into what appeared to be perfect works because they wanted to prevent desire from getting all caught up in the fantasies for which the perfect forms provided the armature? When Ando speaks of his desire to provide "solutions to problems in prevailing circumstances," does he indeed perform a double affirmation?[3] Is everyday life built for, first, and then a symbol made of it? Or does he rather begin with affirming everyday life but then turns it into a ghost, by fixing it onto the abstract image of nature seen in a romantic way? Power is differences—nuances and abysmal differences—each one full of life as it can be. Perhaps, then, and certainly for us in the West, the playful Scarpa, and Siza, when he is not too heavy, come closer to the discipline of boundless affirmation.

1.  Tadao Ando, "From Self-Enclosed Modern Architecture Towards Universality," in *Tadao Ando, Buildings Projects Writings*, Kenneth Frampton, ed., New York: Rizzoli International Publications, 1984, p. 139.
2.  See Jacques Derrida, "Structure, Sign, and Play In the Discourse of the Human Sciences," in *Writing and Difference*, trans. by Alan Bass, Chicago: University of Chicago Press, 1978, pp. 278-294.
3.  op. cit. Tadao Ando, p. 140.

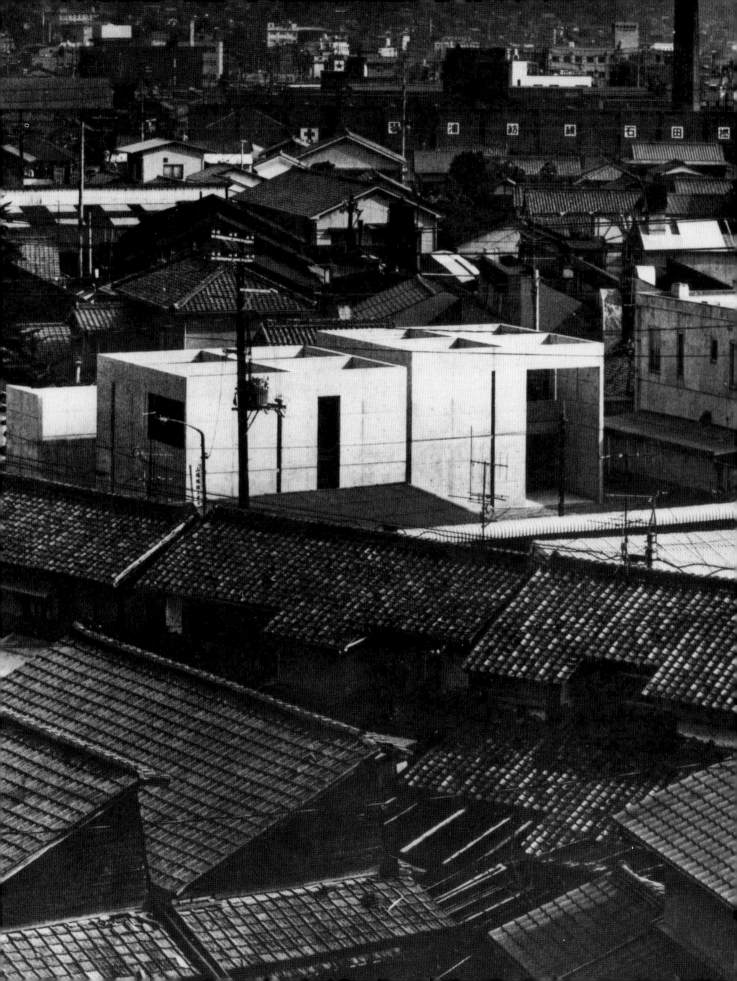

for José Oubrerie.

Rose Mary Badami
Sister Kathy        Phone 713/ 664-0659
3134 Plumb
     Houston, T.X. 77005
We want to build a chapel for
our people who are very special
we need a special architect

José Oubrerie

# Letter to a Client

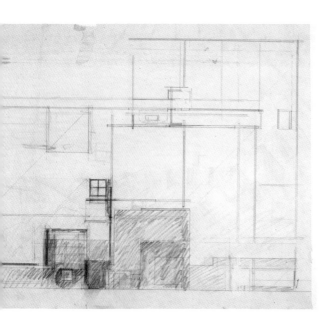

DEAR ROSEMARY / 4/245 SENT MAIL ON
EXPRESS MAIL FEB-14-86

THIS LETTER INTENDS TO MAKE CLEAR
FOR YOU WHAT I HAVE MADE IN
THE DEVELOPPEMENT OF THIS PROJECT
AND HOW, FROM MY POINT OF VIEW,
IT DEVELOPS.

IST- I THINK, AND I ALWAYS UN-
DERSTOOD IT THIS WAY, I STILL THINK
THAT YOU ASKED ME TO COME TO
MAKE A PROJECT FOR YOU IN
SOMEWAY "SPECIAL." YOU LIKED
RONCHAMP ! I DON'T KNOW IF YOU OR REMEMBER
SAW THE FIRMINYS CHURCH EXHI-
BITION AT THE RICE UNIVERSITY
COLLEGE OF ARCHITECTURE'S GALLERY
SOMETHING WAS ALSO PUBLISHED
IN A HOUSTON NEWSPAPER ...ETC...
SO I CAME HERE AND AT THAT
TIME YOU HAD NO/SITE AND
IT WAS DIFFICULT TO REALLY

ENE DAY WE'LL MEET
"VOLCAN M." TO MEET.

245

JO
NY
8
13
86

START SOMETHING WITHOUT A SITE
YOU START RESEARCHING AND TRYING TO
MEANWHILE I MADE THE FIRST
IDEA OF A CHAPEL MADE OF
3 ANGLES WHICH WAS
DIEDRES
CONCEIVED AS A CHEAP BUILDING
MADE LIKE THE STREET ADVER
TISING PANELS PLANES AND TRIDIMEN
SIONAL BEAMS AND COLUMNS ETC...

Chapel

Shelter
with

NO GLAZING FOR THE WINDOWS AND
AIR CONTROL. JUST A KIND OF OPEN
SCULPTURE. OR/AND LATER WITH
THE POSSIBILITY TO MAKE IT MORE
COMFORTABLE ADDING TO IT WHEN
YOU HAD MONEY.
UNDERNEATH THE CHAPEL, AND
AND SO CORRESPONDING TO AN
OLD (AT LEAST (MIDDLE-AGED) "FUNC
TION" OF THE CHURCH, IT WAS
A SHELTER FOR STREET-PEOPLE

COULD BE/EVEN BUILT

BUT FINALLY THE SITE YOU³
AND I, WERE LOOKING FOR WAS NOT
FOR SALE AND YOU WENT LOOKING
FOR THE ACTUAL SITE : AUSTIN.
IN THE FIRST IDEA THE ALTAR
WAS IN AN ALCOVE, WITH A
SPECIFIC LIGHT AND 
PUT IN A SPECIAL SITUATION, ALLOWING
PECULIAR SITUATION, ALLOWING
ALSO TO USE THE ROOM FOR DIFFE
RENT PURPOSES EVEN IF THE
BUILDING WAS CONCEIVED AS AN
ISOLATED OBJECT.
IN THE NEW BUILDING FOR
AUSTIN THE PROBLEM WAS
—TO CONNECT WITH THE EXISTING
BUILDING AND KEEP A COMPOSITIONAL
UNITY AND COHERENCY
—TO ADD A CHAPEL FOR THE
FOWLER'S PIECE OF ART
— TO MAKE ROOM FOR A KITCHEN
+ STORAGE, DINING ROOM AND
ART CLASS
— TO MAKE AN OUTSIDE TERRACE
CONNECTED WITH THE BUILDING
TO MAKE

JO
NY
8
13
00

OUTSIDE MASS, MEETINGS, OUTDOOR⁴
BARBEQUE FOR ALL POSSIBLE OUTDOOR
COMMUNITY EVENTS.
I WAS CONCERNED ALSO BY SOME
ASPECT OF THE SITE

SOME PROBLEMS POSED BY THE EXISTING
BUILDINGS IN THE BACKGROUND ETC
SO CAME THE MAIN SOLUTION OF
HAVING TWO OBJECTS

1 THE EXISTING HOUSE AT AUSTIN
2 THE NEW CHAPEL SHELTER
UNIFIED BY A WALL →3A
WHICH WAS ALSO MAKING
A SCREEN IN FRONT OF THE BACK-
GROUND EXISTING HOUSES
4 — WAS THE OUTSIDE TERRACE
5 — A TREE WHICH WAS CLOSING
THE STREET SIDE OF THE TERRACE

SO THIS PLAN DISPOSITION EXIST
FROM THE VERY BEGINNING

AND EVEN IF THE WALL 3A 5
WAS EXTENDED IN 3B LATER,
AND IF 2 BECAME MORE THE
SANCTUARY WITH A NEW CHAPEL
BUILT IN FRONT OF THE TREE AND
THE TERRACE, THE MAIN PRIN
CIPLES REMAIN.

Fowler's at piece chapel

A SPACE WAS SO PRODUCED
BETWEEN THE STREET 1 2 AND
3 BECOMING A KIND OF INTERNAL
PLACE OF GATHERING AND PLAY
WITH THE TERRACE 4 BUILT
GAZON AND SOLID SURFACE TREE
AND THE DIALOGUE OF THE 2
BUILDINGS, THE WALL 3 AND
THE TREE 5
INSIDE THE BUILDING NATURAL
LIGHT WAS PROVIDED EVERYWHERE
FOR ME AT THAT, ACCORDING TO

DO
NY
8
13
80

YOUR PROGRAM THE PROJECT 6
WAS MADE AND COULD BE DE-
VELOPPED INTO MORE PRECISE
DRAWING. IT WAS STILL GOOD
ARCHITECTURE, WELL FUNCTION-
NING AND CHEAP (AT LEAST
IN ACCORD TO YOUR POSSIBILITIES)
SO ██████ REFUSED THIS PRO-
JECT IN THE AIRPORT AT NEWARK
LIKE INAPROPRIATE PROGRAM ETC...
ETC... AND WE DID A NEW VERSION OF
IT ALTERED. A BASEMENT WAS INTRO
DUCE "DEFINITIVELY" AGAINST THE OPI-
NION OF J-HOUCHINS AND MINE ABOUT
THE COST OF A BASEMENT. (ARGUMENTS
THAT JUST THIS YEAR ██████ ACCEPTED
AND WE HAD RECENTLY TO MAKE A NEW
PROJECT WITHOUT BASEMENT, SO DEVELOPING
THE AREA ON EARTH)
DURING THIS PERIOD WE I HAVE MADE
SEVERAL PROPOSALS THAT HAVE ALL
BEEN REJECTED. D██████ SENT ME BACK
DRAWINGS WHICH FOR ME SHW A
COMPLETE MISUNDERSTANDING AND
ALTERATION OF MY THINKING, EVEN
IF THEY ··WERE PROFESSIONALLY

CORRECT   THEY WERE JUST SHOWING 7
THE IMPOSSIBILITY OF WORKING TO-
GETHER FOR THE ~~SURE~~ ~~OF~~ REASON OF
STANDING IN DIFFERENT AREAS OF
ARCHITECTURE.
SO  I DON'T SEE  HOW WE CAN HAVE
A  POSITIVE ISSUE THE WAY WE ARE
WORKING NOW.   SINCERELY.  I HAVE ALREADY
A PROPOSAL  ILLUSTRATED IN ~~THE~~ ~~DWG~~ SENT
... ~~...~~
TO YOU  FRIDAY.
I INSIST THAT IT IS NOT A PROBLEM
OF CAPABILITY (FOR ME) ABOUT
■■■■ OR MYSELF  IT IS A
PROBLEM OF  SPIRIT, OF MISUNDER-
STANDING  AND  I FEEL OFFENDED
BY ■■■■ ~~TO BE QUALIFIED OF DOING~~ "EXER-
CISES OF STYLE"  THAT MEANS
THAN  I IS NOT SERIOUS  WORK AND
I READ IT  THAT WAY  FROM THE
PART OF  ■■■■
SO  WHAT  ~~DOES~~ ~~HE~~ ~~FEELS~~ THINK ABOUT
RONCHAMP! RONCHAMP WAS
STARTED AND  FINISHED TO BE
BUILT  IN  QUITE  FIVE YEARS!
BUT  THE  QUALITY UPON OF THE
BUILDING DEPENDED ~~~~ THIS PROCESS
MAINLY.

I O
NY
8
13

I THINK  THE  ACTUAL PROJECT 8
DEALS  WITH  MOST  OF  OUR REQUI-
REMENTS  ~~AND~~  PROGRAMMATIC AND
POETIC  WHICH ARE  AS MUCH IMPOR-
TANT.  (POETRY IS  NOT A QUESTION
OF MONEY  BUT  OF SPIRIT) ...
LETS  GO TO THE PROJECT

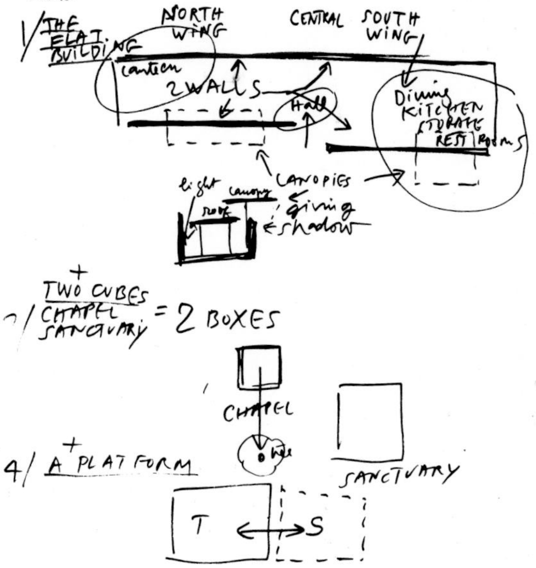

1/ THE FLAT BUILDING — NORTH WING — CENTRAL — SOUTH WING
canteen — 2 WALLS — Hall — Dining KITCHEN STORAGE RESTROOMS
light — canopy — roof — CANOPIES giving shadow

2/ TWO CUBES — CHAPEL / SANCTUARY = 2 BOXES

CHAPEL — Oror

4/ A PLATFORM — SANCTUARY

T ⇄ S

**5/ THE SITE AND THE EXISTING BLDG**

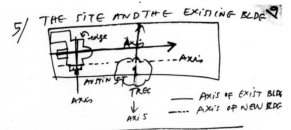

Hedge · Axis
AUSTIN ST
AXIS · TREE
↓ AXIS

— AXIS OF EXIST BLDG
--- AXIS OF NEW BLDG

THE FLAT BUILDING CONTAINS ALL
THE "SERVICES" AND CAN BE REALISED
BY PIECES (AS I SHOWED IN SKETCHES
SENT TO YOU) AND PERMIT A
COHERENT DEVELOPMENT OF THE
PROJECT AT THE DIFFERENT PHASES
OF REALISATION.

THE CENTRAL HALL WAS TRANSPARENCY ① ON
THE BACK AND CLOSE-
NESS ② ON AUSTIN
STREET BECAUSE
IT INTRODUCE YOU
IN FRONT OF YOU
TO THE BLDG GATE
③ AND TO THE
OUTDOOR
MAIN ALTAR
④ AGAINST THE
OUTDOOR MASSES

AUSTIN STREET

SANCTUARY WALL FOR
AND EVENT. THEY ARE FACING
THE SANCTUARY!

50
JY
8
13
or

WALL, WHICH DIALOGUES WITH THE
SOUTH FACADE OF THE EXISTING BUILDING

PENIG
COURTYARD

N

LIKE PRODUCING AN
INSIDE SPACE ON YOUR

SITE (IN THE BACK OF THE SANCTUARY'S
THE COURTYARD IS JUST PLASTICALLY TO UNDERSTAND
THE SANCTUARY AS A CUBE AND IS USED
AS SERVICE COURT)

SO YOU PROGRESS FROM THE STREET
AXIS ⓪ TO ① SIDE OF ENTRANCE
② YOU DISCOVER THE LINEARITY OF THE
SITE AND ③ THE HALL WITH 4 THE
MAIN AXIS OUTDOOR WITH ⑤ THE MAIN
ORGANISATIONAL AXIS INSIDE (PARRALEL TO ⓪
⑦ AND ④) AND WITH ⑥ THE RELATION-
SHIP OF THE CHAPEL WITH THE TREE
AND THE STREET NATURE AND CITY
OPPOSED AND TOGETHER.

ALL THIS SUCCESSION OF SPACES VIEWS
AND DISCOVERIES OF THE BUILDING IS POETI-
CALLY IMPORTANT AND HAS NO COST
MORE THAN

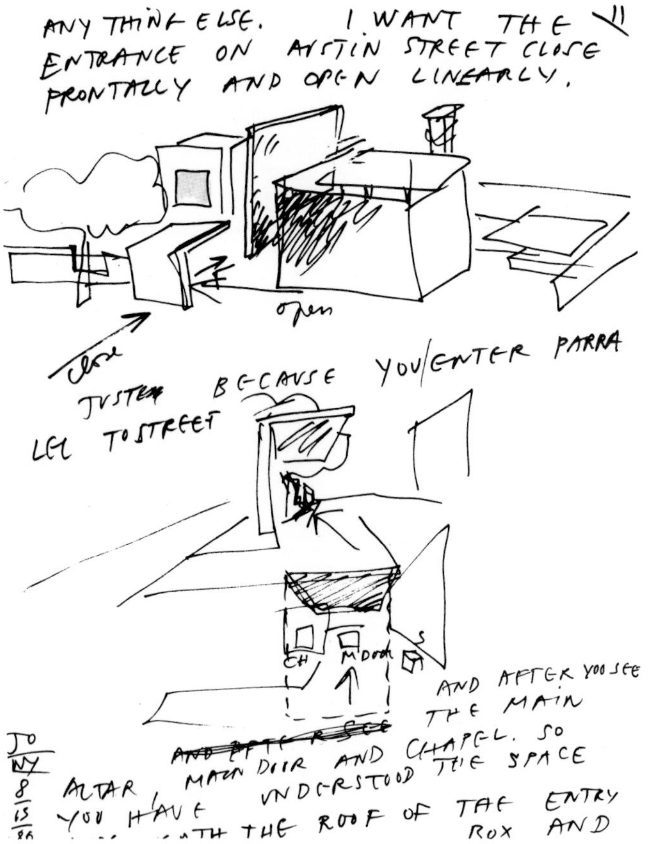

ANY THING ELSE.    I WANT THE V1
ENTRANCE ON AUSTIN STREET CLOSE
FRONTALLY AND OPEN LINEARLY.

open

Close

JUSTE← BECAUSE YOU/ENTER PARRA
LEL TO STREET

CH  M DOOR

AND AFTER YOU SEE
THE MAIN
AND AFTER SEE
MAIN DOOR AND CHAPEL. SO
ALTAR        UNDERSTOOD THE SPACE
YOU HAVE    WITH THE ROOF OF THE ENTRY
ROX AND

TO
NY
8
15
88

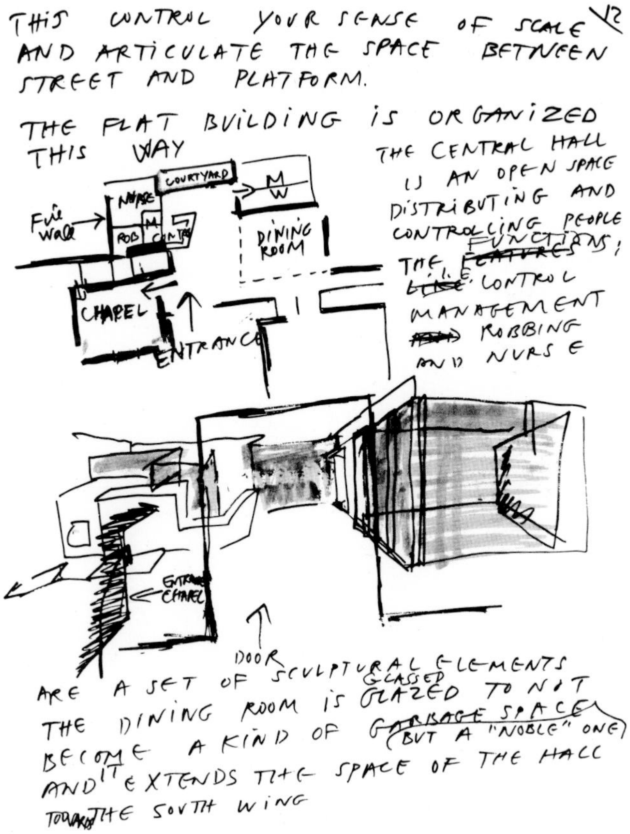

THIS  CONTROL  YOUR SENSE  OF SCALE  V2
AND ARTICULATE THE SPACE  BETWEEN
STREET AND  PLATFORM.

THE FLAT BUILDING IS ORGANIZED
THIS WAY

Full
Wall        COURTYARD        M
NURSE                         W
M
ROD  CENT    DINING
                            ROOM

CHAPEL

ENTRANCE

THE CENTRAL HALL
IS AN OPEN SPACE
DISTRIBUTING AND
CONTROLLING PEOPLE
FUNCTIONS;
THE COFFEES
ELSE CONTROL
MANAGEMENT
ROBBING
AND NURSE

ENTRANCE
CHANEL

DOOR
ARE A SET OF SCULPTURAL ELEMENTS
THE DINING ROOM IS GLAZED TO NOT
BECOME A KIND OF GARBAGE SPACE
(BUT A "NOBLE" ONE)
AND IT EXTENDS THE SPACE OF THE HALL
TOWARD THE SOUTH WING

Oubrerie

THE NORTH AND SOUTH WING
GET THE LIGHT BY THE CEILING
AND SOMETIMES ON THE FAÇADE.

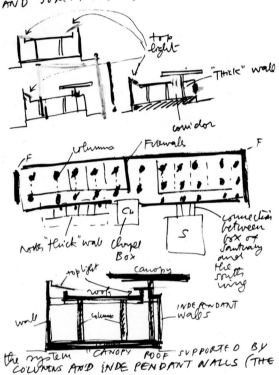

top light

"THICK" wall

corridor

F — columns — Firewalls — F

Co

S

Note "thick" wall    Chapel Box

connection between box or sanctuary and the south wing

top light    canopy

roof

wall    columns

INDEPENDANT WALLS

the system "CANOPY" ROOF SUPPORTED BY
COLUMNS AND INDEPENDANT WALLS (THE

"TOPLIGHTS" BEING THE JOINTS) AIR-COND BEING
BETWEEN THE 2 SIDES) ON TOP OR ON
SIDES OF THE BUILDING ⒜
THERE IS NOTHING DIFFICULT TO BUILD HERE
EXCEPT THE CANOPY, BUT DETAILS HAVE TO BE ARCHI-
TECTURALLY STUDIED
EX: I WANT SOME SPECIFIC DETAILS FOR DOORS ETC.

THE CHAPEL IS A WINDOW ON THE TREC
WITH THE ALTAR IN
FRONT OF IT. IT PRESENT

EXCEPT
THE SIZE
NO REAL
DIFFICULT
PROBLEMS
THE WINDOWS
ON THE ROOF (TOP LIGHT) PERHAPS

lectern    altar    cross    holy south    wall column and beam

AND THE NECESSITY TO BUY A LARGE
SPECIAL GLASS (13 x 13') FOR THE
MAIN OPENING.
THE FACT TO HAVE THIS WINDOW
GIVES THE CHAPEL THE SAME QUALITE
AS THE SMALL CHAPEL OF ST THOMAS
BUT THE WHOLE CONTROL OF THE SPACE
IS BETTER IT IS A MORE COMPLETE
CONTROLLED SPACE

⒜ AIR CONDITIONNING    ON CEILING
HEATING VENTILATION

OR WE CAN CREATE
SMALLS "COURTS" ON THE BACK FAÇADE

TO LOCATE IT.

JO
NY
8
13
86

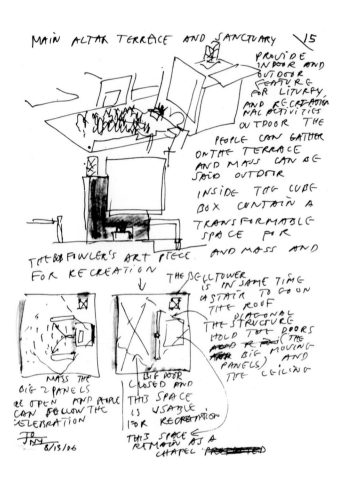

PROVIDE INDOOR AND OUTDOOR FEATURE FOR LITURPY, AND RECREATIONAL ACTIVITIES

OUTDOOR THE PEOPLE CAN GATHER ON THE TERRACE AND MASS CAN BE SAID OUTDOOR

INSIDE THE CUBE BOX CONTAIN A TRANSFORMABLE SPACE FOR AND MASS AND FOR RECREATION

THE BOB FOWLER'S ART PIECE

THE BELL TOWER IS IN SAME TIME A STAIR TO GO ON THE ROOF THE DIAGONAL STRUCTURE HOLD THE DOORS (THE BIG MOVING PANELS) AND THE CEILING

MASS THE BIG 2 PANELS RE OPEN AND PEOPLE CAN FOLLOW THE CELEBRATION

JO 8/13/06

BIG DOOR CLOSED AND THIS SPACE IS USABLE FOR RECREATION

THIS SPACE REMAIN AS A CHAPEL

THE MAIN ALTAR AND BOB FOWLER'S ALTAR LOOKS NORTH THE COURTYARD AND TERRACE ARE WEST AND NORTH GIVING MORE FRESHNESS TO THE OUTDOOR SPACE - THE BACK OF THE SANCTUARY IS CLOSED AND LOOK SOUTH THE WARMEST AND ALSO SERVICE COURT.

PEOPLE GATHERING IN THE SANCTUARY HAVE VIEW ON THE TERRACE THE EXISTING CHAPEL AND THE DING. BECOME FOCUSED ON ONE MAIN SPACE LIMITED ON A WALL. THE STREET BY THE TREE AND MOSTLY A LOW PRESENCE WITH A BIGGER OPENING IN FRONT OF THE TREE CONNECTED WITH THE HOTEL WINDOW.

Chapel window

OTHER FEATURES OF THE SANCTUARY ARE THE SCREEN PANEL, THE ROOF CANOPY, AND THE BELL TOWER.

THE SCREEN PANEL BUILT IN LIGHT MATERIAL (LIKE HIGHWAYS CROSSING- SIGNS OR

## 17

BIG ADVERTISING PANELS PROVIDE
THE DRAMATIC LIGHT with ENHANCING
THE OUTSIDE ALTAR "STAGE".

FIRST IS THE BOX AND THE SCREEN

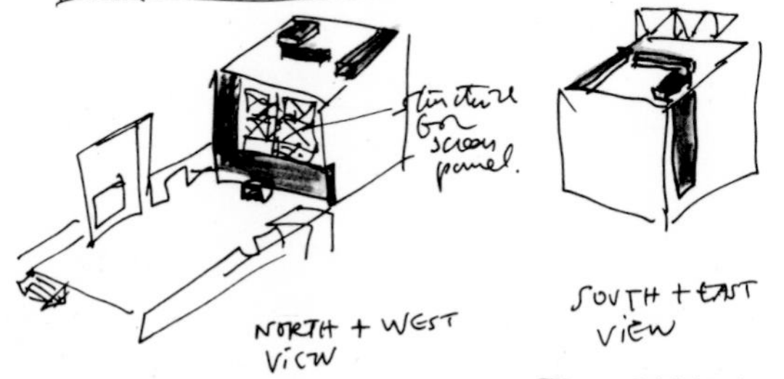

structure for screen panel.

NORTH + WEST VIEW

SOUTH + EAST VIEW

PANEL IS ATTACHED TO IT, THE CANOPY FIXED

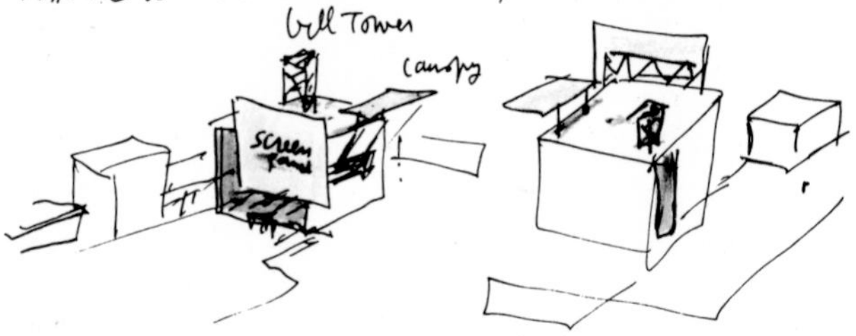

bell Tower

canopy

screen panel

IO
NY
8
13
86

ON THE ROOF PROTECT THE TOP LIGHT
AND SHADOW THE WALL THE BELL
TOWER BEARING BELLS TRADITIONAL OR
ELECTRONICAL. THIS "EXPLODED" BOX

THIS STRANGE ANIMAL WILL BE
CONFERED DRAMATIC AND THEATRICAL
(IN THE positive way GOOD SENSE OF THINGS) PRESENCE
BY THOSE 3 ELEMENTS

ROSE-MARY, NEW I THINK HERE NOW THE THE PRO-
JECT HAS REACHED AN EXPRESSION AND
AN APPROPRIATE LEVEL OF RESPONSE
TO YOUR NEEDS

I DON'T THINK THAN D▮ AND I
ARE MADE FOR COLLABORATION
THERE IS A BASIC MISUNDERSTANDING
WHICH CANN'T BE REPLACED BY GOOD
WILL. JOHN HOUCHINS DEMONSTRATED
A GOOD UNDERSTANDING OF THE
THINGS.

I AM READY TO DEVELLOP EVEN THE
WORKING DWINGS BUT IN WHICH
CONDITIONS?

I NEED AN ANSWER AND TO KNOW
NEED TO KNOW
WHAT WE DO HOW TO CONTINUE

1ST / IF YOU ALL AGREE THAT THIS
PROJECT IS JUST AN EXERCISE OF
STYLE AND UNUSEFULL I HAVE TO
QUIT

2ND / IF NOT GIVE ME THE CONDITION
TO PURSUE THIS WORK.

I THINK LIKE JOHN HOUCHINS' ~~THAT~~ BUILDING IT YOURSELVES, ~~THESE~~ EXCEPT IF IT IS ALL WOOD, WILL BE DIFFICULT, AND SOMETIMES IMPOSSIBLE. ~~AT~~ LEAST FOR THE MAIN STRUCTURAL ELEMENTS.

SO:

I ALSO THINK ~~THAT~~ I PROPOSE SOLUTIONS TO BUILD WELL IN PHASES AT DIFFERENT PERIOD OF TIME WITH COHERENCY AS EXPLAINED IN THE DROWING I SENT TO YOU.

I DON'T WANT TO BUILD A WARE-HOUSE OR A BAD OR COMMON THING ~~IN~~ EVEN DON'T NEED ME FOR THAT.

I THINK IT IS A QUESTION OF DECISION AND POWER FOR YOU AND UNDERSTANDING.

I HAVE NOT ASK YOU MONEY TO WASTE IT I HAVE MADE QUITE 6 DIFFERENTS PROJECTS OR VERSIONS OF THE PROJECT

Jo/NY/8/B/36

IT HAS BEEN "BUILT" BY/WITH THE DEVELOPMENT OF THE PROJECT.

(2) FROM J.PK (4 FR.) P. 1 quates? ITS. a dump of re

## 20

~~SO~~ I AM NOW FINISHING A MODEL AND READY TO DISCUSS WAY OF BUILDING AND DETAILS, IN AN ATMOSPHERE OF COMPREHENSION IT CAN BE QUICK. OTHERWISE IT WILL NOT WORK, UNTIL NOW I HAD MOSTLY UNCOMPREHENSION FROM ▮▮▮ START.

I EXPECT YOUR ANSWER AND HOPE YOU UNDERSTAND MY POSITION AND WITH THIS LETTER YOU HAVE FOR THE FIRST TIME ~~OF~~ ALL THE MEANING OF THIS BUILDING THIS PROJECT ALL WHAT I TRY TO PUT IN — POETRY AND LITTERACY TEXTS ARE MADE OF THE SAME WORDS, THEY DIFFER TOTALLY IN WAY OF BRINGING SENSE, NEW IMAGE "A SURPLUS OF MEANING" (1) THAT THIS BUILDING TRIES ALSO TO DO AS RONCHAMP DID. IT IS NOT JUST A FORMAL PROBLEM ~~AND~~ BUT THE SHAPING OF THINGS IS PRIMARY TO IT.

WITH MY RESPECTFULL FRIENDSHIP

Jay Oubrerie

Oubrerie

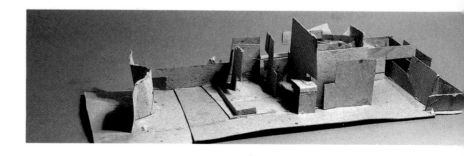

...NEXT I SAW STAGES, MODEL MOUNTAINS AND KABUKI DOLLS BEING CONSTRUCTED FOR THE FESTIVAL...

1 SEPT.

# Reflections Upon

Sylvia Arango

Rogelio Salmona

# Latin American Architecture

*Sensorial*
*Architecture*
*and Contextuality*

The political and social activity of the Latin American architect cannot continue to be contradictory to the mastery of his profession and the skill with which he practices it. On the contrary, there cannot be effective social and political commitment without serious professional support which would be a guarantee of the ideas and choices as well as the quality of the spaces and buildings conceived of and realized. This implies, on the one hand, a rejection of the folklore and fetishism of the past, currently in vogue in Europe and the United States. On the other hand, it implies a rejection of the barren functionalism at the service of monopoly capital which is obscured behind technological pretexts and false necessities, and seeks to impose a spatial and urban order which does not take into account local realities and, even less, the regional differences within Latin America. However, one should not forget that in each project, ideas and solutions can be extracted from both the craft

The most important development in Colombian architecture in the last fifteen years is oriented by the proposals initiated in the late fifties by the "topological" movement, which advanced an architecture of "place." The movement has continued its conceptual and architectonic evolution without interruption. The central issue of this development could be characterized as the will to avoid abstraction. "Concreteness" for this architecture does not rest in particularity or individuality—on the contrary, it is placed at a high level of generalization—but rather on the stress of two aspects: "sensorial perception"

tradition and from the technology which emerged from industrial development.

No philosophy or policy should exclusively favor tradition, i.e. permanence, or solely embrace a systematic search for innovation since, in many cases, the best solution is not the one which uses the most complex techniques but the one which is most appropriate for the site, the economic and the socio-cultural environment.

It is in this respect that brick, for example, may prove to be more modern—given the understanding that it is the spatial solution and not the material itself which makes the work contemporary—and more conducive to progress than the utilization of a newer material such as reinforced concrete. This use of brick can be seen in the work of the Uruguayan Eladia Dieste. In the same way, wood may be more technically efficient than steel. However, this does not mean that reinforced concrete or steel cannot be used under pertinent conditions. In any case, the architectural solution is conceived of and designed in relation to the chosen material which is linked to the spirit of the forms and to the formal, visual, tactile, and spatial qualities.

These reflections do not establish the quality of an architectural work. Fundamentally, one must keep in mind the characteristics of the site and preserve the object from the influence of fashions and styles.

and contextualization. Both are constitutive of what is elsewhere featured as a return to architectural figuration; in Colombia they acquire distinctive traits which we will attempt to specify.

"Sensorial perception" is meant as architectural comprehension or apprehension by direct stimulation of the senses, in contrast to abstract and rational perception. It is an architecture to look at, touch, listen to and explore, appealing more to the body than to the mind. "Sensorial perception" of architecture is located at the core of the contemporary situation, in which the perception of reality has become an unavoidable cognitive mediation with premises of its own that make it a reality in and of itself. But it is also central to a very specific way of being in the world that is unique to Latin America, where sensuality triggers articulation of the spiritual registers of culture.

The models which are present in the surroundings should be taken into consideration not only for their aesthetic and formal aspects but also because they serve as witnesses of the building practices of the place and of the spirit of their use. It is here that one finds the true meaning of integration: architecture should not so much strive to preserve the neighboring forms as respect the organic scale of the space, the ordering principle of the built form, and the patterns of occupation and composition, thus confirming the existing techniques and morphology. These positive elements should, under no circumstances, be destroyed; rather, they should be transformed. When there are remnants or barriers in the existing context which impair this transformation, they should be dampened or eliminated if possible.

Architecture cannot be abstract or premeditated. It is the result of the architect's sensitivity and of his response to each given situation with

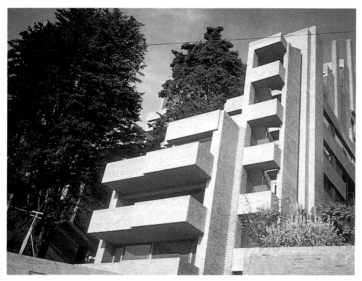

Alto de los Pinos Apartments, Bogota, 1976-81. View of the balconies.

Alto de los Pinos Apartments. View of the court.

"Sensorial" architecture is therefore simultaneously local and universal, contemporary and Latin American.

On the other hand, a sensual architecture is bound to the materials' own attributes, from which concrete sensations emanate. The use of one or another material stops being a technical or economical decision of an aleatory or subordinate kind and becomes an essential premise that determines design. For different historical reasons brick has been the preferred building material in Bogota; while in the fifties this material was to a certain degree contingent, it

regard to his own capacities and those of the environment in which he lives. Unfortunately, this communion is infrequently achieved and the resulting architecture is objectified and alienated from its own and any other site; it lacks identity, for its attempted originality is based on mere appearance.

What can be said of that architecture which assaults the city, boasting of its tiny piece of disjunctive coquetry, or of that other which boasts of nothing which would even distract us from its cynicism but at least has the merit of not confusing us in that it doesn't strive toward architectural dignity? These architectural strategies signal that power which utilizes space for profit or as a field for experimentation. The complicity between the architect at the service of capital and speculative economic forces, which appropriate architecture and transform it into consumer goods, becomes apparent.

### From Theory to Architectural Practice

Raising one's consciousness as a professional is not enough. The architect should possess the capacity to build—as opposed to creating abstracted space or form—and the capacity to know the principles of

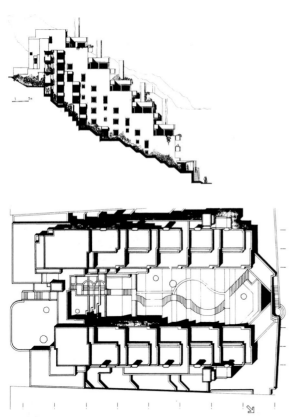

Alto de los Pinos Apartments. View of the chimneys.

Alto de los Pinos Apartments. Site section and plan.

has become essential. This is not the case of an architecture of brick, but rather of an architecture from brick. Within the universe of signs in which we move, the choice of an architecture based upon a certain material acquires specific meaning. It does not attempt solely, as architects of other latitudes have proposed, to capture the "spirit of the materials" but to transmit the formal and semantic possibilities of a constructive alternative. In the Colombian case, in which the available and adequate technology is a semi-industrialized one using mainly brick, rubble-work, masonry, and wood, an aesthetics that refers to the attributes of these materials and techniques has developed. Therefore, it is not craftsman architecture but architecture that connotes craftsmanship.

As a product of economic conditions, the Colombian city comprises a dual structure: the central city of

transformation of material into a useful, harmonious, and benevolent whole. He should know how to pass from theory to practice.

What is most lacking in the Latin American architect—once liberated from imperialistic pretensions and with a genuine knowledge of the cultural, social, and historic problems of his environment—is not so much awareness of the world and society but concrete experience of the terrain and of the realities which his task addresses directly. He runs the risk of making a place which discourages social interaction by dehumanizing the space or stifling it within overly rigorous organizing principles. Architecture should be more radical in its objectives and should transcend the mere fact of its being built in order to become a work which is meaningful for the community. The architect must increase his capabilities by decreasing his pretensions.

The development of a militant architecture in the hands of

Barrio Las Colinas, Bogota.

the rich and the peripheral one of the poor. Nevertheless, the circumstances of its construction process shade this dichotomy, soften the polarization, and offer possibilities for collective appropriation of urban space. A high percentage of the urban population is employed in edifying its surroundings. In daily practice, where "citizen-workers" participate in more labor intensive construction systems, a dynamic develops which enriches construction and spatial quality both of professional or erudite architecture and of popular and spontaneous architecture.

professionals with a political commitment has allowed the profession to come closer to a democratic and modest approximation of its task of giving back to the city dynamic spaces, without stylistic masquerades, which take into account the collective who inhabit them. If this evolution is a positive one with respect to the myths which had intimidated and manipulated us for so many years, it is not sufficient for a reappropriation of space nor does it lead to more radical architectural practices. How many atrocities against the urban place, urban society, and urban culture have been committed in the name of these values? How many absurdities, contradictions, and ridiculous ideological amalgams have been thrust upon space and form?

Although space is not as deterministic as economics, it does have its own laws which have been denied by those who reduce everything to economics without being aware of the purpose and use of space itself. From the moment that public space exists in an adequate form, its appropriation by society follows without any difficulty. Each plot becomes terrain for collective use, open to any social, political, or cultural action. However, without properly designed public space, the occurances of social life become weak and disappear.

A few purely militant positions have attempted to create a dichotomy between the professional architect

In the spirit of the concrete, "contextuality" is understood as the adaptation to a specific spatial and temporal environment. In previous decades there was a tendency to an architecture that would adjust to the immediate circumstances of a place; this notion has expanded to integrate other "distances" of the physical dimension—neighborhood, borough, city, region—with other factors of the physical dimension such as social and cultural expression. This physical environment of complex conformation has peculiar features: a natural geography—tropical climate, exuberant nature, specific luminosity, etc.—and an artificial geography of its own—superposition of various shapes and styles without congruity, contrasts, the indelible marks of poverty and so forth. Something similar happens upon exploring the topic of temporal contextuality; beyond the presence of the past, contextual /

and the politician, between the maker and the critic, thus generating something which is not related to society and which is therefore wrong. Awaiting a radical and complete transformation of society, the "political architect" spends his time proposing or fomenting projects which contribute to repression and are unable to support communities, stimulate collectivity or offer the individual unhindered privacy.

They try to make us believe, or in fact believe themselves, that a built space, by the nature of its design or topology alone, is not capable of stimulating social dynamics, community life, and cultural participation. They think that this is only achieved through false ideologies. A few others sit in the armchair of the "ivory tower" intellectual and lose sight of reality altogether. They theorize and mechanically criticize and cast judgment. It seems strange to be so simple at such a price!

Barrio Las Colinas, Bogota.

historical consciousness possesses a present and a future dimension. Fluctuating temporal contexts force an explicitness of the temporal equation upon each architectural decision: to what extent should the past be respected and to what extent should the future be established as a reference? In an evolving country, the natural and artificial environments and past and future are superimposed in a unique context that informs daily life. Even though contextual "anxiety" is nowadays universal, in confronting specific spatial and temporal circumstances this architecture becomes unintentionally "Colombian."

## The European and Latin American City

The European city is consolidated and circumscribed; it is an historical inheritance and as such it cannot be touched by speculative interests. The image of a communitarian life exists and although it is less intense now than in the past, it maintains its public spaces and places where socialization can take place. Public space is ready to welcome festivities, the act of living together; its enjoyment is blocked perhaps by other factors.

In Latin America, the contrary occurs; the population bubbles over with imagination, creativity, and festiveness but for lack of appropriate places this enthusiasm is aborted by that amorphous conglomerate which calls itself the city but which is, in fact, its antithesis. The privatization of the public sphere illustrates this; the population is dragged along by a convulsive urbanism which obeys only the laws of lustful speculation that finally determine the city's structure. Under these conditions, the community is not afforded the compensation of urban life; they are denied the possibilites of solidarity which might mitigate their poverty.

The galloping urbanization of Latin America does not produce the city, it only creates something which is heterogeneous and unstable; places of segregation and conglomerates. Within these non-places the references and

Torres del Parque, Bogota, 1969.
Approach from the north.

The architect Rogelio Salmona has attempted to synthesize the collective proposals which have surfaced in Colombia in the past decades. Although all his projects express these intentions, we will concentrate on two which are especially meaningful: the rural house next to Tabio, Cundinamarca (1978–81), and the Guest House in Cartagena (1980–81).

The house next to Tabio is a private lodging in the country. The sensual use of surfaces, the washes of natural zenithal light, and the intersecting views discovered inside the house are part of the development of an architecture of "sensorial perception." Nevertheless, these are not the factors that make it special; rather, it is the ability displayed in its contextual interpretation. The starting point for the house was four patios; this conventional

attributes of the city are lost, and there is no sense of focus around which urban life and history can crystallize. It has been forgotten that the ancient rights of the citizen begin with the right to enjoy the city, with the democratic right to live and reside in an urban community imbued with the values and resources offered by cultural exchange.

Urban space is not residual, it is not a result, but is the primordial element in the generation of architecture the goals of which are to shape pieces of the city, to lend it order, and to recuperate urban life. For this reason one of the primary specifications of Latin American architecture is the necessity of creating real space which permits the integration of communities within the city, thus harnessing the richness of the Latin American spirit which is not just disorder but represents the seed of life itself which has not yet found its form.

If we lack communitarian precedents, we must create them

Torres del Parque. Terraced gardens to the south.

type stood only as an organizing element that would then be architecturally re-elaborated: two of these patios are inside (one centrifuges the "noble" area of the house and the other the service area) and the other two are used as transitions between the tamed nature immediately within the house's domain and the outside. This transition includes other levels: the body of the house is circumscribed by a berm that is rotated 45 degrees from the house and which delineates a series of gardens around it. In order to situate the architecture in a controlled natural setting topographic changes were considered, a small lake

without allowing ourselves to be perverted by the models of American or European urban grammar. It is not sufficient for our epileptic city to be ordered "in the fashion of. . . ." We must invent, specify, create, and order spatially, using a grammar which stems from those disparate elements which constitute the references of our culture.

While the European city is a given and crystallized, the Latin American city is made every day; its physical structure is fragile. It lacks the density of important works of the European cities which permit them to more easily ameliorate the impact of bad, coarse, or insignificant architecture.

The foremost quality which our architecture should possess is that of permitting space to be appropriated by the entire community. This architecture must have a unity which transforms itself and projects a different image according to the place in the city from which it is viewed. Architecture should be a surprise because of the richness of its forms, its material, the variety of its spaces, and because of the incidence of light and the landscape upon it. One should be able to discover it for it is more beautiful when discovered than when it imposes itself.

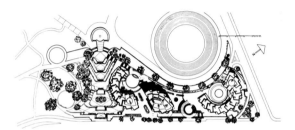

Torres del Parque. Site Plan.

Torres del Parque. View from a balcony.

was built, and certain plantings made. All this was then inscribed in the prairie, whose landscape closes in the distance at the Andes Mountains. These different "distances" are expressed in the "tentacles" that the house extends in communication with the outside: the pergolas, the exterior continuation of the living and dining rooms, the flat roof terraces, and the windows. All of these establish a qualitatively different means of refering alternately to close or far-off landscapes. This hierarchical relationship between architecture and the natural environment expresses, in a metaphorical way, the situation of a country that has not transformed its geography, where man has only exercised his civilizing effect in circumscribed and disconnected areas. The coexistence of tamed and wild, cultivated and primitive, up-to-date and anachronistic is a Latin American trait which stands in contrast to the complete landscape

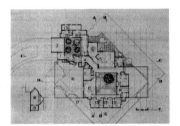

Residence. Tabio, Cundinamarca, 1978-81. Plan.

Residence. Tabio. Interior.

that is the result of continuous cultural elaboration on the European continent. Here the case is one of construction of a new cultural landscape.

The Guest House in Cartagena includes the renovation of the Colonial munitions store of the Manzanillo fort (restored by the architect German Tellez) and a house to accommodate official guests. In designing the house Salmona used local stone and brick vaults. Moving through the house the senses are enveloped by contrasts of light, diagonal views which sometimes open onto the cityscape, and the manifold sounds of water from the sea, the fountains,

Residence. Tabio. View from the lake.

and the narrow streams in the patios and corridors. The munitions store was converted into a dining room and is connected by a ramp to the main house, which was intentionally kept at a lower level so that the armory would stand out from the whole. The enclosing stone walls refer to the walled city of Cartagena and the patios and other formal motifs belong to domestic Cartagenian tradition. Above this analytical contextualization the true integration of old and new architecture is achieved in the interpretation of the basic premises of the natural and historical Cartagenian landscape. In rediscovering what Arabs already knew when building in the tropics, what Spaniards found out upon arriving to the New World, what Cartagenians had elaborated throughout centuries, Salmona succeeds in creating in an architecture that seems to have always been there; one that belongs naturally to its place. This

Guest House. Cartegena, 1980-81.
Ramp and view of old arsenal.

Guest House. Cartegena, 1980-81. South view.

Fortress of Cartegena.

relative atemporality is what allows the impression of a contextuality which surpasses a simple mimesis of the surroundings or a rational decoding of traditional typologies. It is a synthetic contextuality that partially looks back but simultaneously projects itself into the future, adapting to the present landscape while transforming it, and where architecture and nature combine in a unique cultural project. That is the secret of its radical belonging.

Guest House. Cartegena, 1980-81. View of the ramp.

Guest House. Cartegena, 1980-81. Main court.

Guest House.
Patio del Roble Morado.

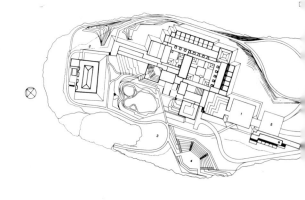

Guest House. Cartegena, 1980-81. Salon.

Guest House. Stair off of Patio del Roble Morado.

Guest House. Passage between Library and Patio del Roble Morado.

Sankai Juku Dance Caravan, Edinburgh. 1981-83.

506.   However, the Japanese
are fascinated by the inner relation of shapes.
They love non-Euclidean concepts, especially
topology.

507.   Japan allows for many
gods. When one god fails or rests, other gods go
to work.

日本人にとっては、ナンセンスも重要なセンスで、ナンセンスのないところにセンスはないと信じられている。人々は時として、真剣にナンセンスを実践するが、それはナンセンスを装ったセンスであって、アメリカによくある、むき出しの芸のないナンセンスではない。また逆に真剣なセンスを装った本当のナンセンスもある。

これらの努力は全て、この世は仮の住まいと考える伝統的感受性の中で、自からの存在を叫び表出するよりは、知的なゲームの一員として同胞に認められようとする努力である。その意味では、日本人は、伝統的に、一貫して、水準の高いポスト・モダニストだったと云える。

一九八七年夏　モントークにて

〔未元〕

311. Descarte caught a big "I" in order to avoid the catastrophy of Nihilism. While in Japan, Dogen ended up with the Nothing of Nothingness. Dogen built up his system of firm belief on the fact that nothing exists. Everything exists only in one's mind. Within this limit, I am what I am. A dog is what a dog is. A pine tree is what a pine tree is.

Metaphysics becomes (super)realism in Japan.

403. Therefore, man-made, rigid principles are regarded as dangerous.

404. For the same reason, individual leadership is regarded as dangerous. Japan is a society that respects one step forward by a hundred people more than one hundred steps by a single genius.

421. Things are not connected by logical lines but are allocated places and grouped on an open field.

504. Geometry is a beautiful toy block for Japanese. However, it is not any part of the supreme truth, nor is it perfection.

505. Euclidean perfections—a circle, a square, or a triangle—are not beauty, nor perfection. Geometrical perfection means:

      boring,

      artless,

      stupid,

      childish.

**"Because I think, I exist" is Descarte's foundation. Descarte found "I," but Dogen, the greatest Zenist, said: "Because I think, this is thinking. I exist only in thinking. Thinking is not actual. That is why I don't exist. There is actually nothing but nothing."**

された。つまり浮世に働き疲れた男達の遊び
につきあう洗練された芸と教養が高い水準で
要求された。

芭蕉が欠如の美学を持ち込む以前の俳句や
連歌、あるいは利休が死をもって完成した佗
茶以前の茶の湯も、もともとは、この「浮き
世」を有意義に過ごす知的ゲームであり、そ
のように定かならぬ世界の連帯感であった。
彼等は、狭い空間に場を限り、誰れにも分
る極限的に洗練された約束の中で、い
かに深い意味を喚起しえるかを競いあった。
5—7—5という節約された文字空間の中
に人生の一片を封じこめるゲームは、今日で
も幾千万かの人口が、日常の生活の中で、ノー
トに書き残しては、新聞や職場で比べあって
いる。それは、おそらくアメリカにおけるク
ロスワード・パズルと同じ位の人口と熱意だ
ろう。クロスワード・パズルは単純に機能的
な時間つぶしだが、日本の俳句は、はるかに
人生をかけた知的なゲームである。

日本の建築雑誌に月々あきることなく繰り
返される様々な風変りな建築デザインの多く
は、この俳句のように、狭い空間で、施主の
プログラムという制約の中で、それ以上の、
あるいはそれ以外の意味やイメージを喚起す
る相互連帯ゲームである。
アメリカのデザイナーのように「表現」を
おもてに立て、それに従って状況を整理する
のではなく、与えられた条件の中で、別な「遊
び」を行う日本人の逃避的傾向は、「遊び」と
いうには、あまりに真剣で求道的であり、損得
の感覚を越えている。今や日本の若い建築家
は、この高貴な遊びの兵士になった観がある。

日本の建築や庭園の多くは、このような制
約の中での意味の喚起、気ずかれないトリッ
ク、見えるものと見えないものの重ね絵、奇
妙で手の込んだディテールといったもので満
ちている。ブルーノ・タウトの再発見した桂
離宮は、機能主義、近代主義風に観るよりは、
様々なトリックに満ちた貴族的な読み物とし
て読まれるべきだろう。

203. The Japanese love tension, especially tension of the mind. Americans prefer relaxation. American athletes, for example a pitcher at a baseball game, often chew gum. That would never happen in Japan. The American player endeavors to keep himself cool and rational when his muscles are tense, while the Japanese counterpart tries hard to move the air with tension from his mind/spirit.

301. Description is a secondary layer of being that has become independent of the foundation. It is now mountainous and manipulative. You can create any "thing" by manipulating this man-made layer.
It is often called imagination.

303. In the West, when you fail to describe, things fail to exist—In the East, when you fail to describe, things emerge.

307. The full moon is the symbol of the existence of non-existence, which the existence of actuality (the sun) supports.

308. Darkness (or lightlessness) is the master that is illuminated by light.

309. Nothingness is the matter that allows existence to be.

Sankai Juku Dance Caravan.
Parc Guell, Barcelona. 1983.

101. There is no doubt that the Japanese have a strong tendency toward nothingness, or dematerializing.

102. Or, Japanese abhor the material presence.

103. I am not certain that Western society really has the ability for compassion with the intangible, such as void space.

105. It is often said that there exists a certain wall between subject and object in Western perception, and not in Oriental perception.

106. Oriental people, or at least I, don't see a clear separation between the self and the other—between self and the object.

107. It seems to me that the Westerner is less capable of becoming other.

110. It seems horrible to the Westerner to transcend the ego and become unified with something unshaped, such as space or time, while it is really a "breeze" to Oriental people.

の覚悟をもって成すという真剣な清らかさこそ、日本の芸能を洗練させてきた主要なモーメントであった。

仏教によって書き換えられた負の浄＝「無常観」を再否定することなく受け入れるところに「遊」の思想が生れる。

この無常の世界観は、初期の軍事的氏族の一方の頭であった平家の興亡を描いた『平家物語』や、内戦にあけくれる世に絶望し、牛車に載せて移せる程に小さいあばら家をもって山中に住み思索を続けた鴨長明の『方丈記』の冒頭にいかんなく表現されている。

祇園精舎の鐘の声、諸行無常の響あり。娑羅双樹の花の色、盛者必衰の理を顕す。奢れる者久しからず、ただ春の夜の夢の如し。……猛き人も遂には滅びぬ。ひとへに風の前の塵に同じ。

『平家物語』

ゆく河のながれはたへずして、しかももとの水にあらず。よどみにうかぶうたかたはかつきえかつむすびて、ひさしくとどまる事なし。………朝に死に、夕に生きるならひ、ただ水の泡にぞ似りける。不知、うまれ死ぬる人いずかたよりきたり、いずかたへか去る。

鴨長明 『方丈記』

この世を無常な「浮き世」と受けとるところから、全ては仮の宿での「遊」と考える態度が生れる。

日本の場合は、この快楽主義的態度は、物欲・性欲を満たす方向よりは、精神的な遊戯性の方向に傾いている。外国に喧伝され、好奇の関心となった吉原に代表される遊廓は、日本の家庭構造、そして多分家屋構造の欠陥を補うヘルス・キッチンの公的制度化だったが、芸者という呼び名が示すように、そこに働く上級の女性には、歌や舞の芸能が必須と

62. Fireworks in Japan are released one at a time with an interval between each to appreciate the *Ma* as well as the beauty of each. Fireworks in America are displayed as many as possible at one time to fill up the dark sky.

It is a power show.

65. There is no rule to *Ma*. But there are principles; contrasts—large and small, heavy and light, dark and light, tension and relaxation, long and short, the expected and the unexpected, continuity and discontinuity.

69. *Ma* is decisive. If the *Ma* is miscalculated, you might get killed.

73. *Ma* is not uniquely Japanese, or anything mysterious at all. It is very common and very universal.

74. The Japanese can, however, claim that they put this psychosomatic time/space in the midst of their art. They have polished it. They have produced arts from these most fundamental, common materials of the human mind. They raise *Ma* to its culmination.

83. The Japanese can also claim a unique development in their reversal of figure/ground relations. They have developed the art of ground while the rest of the world has concentrated on the art of figure.

**A : B : A is prohibited.
It must be**

**A    Ma 1    B    Ma 2    A**

自殺や狂うことを回避するため、いにしえ
の詩人は旅に出た。
西行、芭蕉。

西行は娘をけとばして旅に出たことで、芭
蕉は道ばたに捨てられ助けを求めて泣く赤子
を、助けひろわず立ち去ったことで、人道主
義者から非難されているが、人間のしがらみ
から絶対的に自由であろうとする彼等の死に
もの狂いの浄への志向を読みとることができ
る。

また童話の主人公として愛されている一休
と呼ばれる僧は、自己の純粋にして自由な魂
を守り抜くために、男色、放蕩、殺生を尽く
してみた。

芸術家の狂気に東西の違いはないが、日本
では、その狂気が神聖なもの、高貴なものと
受けとらえている。

一徹な狂気と清く散ることへの共感は、江
戸時代の古典的な仇討劇「四十七士」の物語
にいかんなく表現されている。これは、いわ
れなき理由から殺された(と彼等が規定する)
主人の仇を討った後、四十七人の武士が一人
一人、白衣に着がえて、自から腹をかき切っ
て死んで行く国民的悲劇で、高貴な人々が次
々に死んで行くギリシア悲劇のカタルシスに
似ていて、かつては、新年を迎える時に観た
ものだが、今は、ヴェートーベンの「第九シ
ンフォニー」の合唱部を聴くという不思議な
習慣によってとってかわられた。

一畳半の茶室は、常に死の覚悟と共にあっ
た詩人の狂気をもってはじめて可能な、否定
の上の肯定の透し影の美である。
彼は、常時、死の清浄の中で、生の中で尚
残り得る価値は何か、全てを消しても尚残り
得る美は何かをさぐっていたに違いない。
だから、全ての茶会は一期一会—人との出
会は一回をもって最後とする覚悟をもって成
される自然にして完全な美でなければならな
いという思想—を旨とした。
たかだか湯をわかし、茶を点て、これを客
に贈り、客はこれを受けることを、一期一会

---

46. In Japan, there does not exist an unyielding independent self. There does not exist a true individual, or expression. The bond is in the void between things, events, and people. This is what is called *Ki* (psyche), *Ba* (field) or *Ma* (time and space between). The art of manipulating these bonds is called *Hara* (belly, or navel). Politics, manipulation of others' powers, is called *Hara-gei* (the art of belly).

48. Signification: in a word, the negation of expression. Japanese do not know the concept of ex-pression in the Western sense. It is parallel to the fact that we've never known true individualism.

49. Expression is a process of casting outward what you conceive (inside). When you seek to express, you have to recognize what you conceive, then articulate the whole into elements of expression and reconstruct them into another perceivable whole for the audience or receiver. The expressed is a description of the conceived. This Western process is not a congruent copy of the thing itself. It is a second layer of the world. Japanese distrust this process and avoid it.

50. Haiku is one of the best examples of the abandonment of expression. It is a body of im-pression. Haiku limits its means to convey its message:

51. Without the receiver's ability to extract meaning, there is almost nothing significant. Each receiver is required to create their own picture. This is a test for the receiver. Receivers are then required to establish the value context for this scene.

61. The Japanese tend to believe that a purified form can convey more message. They polish shapes with the highest sensitivity and craftsmanship. During this process the disparity between form and message becomes greater and greater. This is one source of Japanese mysticism. The Japanese tend to forget the fact that forms in art are the means by which one conveys what one thinks. Avoiding descriptive effort and polishing media creates a better message only in its own culture.

**Haiku:**

Fu ru i ke     ya
1 2 3 4     5

[An] old pond     !

Ka wa zu     To bi ko mu
1   2   3      4  5  6  7

[A] frog jumps into

Mi zu     no     o to
1   2      3      4  5

water of sound.

私が「狂」と名付ける性向を表現している。

利休は、この極小の、百姓の小屋を模してそまつを装った、神経と趣味が気ずかざる仕方で高密度に張りめぐらされている空間をもって、時の将軍秀吉の豪華壮大な宮殿に対抗した。

この天才的芸術家と、百姓の息子から権力と富の頂点に登った天才的軍事家・政治家は、芸の力をもって結ばれたが、この危いバランスは、将軍の不信と芸術上の嫉妬をかって、利休の切腹となって終った。

岡倉天心の『茶の本』は、この利休の最後の茶の会の美しさを描いている。
それは、日本人が、清く散ることの美しさをいかに賞讃するかをいかんなく表現している。

日本の国花は桜であり、それは形あるものが、汚れる前に、美しく散ることへの尊敬を表現している。それは神風パイロットのシンボルであり、三島由紀夫の自作自演の切腹の思想と美学である。
これは全て、日本芸術の狂への志向である。

「狂」は、浄、つまり生命の本来的な姿が抑圧されたところに、それをなお求めてやまない精神に顕われる。
真に優れた仕事を残した日本の芸術家は、自殺するか、早死するか、精神分裂症になっている。思いつくままの例ー

自殺ー三島由紀夫（切腹）
川端康成（ノーベル賞受賞作家　ガス自殺）
芥川龍之介（睡眠薬自殺）
太宰治（入水自殺）

早死ー宮沢賢治
石川啄木
中原中也
立原道造（詩人建築家）

分裂ー夏目漱石
芥川龍之介

32.   Hegel's phenomenology starts with the examination of "here."  But the Japanese mind starts with the farthest horizon, such as the universe, the world, the twentieth century.

33.   The themes of Tange's architecture are good examples of this mental attitude, such as "World Peace" for the Hiroshima Peace Center; "Economic Growth and Take Off" for the 1960 Tokyo project; "Information Society" for the Yamanishi Broadcasting Center.

34.   Compare him with Kahn. Kahn also was conceptual.  But he always stuck to the design object, as in asking "What is School?" or "What is House?"

35.   Tange questioned the major context in the field, Kahn questioned the essence of the design object.

38.   The competition in Japanese art is a race to conserve expression.

39.   Japanese art is not individual works but communal endeavours of a society—an individual way of expression versus the expression of an individual.

42.   The Japanese don't have the capital "I" (the individual ego).  The Japanese "I" is "i" or " . " or even (  ).

多分に浄の概念に影響を受けている日本の禅は、この仏教的無常の無を、はっきりと、再び、自然の恒常の無として定立し直し、この絶対的無の上に絶対的有を定立し直した。サルトルに先だつ七〇〇年前、道元は、恒常的で絶対的な無の上に、相対的にして絶対的な自己定位の理論をうちたてた。これは「浄」の思想の絶対的表現である。

「わび」「さび」という、今では外国人にもなじみになった日本伝統芸術の中心概念は、日本本来の清浄で健康な無の概念を、一度仏教の無常観で否定化し、それを再び絶対的なものとして肯定し直した禅の思想に色濃くそまっている。

「わび」も「さび」も欠如の美学で、欠けたることの美しさを言う。「わび」は物質的欠如感、「さび」は心理的欠如感を言う。いずれも、否定の上の肯定という二重の価値の重ね焼き構造が、世界に、言葉にはしづらい奥ゆきをもたらしている。

それは、次の藤原定家の歌に示される情景と、これを眺める詩人の心象に代表されると言われてきた。

見渡せば
花ももみじもなかりけり
浦のとまやの
秋の夕暮れ

あるいは、もっとも決定的な瞬間としては、芭蕉の次の俳句

古池や
蛙飛びこむ
水の音

がよく例として挙げられる。
いずれも、ほとんど何もないところに、わずかなことが起ることの響きの美しさを歌ったものである。

「わび」「さび」の建築的な結晶は、千利休の一畳半の茶室である。これは、日本人の内にやみがたく存在する極限を究めようとする、ものである。

29. In Japan the most esteemed achievement is not to pile up money or possess power. The more serious competition among people focuses on how deep, how high, how far one can reach in the everlasting values—aesthetics and ethics. This endeavor is called *Michi* or *Doh*—the Way or the Path.

## ON THE DIFFERENCE BETWEEN PLANT AND ANIMAL

**The West is an animal existence**
                    **—the East is a plant existence.**

**The animal is active**
                    **—the plant is passive.**

**The animal moves toward what he wants**
        **—the plant waits for the proper situation**
                    **to obtain what she wants.**

                    **The plant cultivates the**
                    **hostile land.**

**The animal must be absolute**
            **—the plant must be relative.**

**The animal thinks**
                    **—the plant senses.**

26. The Katsura Detached Palace holds the symbolic position of this tradition. It was the retreat of a heartbroken prince who lost his kingdom. The disappointed prince therefore designed his own Eden outside of Kyoto, a place well known for its heavenly and beautiful moon. The story and image of this Buddhist paradise was created and symbolically represented by trees, water, and stones.

27. The pleasure quarters for men, the *Iyu-kaku*, were regarded as the place where men polish the art of play. Architecture there explicitly displays the joy of color, shapes, and materials.

Salk Institute. La Jolla, California.
Louis Kahn.

茶の湯にしても、俳句にしても、能にして
も、ぎりぎりの立て組みにまで還元されてい
る。

西洋から輸入された「技術」が日本におい
て、いよいよ精度を上げ、効率をあげ、小型
化されて行くのも同じ浄の精神的仕組から来
るものである。

伊勢神宮は、「浄」の概念が、建築的に具体
化された姿と考えてよい。
私は、国粋主義者ではないが、伊勢神宮の
美しさと力強さにいつも驚く。
それは静かに美しい。
それは死して静かなのではなく、健康にし
て静かである。

多くもなく、少くもない。
それは合理的であり同時に象徴的である。
それは完璧に構築的（テクトニック）であ
ると同時に完璧に建築的（アーキテクトニッ
ク）である。

この建築の様式である高床式の住居や倉、
厚いかやぶき屋根、それをおさえる千木や勝
男木なども、やはり輸入品で、きっと東南ア
ジアのどこかにあるのだろうと思うが、重要
なのは、その雑多な構法的源流や象徴体系を
一つにあみ上げ、洗い清め、その生命的な本
質だけを浮び上らせた、その異常にして健康
な精神の姿である。

この伊勢神宮に比べると、日本建築史の大
半を占める寺院建築は、陰気で、重々しく、
美しくない。私には不浄なものに見える。
仏教は、中国の壮大な思想と制度と建築と
都市を日本にもたらしたが、以来、日本人は
自然にのっとった明るさを失った。
浄は自然の無の概念と結びつき、有機的な
無と有のサイクルを大切にするが、仏教（少
くとも日本の仏教）は、この自然界の健康な
休息としての無を、湿った陰々たる人間界の
無常感に置きかえてしまった。仏教は、日本
に色彩と救済思想をもたらすと同時に、苦悩
と無常観をもたらした。

21. For those who cannot possess *Jyo* or *Kyo*, there remains the way of *Iyu* (playfulness).

22. *Iyu* in Japan is not always pleasure or leisure. *Iyu* is also a serious quest towards a way of life. Isozaki is heavily tinted with the concept of *Iyu*, though often he shows traces of *Kyo*.

23. Both insanity and playfulness of artists are common in the West, too. The difference is that the West appreciates the content pursued. In Japan we appreciate the attitude itself more.

24. Things of *Iyu* are described with the word *Omoshiro* (interesting). In Japan being interesting dominates being right. The value scale is thus

to be beautiful (*Jyo*)
to be true (*Kyo*)
to be interesting (*Iyu*)
to be right.

25. The attitude of *Iyu* is fixed in the social mechanism that embodies the philosophical tradition of *Ukiyo* (a floating or depressing world) or *Muzjo* (a world of uncertainty). This tradition is believed to have come from the Buddhist belief that this world is a temporal and transitional one. Taoist and Zenist thought also tells us that nothing is absolute, that everything is relative.

*"Where there is no nonsense, there is no sense."*
—Unknown

Wall at Ryoan-Ji, 1985.

な森林と潤沢な清流、温和で変化に富む日本の自然の中で純化したものであろう。

浄の概念は、本来自然の内に存在する生命の生成、成長、合理化を促進する環境の状態で、それに反するもの及び状態、不自然、不合理、環境汚染等は不浄と呼ばれる。

この清浄感は、一次的には物的なものとして表現されるが、一層重大なのは、内面的な清浄である。日本人が修業を好むのは、秋の空のように澄きった、そよ風のようにさわやかな、清流の如く濁りなくとどこうらない「心」を得るためなのである。

「浄」の概念は「正」しさの概念と結びついているが、それは理性的合理にもとずく正義や教学とは違って、「自然」との合同的合致を云う。

詩歌の言葉は、言霊と云って、自然の霊を呼びさますものと考えられ尊敬をもって取扱われるが、理屈を組み上げて自己の立場や利益を守るための言葉は不浄と考えられる。

理屈、言訳、説明、自己主張は日本社会では大変嫌われる。すべからく自然は明らかであり一切の説明や言訳は不要でありムダであり、汚染である。それをあえて行うのは不浄であり「美しくない」。

日本人は、説明が必要なのは、何かが明らかでなく、従って何かが間違っていると考える。

社会的な不浄感は、後に儒教と結びついて、「恥」という形で社会心理化され、人々はこれをつぐなう為に、自から腹をかき切ることを儀式化した。人は自からが自からに与える苦痛に堪えることで自からの不浄を断ち、同時にそれを宿した自からの身を社会から消すことによって、社会の浄をとりもどした。

日本芸術は、内容的には全て外国から輸入されたものであるが、形式的・機能的には、日本人特有の「浄への志向」によって洗い清められ、無理と無駄が除去され、人間的な混濁のない、自然そのものに還元されている。

19. Inch by inch, foot by foot, like nature, Rikyu's design keeps diverting from itself, reserving the conclusion for the final destination in the infinite. Rikyu's imagination must have solved thousands of simultaneous equations to find the equilibrium among millions of variables in this microcosmos: textures, colors, shapes of elements, light and shadow, even scratches on the walls, utensils, connotations and ritual rules, customs, functions and constructions.

20. It was beautiful for Rikyu to suddenly terminate his own life. The sudden death is the most vivid moment of life and the very catalyst against the gradual looseness and decomposition (of life). This death makes the calculation of life simplest and the priority clearer.

*Lying sick on a journey,*
*My dreams are still wandering*
*on withered fields.*

Basho's haiku on the verge of passing away.

15. "Truth" lies just behind beauty in Japan. The very truth comes to *Kyo*. Artists of *Kyo* traveled, died young, or committed suicide: Saigyo (a monk poet), Basho (a haiku master of the nineteenth century), Rikyu (a teamaster of the nineteenth century who committed *hara-kiri*), Akutagown (a twentieth century novelist who committed suicide), Takuboku and Kenji (twentienth century poets who died young).

16. There is a sparkling glimpse of truth (in the tea room by Rikyu, the haiku by Basho, and the children's story by Kenji) which can be seen through the eyes of people of *Kyo*.

17. The tea room is an architecture of *Kyo*. It is improper to analyze it, though it is not impossible. Its ideograms might be read as the House of Pleasure, the House of Personal Taste, or the Odd Fate House. It is an absolutely arbitrary world of personal taste, in which the masters competed to achieve the highest order of harmony.

18. A different insanity, which has eyes to examine a 0.1 millimeter detail, is necessary to analyze Rikyu's insanity. Rikyu's tea room shows a concealed insanity. Nothing is unusual there except its extreme smallness. It is extraordinarily ordinary, the most artfully artless, as natural as nature. Nothing is formally concluded—no symmetry, no repetition. It manifests the idea that completion is death, that repetition is sabotage.

自国にいるときも、外国人が驚くほど高価で清潔なものを身につけている。それは経済的な豊かさである以上に内的規範に命じられる限りない進行なのである。

彼等はいわしのかんづめのような通勤列車にもめげず、母や妻が毎朝磨いてくれるピカピカの靴をはき、おろしたてのようなスーツを着ているし、アメリカの雨に比べたら遥かにやさしい雨にも濡れまいと努力する。彼等にとって、それは靴がいたむからとか、クリーニング代がかさむという功利的な理由からではなく、ほこりが靴につくこと、スーツが雨に濡れることは「不浄」つまり「浄」が犯されることであり、いむべきことだからなのである。

多くの宗教団体が、掃除を修業の重要な徳目としているし、小学校から高校に到る義務教育期間中、生徒は自らの教室のみならず、廊下、庭、窓ガラス、さらに便所に到るまで掃除の義務を課せられ、それを怠ることは罰則をまぬがれない。それは人件費節約以上に人格修養の意味が深いからだ。

家の内で靴をぬぐことは、日本の生活習慣の著しい特色だが、これは単純に家の中にほこりを入れないとか、いたみやすいタタミを守るといった物理的な理由でなく、「外」は不浄、「内」はそれから守られた「浄」でなければならないという精神的な内在的規範で、それが犯されると、西洋人が嘘をついた時に感じるような罪の意識に似たものを感じるのである。

人格を形容する場合も、「清潔な人」「高潔な人」といった表現が使われる。政治という最も汚れた世界でも「清潔な政治」が叫ばれ、ロッキード・スキャンダルで時の首相が逮捕された時は、「みそぎの政治」が提唱された。「みそぎ」とは、不浄を清め、再び浄の世界に戻る儀式である。

このように病的に内在化している日本人の清浄への指向は、神道あるいは神道を産んだものに由来する。それは何か分らないが、水稲を携えて、いずこからか日本にやって来た支配民族が、彼等のアニミズムを、広大深奥

09. *Jyo* is embodied architecturally in the Ise Shrine. Tange's work before the Expo shows traces of *Jyo*. Kahn and Mies have a similar quality. Shinohara and Ando started their resistance with *Jyo*. Their great effort is to keep away stained ideas, stained attitudes, stained culture.

12. The world of *Jyo* is a pre-logos world. A closed self is regarded as an unfortunate disease. Self-consciousness in a stable fortress fighting with other fortresses will not be allowed to exist. The man-made principles of offense and defense are of no use.

Fresh Eels. Japanese Coast, 1985.

13. The state of *Jyo* can be described by the word beautiful. Beauty is the very top in the heirarchy of Japanese values.
To be beautiful doesn't mean visual or audible "handsomeness," nor formal perfection, but instead, beauty is the unspoiled intention and dedication behind the presentation. Visual harmony and formal perfection is just additional proof.

14. In the actual society, for the artist who does not possess this impossible *Jyo*, there remain two choices. One is the way of *Kyo* (insanity) where they shall quest for the goal without compromise. The other is *Iyu* (the way of playfulness) where they accept the status quo.

**Example: toro and hamachi for sashimi must be the freshest tuna and yellowfish. But they will be deprived of the original meaning as the meat of fish. They are not a diet food as Americans appreciate sushi, either. In the most extreme meaning, they are selected as materials to welcome the guest. They become the material to celebrate this occassion with treasures from the sea.**

## 浄・狂・遊

工藤 国雄

日本の芸術家は、古来、三つの目標を追求して来た。

それらは、「浄」、「狂」、「遊」という三つの漢字で規範化できる。

日本語の含みを考えず、字義通り訳せば、"Purity." "Insanity." "Playfulness." となる。

そして、この三つのベクトルの初点に「無」がある。

「浄」という概念は、芸術用語として使われたことがない。日常生活でも、時たま御不浄という言葉が使われる位に、今日ではあまり使われない。その概念は「清」という漢字でおき換えられ、その意味するところも、清潔もしくは衛生に近くなっている。

この「浄」を依持したり回復するために、今日でも、正月に「しめなわ」を張ったり、角力の力士が「塩」をまいたりするが、若い世代は、その由来する意味を知らない。

「浄」は概念としても儀式としても完全に忘れ去られているが、それは日本人の病的な潔癖感として日常化している。

ニューヨークで日本からの旅行者を見わけるコツはそのはきだめの鶴にも似た清潔な服装と新しい靴である。彼等は心象的に、外の国に、着古した服と靴では上れない。それは礼儀に反するし、人の道に反する。

01. There are three ultimate destinations which the Japanese have quested after in aesthetics and ethics since the beginning of their history. These absolutes are *Jyo*, *Kyo*, and *Iyu*, literally translated as purity, insanity, and playfulness, respectively. The quest for *Jyo* is the strongest current that dictates the conscience of the Japanese people.

02. *Jyo* is an unstained state of things, in life and mind. An order of unpolluted nature and innocent life. Philosophically, it comes directly from the Shinto, Japan's native religion. *Jyo* derives from the purifying function of nature which protects and fosters the well-being of life—the cycle of birth and rebirth.

03. In the world of *Jyo*, expression in the Western sense is abhorred. Human desires and thoughts are seen as pollutions of nature.

04. In order to maintain and restore this state of *Jyo*, people burn away the "stained" by acts of fire; or they throw it into the clean stream; or they bury it in the ground and spray salt over it.

05. …Innocent children, fresh snow, virginity, the first day of the year, untouched forests…

06. It is related to the fact that the Japanese try to be meticulously clean. They feel themselves stained by a single drop of rain or by the slightest dust on their shoes. The raised wooden floor and the intricate custom of taking off one's shoes are physical expressions of this belief.

Taxi Driver. Tokyo, 1985.

Purity

Insanity

Playfulness

Kunio Kudo

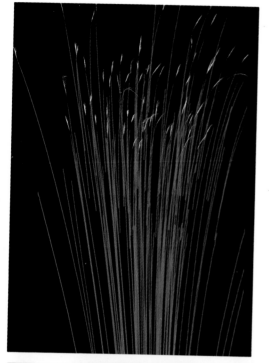

# St. Martin

"*I did not move to St. Martin to live a guarded life or as if I had expected of nature any revelations. If you live in the countryside it is good to know ahead of time what you want to do there. The everyday living in the country and the work of a sculptor are actually very close. I have found in St. Martin the conditions which are the most favorable for me. I have excellent working facilities on the ground floor which leads to a big inside court. I have enough material in hand, material I never could get living in the city. I am able to acquire techniques of construction and trade which are almost forgotten and the location of this property which is at my disposal is just ideal for my projects. Also, in such a surrounding, times are quieter and one learns to take it easier with the days. One can sense that time is a working material like mud, wood or metal.*"[1]*

**-Walter Pichler**

Walter Pichler's earliest work was embedded in an explicit critique of the modern urban environment. In one of his first gallery shows in Vienna in 1963, with Hans Hollein, Pichler exhibited a series of drawings of compact underground cities. Overtly abstract and sculptural, they posed a debilitating blow to the bourgeois conception of the city. They initiated a desire to reintegrate the form of the city within the folds of the great earth itself. These later trans-

Ruderer, 1978                    *Rower, 1978*

Ein und derselbe, l986                    *One and the Same, 1986*

Frontispiece:

Haus für den Großen und den Kleinen Wagen, 1974    *House for the Large and Small Wagon, 1974*

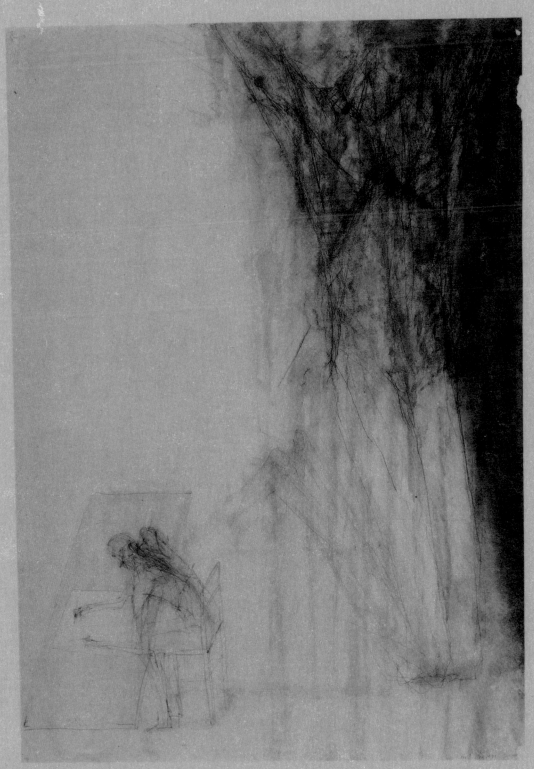

Hängender und Zeichner, 1979                    *Hanging and Drawing , 1979*

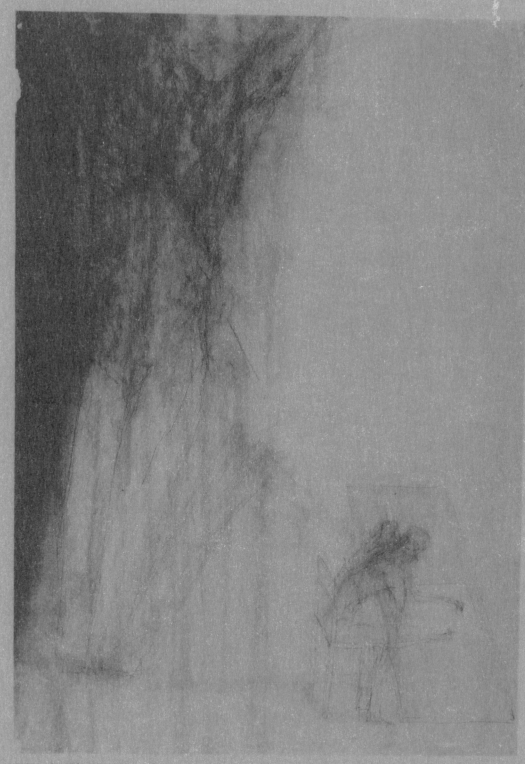

Hanging and Drawing, 1979

Hängender und Zeichner, 1979

Stausee, Kupferhaus und Boot, Grundriß, 1986

*Pond, Copperhouse and Boat, Plan, 1986*

formed into a series of foreboding, yet exquisite, sculptures made of poured concrete and formed steel. It is here that the first trace of Pichler's interest in joinery and details manifests itself. The poured concrete replaces the earth of the drawings, the formed steel becomes the replica of the city; the tense connection between the two signals the scope of meaning residing in the detail.

Pichler gradually began moving away from such explicitly urban critiques toward an investigation centered on the individual's relationship to various forms of modern technology and communications. Beginning with his *Intensive Box* of 1967, in which a bulbous room contains all the necessary artifacts of modern urban life—a chair, a TV, a light fixture, and climate control—Pichler produced a series of grossly erotic and exaggerated pieces that serve to remind the viewer of the alienating and hostile effects that technologies impose on the body. Having discovered through these investigations the limits of technology, Pichler immersed himself in his Catholic roots and began a series of works grounded in religious notions of sacrifice and pain as experienced by the body both in life and in death. The body no longer remains a subject governed by the forces of an alien technology; it now subjects the world and forms around it to the specific demands of its own gestures, its own memories, its own emotions. Through a number of ritualistic performance works, Pichler discovers and promotes this body as the "degree-zero" of meaning, as the locus and generator of all physical forms and as the warehouse of

Stausee, Kupferhaus, Seitenansicht, 1986

*Pond, Copperhouse, Side View, 1986*

Coat, 1982

Coat, 1982

Stausee, Kupferhaus, Vorderansicht, 1986                    *Pond, Copperhouse, Front View, 1986*

the human spirit. Returning to drawing and sculpture, Pichler finds within this privatized body a means to escape the abstraction of his earlier work; his form of expression becomes more specific as it begins to resonate with levels of progressive intensity. One senses an expansion of knowledge occurring, as the drawings, rendered with a new passion, attain a greater density of resolution. Increasingly unable to reconcile the disjunctive realities of urban life with the implications and demands that this work now suggests, Pichler finds it necessary to move to a farm in the sparsest, most isolated corner of Austria.

The farm in St. Martin can be seen as a continually evolving synthesis of his life's work. As the everyday life on a farm demands a specific set of tools and shelters for existence, Pichler obsessively begins a series of studies and sketches for wagons, mowing machines, storehouses, boats, as well as numerous individual sculptures. He follows these with exquisitely rendered studies and drawings that describe the process of their construction. Whether built to

house a specific piece, such as the house for the wagon and mowing machine, or for more general purposes such as the

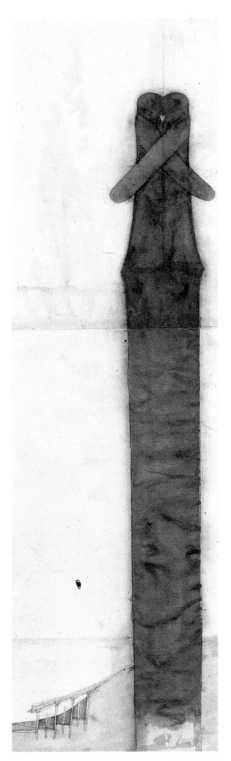

Paar, 1982                    *Pair, 1982*

Gespräch mit einem Radfahrer, 1982

*Speaking with a Bicycle Rider, 1982*

Speaking with a Bicycle Rider, 1982

Gespräch mit einem Radfahrer, 1982

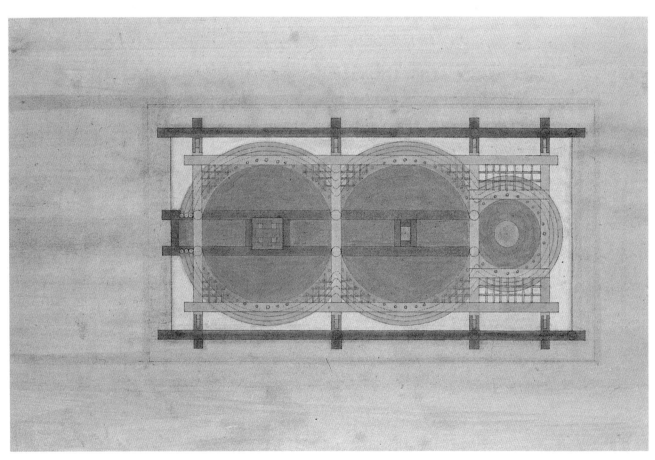

Lehmhaus für die Paare, Grundriß, 1985

*Clayhouse for the Pair, Plan, 1985*

workshop or chapel, each addition expands on his growing understanding of the secret affinity between bodies and objects, and nature and artifice. The specificity of each new sculpture or tool he designs in turn governs the specificity of the architectonic form built to house it. Entrances and passageways reintroduce his passion for joinery through a complex articulation of hinges and thresholds. This renewed interest in the joint no longer signals his previous preoccupation with the interaction of two ultimately incompatible realities, but now reveals a structural convergence of these worlds as architectonic, natural, mechanical and anatomical systems become joyously and desperately intertwined.

There is clearly more at issue here than the mere development of an "architectonics" or a catalogue of buildings. Varying emotions, fights, gestures, ruminations, and memories surface during the making of these constructional drawings, and as with Carlo Scarpa (who had an undeniable Viennese love for the fragment and detail), their presence is never silenced. Rather, they remain so as to remind and inform Pichler of the purpose and source of that detail or form. Pichler shatters the ancient tradition of architectural representation by invading the language of public information with scenes from private life, insisting that to split the two renders them both ultimately meaningless. Unlike Laugier, whose return to the archaic only reaffirmed the abstract and grand historical forces that preoccupied the Enlightenment (reshuffling, never violating, the estab-

Lehmhaus für die Paare, Schnitt, 1985

*Clayhouse for the Pair, Section, 1985*

Die silberne Schürze meiner Mutter, 1979

*The Apron of My Mother, 1979*

Lehmhaus für die Paare, Seitenansicht, 1985

*Clayhouse for the Pair, Side View, 1985*

lished heirarchies defining Man, God, Technology and Nature), Pichler exposes the interchangibility between, and the ultimate contamination of one by any of the others. Lurking beneath the apparent simplicity and resolution of his forms, one senses a world of tension, of a system of desires

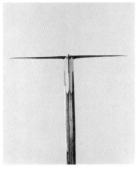

and forces all anxious to be recognized and released through the magic of sight, touch, or use. Through the rigorous application of technique and craftsmanship, and nourished by the cultivation and unleashing of a private mythology, Walter Pichler unearths the metonymic nature of all appearances.

On the Viennese avant-garde Franco Raggi remarks, "On the whole... these men offer no solutions and provide no project models...The complexity of reality is unknowable; the methodological Utopia which claims to control the connexions and causes is frustrated by the continual reproduction of relations...To recover the dimension of oneself through behavioural operations like primordial forms communicating awareness, is a characteristic common to the search for new operational spaces. The architecture of oneself before that of things."[2]

**Marwan Al-Sayed**

Lehmhaus für die Paare, Axonometrie, 1985          *Clayhouse for the Pair, Axonometric, 1985*

Lehmhaus für die Paare, Vorderansicht, 1985

*Clayhouse for the Pair, Front View, 1985*

Clayhouse for the Pair, Front View, 1985

Lehmhaus für die Paare, Vorderansicht, 1985

Schlafender,1985

*Sleeper, 1985*

Pichler

...I WAS INVITED TO JOIN A COMMUNITY
GROUP ASSEMBLING ITS FESTIVAL WAGON
AND *HARIBAN* (THE TEMPORARY ALTAR AND
GREETING PLACE FOR THE COMMUNITY)...
6 SEPT.

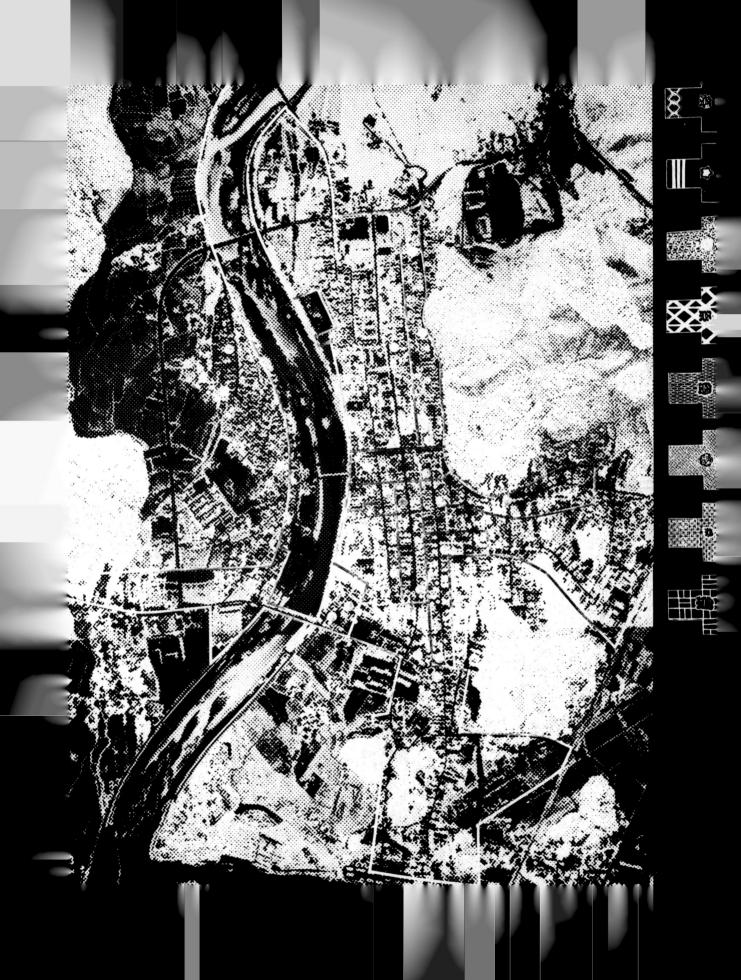

# DAS ANDERE

EIN BLATT ZUR EINFUEHRUNG
ABENDLAENDISCHER KULTUR
IN OESTERREICH: GESCHRIEBEN
VON ADOLF LOOS        I. JAHR

**Nr. 2** ENTHÄLT UNTER ANDEREM:

## ÜBER DEN GEBRAUCH DES KLOSETTPAPIERS

MODERN ODER SEZESSIONISTISCH?

ABENDLÄNDISCHE RESTE IN WIEN

## GESCHLECHTSVERKEHR ODER MASTURBATION
: ASYL FEUERSTEIN :

## TRISTAN und ISOLDE

VENEDIG IN WIEN —
EIN FAMILIENPLATZ?

## BRIEFKASTEN FÜR

## FORM
## KLEIDUNG
## WOHNUNG

## IN ALLEN TRAFIKEN 20 h

Cover of *Das Andere 2.*

Beatriz Colomina

# A d o l f   L o o s:
## *das andere*

My uncle is a watchmaker in Philadelphia, on Chestnut Street, between Eighth and Ninth streets. The location corresponds to our Karntner-strasse. When I visited him in America, he was living on Park Avenue.

His wife, my aunt, was born in America. She had a brother, Uncle Benjamin, a farmer near the city.

I was living in the house of my uncle and one day I was told that I should visit my uncle Ben and his wife, Aunt Anna. One of my cousins came with me. We took the tram and then we walked for an hour. There were many villas along the way. Charming little houses of one story with tower, gable, and veranda. They were the houses of the farmers.

My Uncle Ben was living in one of these houses. We went in and my aunt Anna was very happy to meet the "cousin from Europe"—from Austria, precisely. She had been there, many years ago, on a trip to Europe.

My aunt was wearing a cotton skirt, a white shirt, and an apron, also white. She was a slender woman, quite old, gentle, without children, with her hair parted in the center. We sat around the table for lunch; she cooked and personally served us oatmeal. Then we went to the fields to look for Uncle Ben. After a quarter of an hour we saw an old man sitting in the middle of a field peeling onions. He was wearing high boots, trousers made of raw fabric, a shirt of colored flannel, and a hat like the ones that our sea guards wear. He was Uncle Ben.

Four weeks later, the cousin who had accompanied me to see Uncle Ben died of typhoid fever. All of my aunt's relatives were expected to come. Everyone was willing to come from the countryside to bring their last greeting to their dead nephew.

Two hours before the funeral I was asked to go to the city to buy some black linens. When I sat down on the horse trolley to go back home an aged lady, elegant, all dressed in black, addressed me. I felt greatly embarrassed since I knew that she did not know me because of the fact that I hadn't met anyone during my six week stay. I was trying to explain this to her, with my limited notions of English. But she kept talking to me and finally, yes, god, it was she! Aunt Anne. The farmer, the American farmer. I tried to excuse myself by referring to her different style of dress. "Yes," she answered, "the dress is also Viennese, by Drecoll."

When we arrived at the funeral, the participants had already gathered together. I wouldn't have recognized Uncle Ben either. He was wearing a tall hard hat with a wide band on it, a distinguished redingote, and a pair of tight trousers; which I judged, in comparison with my wide trousers, out of fashion (it was 1893). Only later I knew that he was not "still" wearing tight trousers, but "already." At the time this was all for the best, for otherwise my European pride would have been totally crushed.[1]

Thus starts the first issue of *Das Andere: Journal for the Introduction of Western Culture into Austria*, the magazine that Adolf Loos published, albeit for only two issues, in Vienna in 1902-03. As with his other titles, *Spoken into the Void* and *In Spite of Everything*, Loos seems to define his object with a dialectic between presence and absence, fullness and void, a relation of difference. What is this "Other" that Loos never names? In what follows I will attempt to trace the possible meanings of the Loosian concept of *das andere*.

## 1. *Kunst und alles Andere*

*Das Andere* was published as a supplement of the magazine *Kunst, Halbmonatschrift fur Kunst und alles Andere* ("Art, Fortnightly Review of Art and all the Other"). Note that "the other" is already incorporated into the subtitle of this magazine and provides a first possible interpretation of *Das Andere*, "the other," in the subtitle of *Kunst*.

*Kunst* was edited by Peter Altenberg, a close friend of Adolf Loos and Karl Kraus. (His portrait appears in some photographs of the Kartner Bar).[2] Five issues appeared and were written entirely by Altenberg (as Loos wrote *Das Andere* and Kraus, *Die Fackel*, from 1911 on). In the first editorial note of *Kunst* Peter Altenberg writes , "Art is Art and Life is Life but to live artistically: that is the art of life." This statement indicates that the association between Loos and Altenberg was rather ambiguous; rather than attempting synthesis, Loos was determined to distinguish between Art and Life.

*Kunst* is a magazine of stories, anecdotes, curiosities, and café talk; its literary form is the *feuilleton*. In *Kunst*, aside from rather conventional artwork, one can see such things as photographs of a woman's hands alongside a poem by Peter Altenberg extolling their beauty; "artistic" objects from other cultures (that is to say, objects which, *in situ,* are precisely nonartistic but are ritual objects, objects of cult); and photographs of women on transparent colored paper. All these

KETE PARSENOW

objects stand for "the other" in the subtitle of *Kunst,* rather than the supplement *Das Andere.*

Altenberg's is a rather regressive operation. Consider, for instance, the photographs of women on transparent colored paper. This type of production is a form of representation typical of art books at the turn of the century but in *Kunst* this form is utilized to reproduce the image of women. In addition, the photographs are typographically framed, treated as paintings. This is the attempt to attribute "aura" to photography and, furthermore, to turn photography into a fetish: the photographs can be pulled out, collected.

Peter Altenberg's "other" could be said to be characterized by the object that Lacan designates with a lower case "a" as opposed to the capital "A," which stands in Lacan's writings for the *Autre,* the radical "other." The object "a" sets itself in the place of that of the "other" which cannot be glimpsed. The object "a" somewhere fills ..."the role of that which comes in (the) place of the missing partner."[3] As Jane Gallop has noted, the structure is analogous to Freud's mechanics of the fetish object: "For Freud, the fetish object appears in the place of the Mother's absent phallus (the attribute of the other which cannot be glimpsed)." Phallic sexuality is the relation to this object which obstructs and replaces the relation to the other.[4]

*Das Andere* is not "the other" in the subtitle of *Kunst* but is rather the "other" of the magazine in its entirety.

## 2. Fashion

"My uncle is a watchmaker in Philadelphia...." The most striking thing about this opening passage of *Das Andere* is Loos's attention to clothing, to fashion. But what is behind this interest? How does Loos come to fashion as a relevant topic? This interest was already manifest in the earlier series of articles published in the *Neue Freie Presse* between 1897-1900[5] and it is interesting to note that some studies of nineteenth century culture have noted a shift of attention around 1890 from the dwelling (first need after food) to clothing.[6]

This shift had to do with the emergence of metropolitan life and the abandonment of a traditional, rooted culture in the anonymity of the big city. In *"Die Grosstadt und das Geistleben"* ("The Metropolis and Mental Life"), 1903, Georg Simmel wrote: "The deepest conflict of modern man is not any longer in the battle with nature but in the one that the individual must fight to affirm the independence and peculiarity of his existence against the immense power of society, in his resistance to being levelled, swallowed up in the social-technological mechanism."[7] In his "Fashion," 1904, he wrote: "The

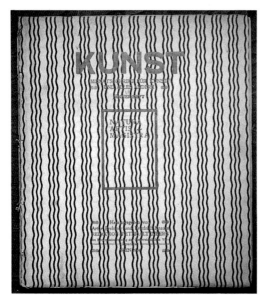

Cover of *Kunst.*

Left: Goldman and Salatsch tailoring studio.

Previous Page: Photograph of a woman on transparent paper from *Kunst.*

Photograph of a women's hand with a poem by Altenberg. From *Kunst.*

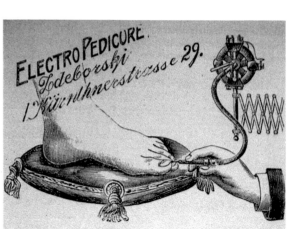

Die Schönheit des Fusses

**Der Elektropedigraph,** die sinnreichste Erfindung dieses Jahrhunderts, mit dessen Hilfe es erst ermöglicht wurde, eingewachsenen, verkrüppelten und hässlichen Nägeln ohne den geringsten Schmerz und ganz gefahrlos die schönste Form und einen herrlichen Emailglanz zu geben, wird täglich von 9–4 Uhr von dem Erfinder

**C. Zdeborski** in dessen Atelier, I. Kärntnerstr. 29, II. St.

demonstriert, wo auch die schmerzhaftesten Hühneraugen, Frostballen etc. in unerreicht dastehender Weise behandelt werden. Das Atelier ist auf das eleganteste mit Lesezimmer ganz neu eingerichtet, separiert für Herren und Damen. — Der Elektropedigraph ist ausser in meinem Atelier sonst in der ganzen Welt nicht zu sehen.

Advertisement from *Kunst*

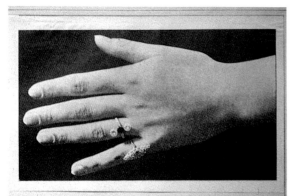

Hand, Hand, edelstes, allerzartestes Gebilde, du Kunstwerk Gottes, wann erblickt man dich?!? Jahre und Jahre sieht man Tatzen und Pratzen, plumpe, klobige Gebilde, wie von kindischen Bildnern aus widerspenstigem Fleische geformt! Wo, wo sieht man eine Hand nach Gottes Plänen, zart und beweglich, jedem Hauch des Inneren nachbebend und Seele und Geist zum zarten Ausdruck bringend in Beweglichkeiten?! Nicht schieben soll die Hand in plumpem Ausdruck an schwerbeweglichem Geiste, sondern, leicht erbebend, tanzend, das letzte körperliche Schwingen von Geist und Seele sein! O schöne, leichte, zarte, sanfte Hände, edelste Kunstwerke der Natur, wo seid ihr?! Schönen, edlen, zarten Händen soll man Altäre errichten, denn sie sind Gebilde, herrührend vom Geiste Gottes! Frau Risa H., Gottbegnadete, heil deinen adeligen Händen!

*Peter Altenberg*

commonplace is good form in society….It is bad taste to make one's self conspicuous through some individual, singular expression…. Obedience to the standards of the general public in all externals [is] the conscious and desired means of reserving their personal feelings and their taste."[8] Fashion, for Simmel, is a mask that allows the metropolitan individual to preserve his individuality by protecting it rather than trying to find forms of its expression.

Adolf Loos's man is the man of Simmel. He writes: "We have become more refined, more subtle. The herd must distinguish themselves by the use of various colors; modern man uses his cloths like a mask. His individuality is so strong that he cannot express it any longer by his clothing. He concentrates his own invention on other things."[9]

No longer able to find identity in fixed, stable things such as the house where one lives, the name of the family, modern man finds himself surrounded by objects without meaning. Unlike Van de Velde, Olbrich, and Hoffman, Loos did not attempt to force these objects to speak. In any case, that effort, Loos thought, would never produce a language, but at most an *Esperanto* (an artificial language). As the conscious design of the everyday object is pointless, the modern everyday object exists already in the traditional craft object or in the industrial product, so fashion and formality in society are the existing forms of language in industrial civilization, the language of behavior. This language does not express the soul, and it is precisely because it does not unveil one's feelings or taste that it provides a form of protection, a mask. Loos writes: "How should one dress? Modern. One is modernly dressed when one stands out the least." In another passage he continues:

> For both the English and the Americans demand of an individual that he be well dressed. But the Germans do them one better. They also want to be *beautifully* dressed…but the English mock the German's craving for beauty. The Medici Venus, the Pantheon, a picture by Botticelli, a song by Burns—of course, these are beautiful! But pants? Or whether a jacket has three or four buttons? …Germans from the best society side with the English. They are satisfied if they are dressed *well*. They adjure claims to *beauty*.…But what does it mean to be dressed well? It means to be dressed correctly. It is a question of being dressed *in such a way that one stands out the least.*[10]

For Loos, dressing is a language, not a form of art. Therefore, all claims to beauty, originality, and creativity in this realm are misplaced. Fashion is both "the other" of art and "the other" of the expression of one's inner feelings.

### 3. The House

"When I was finally given the task of building a house, I said to myself: in its external appearance, a house can only have changed as much as a dinner jacket. Not a lot therefore....I had to become significantly simpler. I had to substitute the golden buttons with black ones. The house has to look inconspicuous.... Have you never noticed the strange correspondance between the exterior dress of people and the exterior of buildings?"[11]

When Loos writes about the house, he does it in the same terms that he writes about fashion but first he has to make a distinction between the exterior and the interior of the house. Thus in *Heimat Kunst* (1914) he writes: "The house does not have to tell anything to the exterior; instead all its richness must be manifest in the interior."[12] This silence of the house to the exterior speaks of the modern condition, of the split between what we think and what we do, between our intimate and our social being. The interior speaks the language of culture, the language of the experience of things; the exterior speaks the language of civilization, of information. The interior is the other of the exterior, in the same way as information is the other of experience.

Massimo Cacciari has related the thematic of Loos's interiors to that unfolded by Lou Andreas Salome in *Zum Typus Weib.*[13] This extraordinary text, a "stroll in thought," in Salome's words, begins with her very first memory: "I was sitting on a flowery carpet, before me an open brown box, where, when I had been very good or when my old nanny did not have time for me, I could rummage in among buttons of glass and bone, many-colored and of fantastic shapes." She compares this experience with a later one "which also has as object small round precious pieces: coins." It was around the time when she started getting some pocket money (eight years old) which consisted of a silver coin. One day, taking a walk with her father, they encountered a beggar to whom Lou would have liked to give the silver coin that she had. Her father says, "Half would be enough," and he exchanges her coin for two others so that she can give one to the beggar and keep one for herself.

For Salome, the buttons remained for a long time "the quintessence of that which, considered precious, is not given away but kept... of the inalienable, in a certain sense fragments of my very mother [of her dress]. In contrast, the substance of money consists in being divisible."

Salome identifies money as representing "the sphere of social exchanges" and the buttons that of "the anal interests [repressed through education]." The buttons were "now systematized in a fable representation of erotic origins." But, as Cacciari has noted, the buttons in her text are "not only memory, but...in-fancy that operates continuously in the very growth and transformations of the language. But how to keep [collect] the buttons? and where to keep them?" This is the problem of the interior in the metropolis. The interior as the place of the "withdrawal," as the place for everything that can not be given away, that does not circulate, that resists as infancy. The difficulty of defining this space results also from the fact that it has to exist in the productivity of the metropolis. "The interior that guards the buttons can only exist as absolute difference with respect to the exterior. The exterior should not translate what is kept in the interior....The exterior must be pure money....The exterior of the possible place of "withdrawal" is pure language which has its history....[and its problems to resolve]—but not transparency....The exterior does not express anything (if it did there would be no interior)."[14]

Loos's architecture is about the "difference" between living in the interior and dealing with the exterior. The Raumplan is perhaps the more obvious design consequence of this premise. The Raumplan is a way of creating space from the inside out, spaces defined precisely from the difference between inside and outside.

## 4. The Window and the Mirror

In a passage from *Urbanisme* (Paris, 1925) Le Corbusier wrote: "Loos told me one day: a cultivated person never looks out of the window; his window is a ground glass; it is there only to let the light in, not to let the gaze pass through."

In every house by Loos, windows are either opaque or covered with sheer curtains. Moreover, the entire organization of the spaces, the disposition of the built-in furniture *(the immeubles)*, seems to be done in a way to prevent physical access to the windows. Very often, a couch has been placed just at the foot of the window in such a way as to position the occupant with their back to it. This happens , for instance, in the alcove in the dining room of the Alfred Kraus apartment (1905), the bedroom of the Hans Brummel House in Pilsen (1929), the music room and raised sitting area in the living room of the Moller House, and the living room of the Straser House.

Even in those "windows" which do not mediate between interior and exterior but rather look into other interior spaces as, for instance, the window in the ladies' sitting area of the Müller House (1930), there is a couch placed against the window. One could go further and suggest that upon entering a "Loos space" one's body is being continuously turned around to face the interior space, the space one just moved through, rather than to contemplate the exterior or the upcoming space. One is also stopped; it is easy to imagine oneself in precise, static positions, usually indicated by the unoccupied furniture, in the photographs of Loos's spaces. These spaces are intended to be comprehended by inhabiting them.

Sitting in the alcove of the Moller House, for example, the light comes from behind. We do not see out of the window but the window's presence is definitely noted in, for instance, a comfortable position for reading; this is further indicated by the bookshelves. Comfort here is not only a sensual experience, the exact amount of light needed, at the correct angle, the texture of the sofa's fabric, etc., but perhaps there is, in addition, a more psychological

Left: Mirror in Freud's study.

Steiner House: View of the dining room.

Reading area in the Moller House.

Left: Street facade of the Moller House.

Previous Page: Street facade of the Tristan Tzara House.

Following page: Adolf Loos: *The Bedroom of My Wife* in *Kunst.*

Raised sitting area in the Müller House.

Moller House: View of the music room from the dining room.

Moller House: View of the dining room from the music room.

component: the privacy granted by the placement of the sofa against the light. Anyone entering the living room, following the passage of ascending stairs from the entrance—a rather dark space—will take a few moments to recognize a person sitting in the space. And, vice versa, any "intruder" will be immediately detected by a person sitting in this area, as an actor entering the stage is immediately seen by the spectator in a theater box. The window here is a source of light, of sensual pleasure, and perhaps provides psychological protection. The gaze is turned toward the interior. While there is a possible view to the exterior from this position, the view is toward the back garden, and the gaze has to traverse the whole depth of the house (from the alcove to the living room and from there to the music room). The exterior view is dependent upon a view of the interior first.

The raised sitting area of the Moller House constitutes the most intimate space in the sequence of living spaces but, paradoxically, rather than being at the heart, it is located at the periphery and coincides with the most expansive window (almost a horizontal window) of the street facade.

The inwardness, the gaze turned upon itself, of Loos's interiors can be noted in other projects. In the Müller House in Prague, for instance, the scenic sequence of spaces follows an increasing sense of privacy from the living room, dining room, and study to the "ladies' room" *(Zimmer de Dame).* But the window of the raised sitting area in the "ladies' room" looks back into the living space. Again, the most intimate room in this house is like a theater box placed just over the entry to the living rooom; any visitor could be watched from that point.

Loos's play with the limits between inside and outside is also manifest in his use of mirrors. In the dining room of the Steiner House (1910), for instance, a mirror is placed in the same plane as the window to the exterior. The opaque window is, again, only a source of light. The mirror at eye level returns to the gaze the interior with the lamp over the dining table and the objects in the built-in sideboard.

One is reminded of the image of Freud's studio in Berggasse 19 where a small framed mirror has been hung in the plane of the window, reflecting the light of Freud's working table. In Freud's theory the mirror represents the psyche. The reflection in the mirror is also a self-portrait projected to the outside world. Freud's mirror, placed in the frontier separating interior from exterior, undermines the status of this frontier as a fixed limit. Similarly, Loos's mirrors undermine the status of the fixed boundary between interior and exterior. The play between reality and illusion, between the actual and virtual scene is constantly enacted. Does Loos's work amount to a critique of classical representation? I shall return to this question. Meanwhile, I shall address one related to it: Why this obstinate split between sight and the rest of the senses?

This split is not only manifest in the opaque and carefully placed windows in Loos's interiors; the physical and visual connections between the spaces are often kept separate.  In the Rufer House, in Vienna (1922), appearance into the living room takes place as if from behind the scenes, through a peculiar cut in the wall.  This theatrical effect is reinforced by the raised disposition of the dining room in relation to the living room and communicated visually through an opening that, however, does not coincide with the physical connection.  Similarly, in the Moller House there is no visible way of getting from the music room to the dining room (raised some 70 cm above); the only means of direct access is to take out the folding steps hidden in the base.

This general strategy contributes to the formality and theatrical feeling of the place.  The photographs give the impression that somebody will enter the room in the next moment, that a piece of family drama will be enacted, the characters represented by the unoccupied, conspicously placed pieces of furniture.  (In photographs of the houses of Le Corbusier, the impression is that somebody has just been there, leaving as traces a coat, or a hat lying on the entrance table, some recently cut flowers in a vase, a fresh fish in the kitchen, etc.)[15]

For Loos, the interior is still anthropological space—before language, space is felt—as clothing, that is, before clothing as *pret-á-porter,* when one first has to choose the fabric.  Every room of Loos's interiors is a character, a costume in a theater of the family of which perhaps a key could be found in Freud's studies.

In his writings about the house, Loos himself has depicted a few family "dramas."  In *Das Andere ,* he makes the argument that the house is not a work of art, that there is a difference between a house and a series of decorated rooms; he writes:

> Try to describe how does  the house unfold and unravel birth and death, the screams
> of pain for an wounded son, the death rattle of a dying mother, the last thoughts of a woman
> who wants to die. Just an image; the young woman who has put herself to death. She is lying
> on a wooden floor. One of her hands still holds the smoking revolver. On the table a letter,
> the farewell letter. Is the room in which this is happening of good taste? Who is asking this?
> It is just a room!

Here is very clearly expressed the dialectic Art/Life.  More from less possibility of existence, of life and death.  Against Olbrich and Van de Velde who tried to find everywhere synthetic forms,  for Loos, between art and life, there is no possible bridge.  Life is the "other" of art.  The house is the place where one gives birth, lives, and dies.   The house is "the other" of art.

### 5.  Representation

The split between sight and the rest of the senses that can be observed in Loos's interiors was already made explicit in Loos's definition of architecture.  In "The Principle of Cladding" he writes:  "The architect's general task is to provide a warm and livable space.  Carpets are warm and livable.  He decides for this reason to spread one carpet on the floor and to hang up four to form the four walls.  But you cannot build a house out of carpets.  Both the carpet on the floor and the tapestry on the wall require a structural frame to hold them in the correct place.  To invent this frame is the architect's second task."[16]

Loos detested the aestheticising tendencies of the architect's drawings and wrote: "The sign of a truly felt architectural work is that in plan it lacks effect."  By "truly felt" Loos meant a perception of space involving

not only the sense of sight, but also the rest of the senses. But Loos was not only opposing sensual experience to abstraction, he was also intent on the intranslatability of languages. He wrote: "Every work of art possesses such strong internal laws that it can only appear in its own form....If I could erase from the minds of my contemporaries that strongest of architectural facts, the Pitti Palace, and let the best draughtsman present it as a competition project, the jury would lock me in a lunatic asylum." The architect's drawings should be no more than a technical language, "the attempt (by the architect) to make himself understood by the craftsman carrying out the work." The architect's drawings are for Loos only a consequence of the division of labor. Without attempting to negate this condition, Loos thought that the destiny of architecture could not be left to depend on those documents: "But it is a terrible thing when an architectural drawing, itself...a graphic work of art, is built in stone, steel, and glass, for there are truly graphic artists amongst architects."[17]

Loos's Raumplan is a way to think space as it is felt. Symptomatically, Loos has not left any theoretical definition of it. Kulka has written: "Loos will make many changes during construction. He will walk through the space and say: I do not like the height of this ceiling, change it! The idea of the Raumplan made it difficult to finish a scheme before construction allowed the visualization of the space as it was."[18]

Loos's antipathy toward the architectural drawing extended itself to photography and professional journals. In "Architecture" (1910) he writes: "My greatest pride is that the interiors I have created are entirely unphotogenic....The inhabitants of my spaces do not recognize their own houses in the photographs, just as the owner of a Monet painting would not recognize it at Kastan's. I have to renounce the honor of having my works published in the various architectural magazines."[19]

One could read these passages following Loos's indications and conclude that there is no possible reproduction of a spatial effect, of a sensual experience. But there is something about the photographs of Loos's interiors that seems too deliberate to leave it at that. Particularly the strategy of framing with a two-dimensional surface a spatial volume, as happens, for instance, in the bedroom of the Khuner Villa or in Loos's own apartment, a strategy which has the effect of flattening the space beyond the frame. Or in Loos's repeated play with openings and mirrors, wherein mirrors appear as openings and actual openings appear as mirror. The question can be raised of how much these optical effects are more appreciated in photography than in the houses.[20] Perhaps we can venture the idea that the photographs are deliberately taken to play on this effect, particularly since there is more than one indication of Loos's involvement in the photography of his own work. Kenneth Frampton has pointed out the conspicuous presence of an Egyptian stool in every Loos interior. The archives of the photographer who holds the negatives of the photographs published in Kulka's book reveal a few tricks: The view out of the horizontal window in Khuner's Villa, for instance, is a photomontage as is the violin in the cupboard of the music room of the Moller House. A floor was added to the photograph of the street facade of the Tristan Tzara house, and a number of objects were erased.[21]

Loos's critique of the photographic representation of architecture is not nostalgia for the "complete" object. What Loos accomplishes with his play with reflective surfaces is a critique of photography as a transparent medium, and by extension a critique of classical representation. Loos's mirrors undermine the referential status of the photographic image and its pretension to represent reality as it is. These photographs make the viewer aware of the artifice involved in photography. They are the "other" of the images of consumption offered by the architectural magazines.

### 6. The House for Josephine Baker

"Africa: that is the image conjured up more or less firmly by a contemplation of the model." Thus begins Ludwig Münz writing about the house for Josephine Baker, a project that Loos developed in Paris in 1928. What is most striking in this passage is the moment of ambiguity of whether Münz is referring to the model of the house or to Josephine Baker herself. Münz does not know why he is invoking this image and he speculates on it in terms of the "the flat roofs," "the window openings, some of which are small and low," and "the black and white horizontally striped marble facing...." He continues: "none of which are stylistic imitations though they look strange and exotic."[22]

This project provides the occassion for the last possible reading of "the other" in Loos's work to be developed here. "The other" here is not only a woman, it is the famous black dancer and cabaret singer of the twenties.

"The interior cannot be guessed at by looking at the outside," Münz writes, and yet we have seen that this

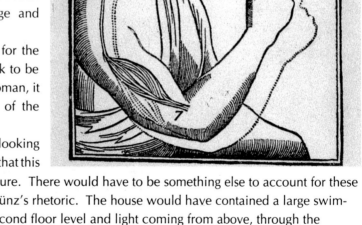

is not an unusual characteristic in Loos's architecture. There would have to be something else to account for these anticipatory remarks, for this sudden change in Münz's rhetoric. The house would have contained a large swimming pool—two stories high—with entry at the second floor level and light coming from above, through the ceiling:

> The reception rooms on the first floor, arranged around the pool—a large salon with an extensive top-lit vestibule, a small lounge and the circular café—indicate that this was intended not for private use but as a miniature entertainment center....On the first floor, low passages surround the pool. They are lit by the windows from the outside and from them, thick, transparent windows are let into the side of the pool—so that is was possible to watch swimming and diving in its crystal-clear waters, flooded with light from above: an underwater revue, so to speak.[23]

As in previous houses, the interior has its back turned to the outside world, the gaze turned toward the interior space. However, in this house there is a reversal of the subject and object of the gaze. The inhabitant is now the object of the gaze and the visitor, the guest, the looking subject. The most intimate space—the swimming pool—occupies the central space of this house and the focal point of the visitor's gaze. As Münz writes, "The entertainment consists of looking." But between this gaze and the object of it—the body—there is water and glass, and therefore the body is inaccessible. The swimming pool is lit from above, through the ceiling. Between this *celibataire* machine and the outside, there is no relationship.

In the *Traité des Passions de l'ame* (1649), Descartes contended that emotions were psychological at base and argued that the control of the physical expression of emotions would control the emotions themselves. Where Descartes treated the body as a machine, with a perfect cycle without losses, Loos transforms this house into an erotic system, a machine of desire— Marcel Duchamp's *Large Glass* comes to mind. In the house of Josephine Baker, as in the *celibataire* machine, all the "apparatus," all the *"mise-en-scene"* constitutes the epical narration of an "impossible" relationship.

Previous page: Descartes, Diagram from the *Traité des Passions de l'ame.*

**Notes**

A preliminary version of this text was first given as a lecture at Columbia University, Spring 1986, as part of a series organized by the editors. The final form has benefited from the encouragement and criticism of the editors and especially that of David Smiley.

1.  Adolf Loos, *Das Andere 1*, 1902: p.1. Reprinted with Italian translation and an introduction by Massimo Cacciari. Milan: Electa, 1981. There is also a reprint with Spanish translation in *Carrer de la Cuitat: 9-10*, (January 1980), a special issue devoted to Adolf Loos.

2.  Altenberg's real name was Richard Englander (1859-1919). He was a doctor but lived as a bohemian man of letters. He not only frequented the Café Central as did his friends Loos and Kraus, but actually lived in a room upstairs. When he died, Loos wrote an unsentimental text in his memory that, apart from being one of Loos's most beautiful pieces of writing, provides insight into Altenberg's personality. Adolf Loos, "Abschied von Peter Altenberg," (1919) in *Trotzdem*, Innsbruck, 1931. See also Jose Quetglas, "Das Andere," in *Carrer de la Ciutat: 9-10* (January 1980).

3.  Jacques Lacan, *Encore, Le Seminaire XX*, Paris: Editions du Seuil, pp. 58.

4.  Jane Gallop, *The Daughter's Seduction: Feminism and Psychoanalysis*, Ithaca: Cornell University Press, 1982, p. 40.

5.  Adolf Loos, "Men's Fashion," "Men's Hats," "Footwear," "Undercloths," and "Ladies Fashion," in *Spoken into the Void*, Collected Essays 1897-1900, Cambridge and London: The MIT Press, 1982. Translated by Jane O. Newman and John H. Smith.

6.  George Teyssot, "La casa per tutti," introduction to the Italian translation of Roger Guerrand, *Les origins du logement social en France*, Officina ed., p. XLIX. Teyssot is referring to the case of France and mentions as possible factors the coincidence in time with the moment in which building construction ceases to be the main activity of the country after agriculture, making way for the textile industry to occupy second place. See also T. Zeldin, *Histoire des passions francaises, III: "gout et corruption,"* Paris: Encres Recherches, 1979, p. 308.

7.  Georg Simmel, "The Metropolis and Mental Life" (1903), in *Georg*

Simmel: On Individuality and Social Forms, edited by Donald N. Levine, Chicago and London: The University of Chicago Press, 1971, p. 324.

8.  Georg Simmel, "Fashion" (1904) in Georg Simmel: On Individuality and Social Forms, Op. cit.

9.  Adolf Loos, "Ornamnet und Verbrechen" (1910) in Trotzdem, Innsbruck: 1931.

10. Adolf Loos, Das Andere 1, 1902, p. 8.

11. Adolf Loos, "Mens Fashion" (1898) in Spoken into the Void, op. cit., p. 11.

12. Adolf Loos, "Architektur" (1910) in Trotzdem. English translation in The Architecture of Adolf Loos, Catalogue of an Arts Council Exhibition, London, 1985.

13. Lou Andreas Salome, "Zum Typus Weib" in Imago, vol. 3, no. 1, 1914.

14. Massimo Cacciari, "Note su Loos, Roth e Wittgenstein," in Nuova Corrente 79/80, 1979, pp. 368-381.

15. Alexander Gorlin, "The Ghost in the Machine: Surrealism in the work of Le Corbusier," in Perspecta 18, 1982, p. 55. See also Thomas Schumacher, "Deep Space, Shallow Space," in The Architectural Review, January 1987.

16. Adolf Loos, "The Principle of Cladding" (1898) in Spoken into the Void, op. cit., p. 66.

17. Adolf Loos, "Architektur" (1910), in Trotzdem, Innsbruck, 1931.

18. Heinrich Kulka, Adolf Loos, Das Werk des Architekten, Vienna, 1931.

19. Adolf Loos, "Architektur" (1910) in Trotzdem.

20. See my earlier article, "On Adolf Loos and Joseph Hoffman: Architecture in the Age of Mechanical Reproduction," 9H 6, 1983.

21. I am indebted to Dick Van Gemeren who first pointed out this material to me.

22. L. Münz, G. Kunstler, Der Architekt Adolf Loos, Vienna: 1964. English translation, Adolf Loos, Pioneer of Modern Architecture, London: 1966.

23. From the letter by Kurt Ungers to Ludwig Münz, quoted in G. Kunstler and L. Münz, Der Architekt Adolf Loos, op. cit.

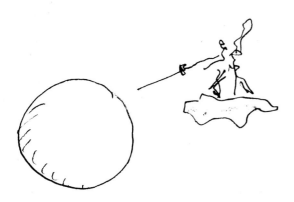

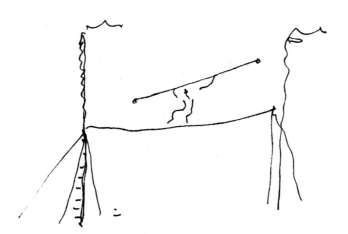

**P.S.**

After having finished my five stories, I got your letter mentioning my approach to details and construction. My answer will be some sketches...I always draw before my lectures—the animal, the acrobat, and Issac Newton.

Sverre Fehn

# FOUR STORIES

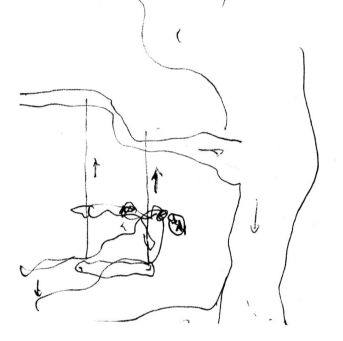

## The Labyrinth

I once made a house which everybody claimed was inspired by Palladio. To be honest, Palladio was not in my mind at that time. But later, I met him. By seeing the plan of my house, he said to me: "You know, the Rotunda was a joke...at that time we lost the horizon as a mystery. It was a shock for all of us when we realized that the world was a globe—it was measurable. So I made the earth a labyrinth with a single house of four fronts. When you leave the house facing west and walk around the world, you come back to face the same front. Before my structure, the big labyrinth was the desert—if you are lost in that landscape, trying to get out, you always return to the same spot."

## The Client

I once got a client who had three fortunes: a site with an extraordinary view, a magnificent art collection, and a beautiful wife. While deciding how to design a house so that these fortunes could be present at one moment, the "triangle plan" was born. From one place you can see the art and watch the sunset as your wife passes by.

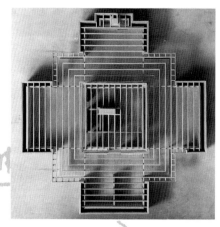

Norrkøping House. Sweden, 1964.

Living Room, Norrkøping House.

Glass corner, Norrkøpir

Lower and Terrace level,
Arne Bødtker House.

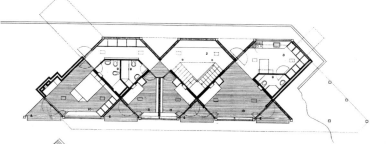

The Arne Bødtker House. Oslo, Norway. 1965.

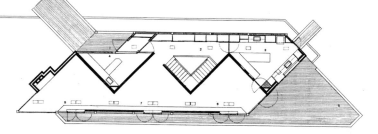

The Arne Bødtker House.

**The Child and the Old Man**

When I was a young architect of twenty-six, I designed a home for elderly people. Twenty years later I was asked by the government to build a school for deaf children. Confronting the elderly as a child you concentrate on the physical differences in their bodies: the joints are weak, the bones are fragile, and the heart beats slowly. Stairs are like mountains. After observing these simple facts, it was natural to construct a one-story building. Meeting the child as an old man you realize that nature must be conquered by the child. So your buildings must be set into the landscape as gently as when the little child makes his first step into the woodlands.

The wall is the partner that returns the ball to the child and gives shadow to the elderly. Both sense the nearness of the elements of architecture. Distance lives only in the memories of the old and the fairy tales of the young. When a child mixes sand and water with his hands, making a cake of mud to transform his face into a mask, it is the child's homage to earth. If you hide the concrete column, you rob the child's possibility of having a conversation with architecture.

Økern Home for the Elderly. Oslo, Norway. 1955.

Concrete column, Skådalen School for Deaf Children. Oslo, Norway. 1972.

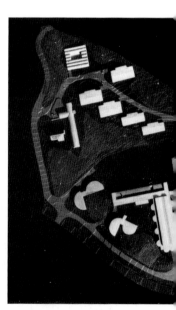

Site model,
Skådalen School for Deaf Children

Atrium, Økern Home for the Elderly.

Ramp entry, Økern Home for the Elderly.

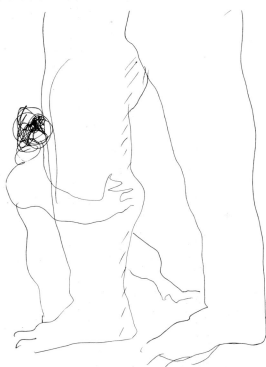

Skådalen School for Deaf Children:
The identity of the hill, vaults, child's window.

## The Voyage

The archaeologists started nearly 150 years ago to open up the earth searching for the past. They looked into the large museum of the globe itself. The artifacts were brought into the present and their journey to eternity was interrupted.

Near the hill of Li in the province of Shaanxi, nine soldiers and two horses were taken from the grave of the Chinese emperor Qin Shihuang. The terra-cotta figures were part of a great army of 7,000 and were to be placed in a modern museum at Høvikodden near Oslo.

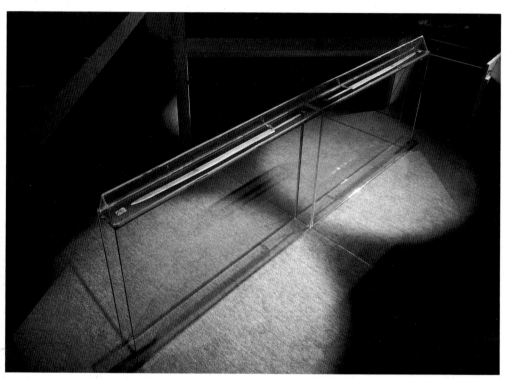

Exhibition installation. Høvikodden, Oslo, Norway. 1972.

By making columns of mirror, each five meters high, the soldiers' eyes of burned clay faced an endlessness of other soldiers in the surface of illusion. In the center of the room, sword pointed against sword and the duel began in a space of double nothingness.

In the harbor of Stockholm, a 300-year-old battleship was found by a diver thirty meters under water. When the ship left the slip in 1628, the voyage lasted only thirty minutes and then the ship sunk. The truth was that the boat constructor had never built a vessel with four decks. The town was very proud of their battleship and decided to build a museum near the place where the ship was found and where a great museum, the Nordiska Museum, already existed. The idea of the new museum was to make a building which in itself had a continuity with the tragic story.

The lawn is the skin of the earth. As the surgeon opens the body from the breast to the navel, so the architect opens the earth from the Nordiska Museum to the old dock where the ship will be placed. By doing so, a journey is created where the objects can return into a silent shadowless world to continue their conversation.

Sketch of the ship, Wasa Ship Museum. Stockholm, Sweden. 1

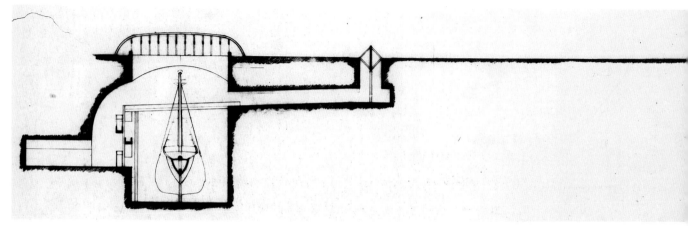

Section, Wasa Ship Mus

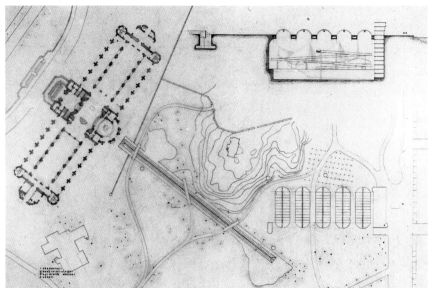

Section and site plan, Wasa Ship Museum.

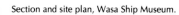

Plans, Wasa Ship Museum.

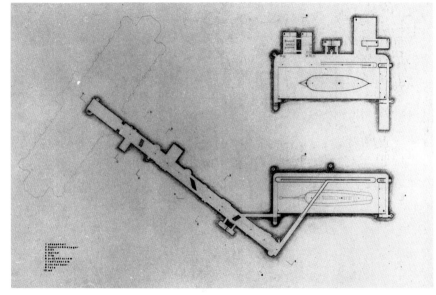

Section showing connection to Nordiska Museum, Wasa Ship Museum.

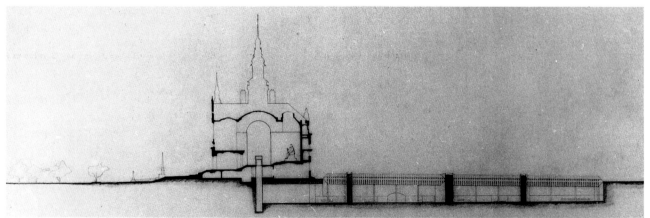

Fehn

If religious sentiment can be expressed in the form of symbols, it is to be found in the *yorishiro*, the god seat, (which is a model mountain) or *yama* on which the god, *kami*, is supposed to alight at the time of the festival. The *yama* is a man-made image of the deity's dwelling place constructed to temporarily receive the *kami*. This *yama* receives its blessing from the Shinmei-sha shrine even though the visible core of the festival, the holy wagon pulled through the streets, has nothing to do with the Shinmei-sha shrine or the Shinto of *Amaterasu*, the Sun Goddess, which it represents. The mountain borne on the wagon refers back to the mountain deity, the *yama-no-kami*, of the original village of Katsuraku enshrined in the Yakushi-do.

Portable shrines were once used to invite the deity into the rice fields to insure fertility and a good crop. Before being placed in the field, these shrines were carried through the streets of the community with frequent stops for festivities. In time, the portable shrines became wagons.

There are two types of *yama*: *oki-yama*, which is fixed in a certain place in the town, usually in the economic area of town as well as in front of the Shinmei-sha shrine; and *haki-yama*, which are mobile and are pulled around the town. The construction is entrusted to the chief carpenter and begins after the ceremony of *oharai*.

Each wagon is decorated with man-made objects that serve as *yorishiro*, which are signs to the *Kami* of a place to descend upon. The full-sized *Kabuki ningyoo* dolls placed in front of the model mountain, *yama*, are *yorishiro*.

# Inside Out:   *Adrian Stokes and*

There is generally in Venetian buildings a thrust upwards from canal or pavement, even where there are heavy crinkled moldings on ground level as is often the case. Such moldings seem to provide a building with a clear spring just as the swirls of water in the Grand Canal release upon the air the spiral-coloured poles for tying gondolas.

In this context, look at the pilaster capital visible above the canal like the fluked tail of a dolphin. Santa Maria dei Miracoli is the only church in Venice with a side upon a canal. Pilasters rise from the water all along this side. The thrust is of a rock from water. The tip of the rock-mass as seen in the photograph is not the dome which disappears out of it, as much as the roof of the attic window on the building beyond. The shutters have air-slits: respiration is also suggested by the black spaces of the open

Peggy Deamer

# orporeal Criticism

windows beneath. Interior life is dark within these wide con-

nexions with the outside world. Like the sense apparatus of the

human body, windows bring what is inside in communication

with what is without: like consciousness they are the exit upon

the external world of the life within. Such, as it were, is the plain

physiology of ordinary building of which we are the more aware

in Venice not only because of the length and darkness of the

apertures in the strong light of Italy, but also because they are

framed so simply and beautifully by the *liston* of Istrian stone

and because at the receptive moment of summer evening as

of early morning, the shutters are thrown wide: the houses

breathe, the tenants show themselves... Adrian Stokes, *Venice* [1]

Adrian Stokes, the early twentieth century English art and architecture critic, approached his criticism as if the objects to which he was attending provided him with a required sensuous gratification. His discussion of buildings, as well as his discussions of Italian sidewalks, olive groves, or Cézanne's *Bathers,* always indicated, in style as much as in substance, his physical identification with the object. Never neutral, never "objective," and never supposing that his rapport with the object was of less than paramount epistemological importance, he wrote less about the buildings per se than about the sensuous image they evoked in his mind's eye.

Let us consider this earth of Venice. Here it is, a few stones and two steps at the entrance to San Michele: the little campo between the church and the lagoon.

It is easy to see the white portal of the church as a purification of the pavement at its base. The great circular step, though the doors are closed, makes of them a big gaping dark interior. It is as if the step were a short, strong, thick projecting tongue with enormous suction power, with enormous power to envelop us with in. Thus dramatically a bridge is made not only between ground and verticle plane, circular and rectangular, but also between, the church's inside and outside. (II, p. 107-8)

Stokes's criticism depended on a particularly intimate position held vis-a-vis the object; the distance required for "objective" observation was effectively annihilated and replaced by a sensual, tactile engagement. It was a position that allowed him simultaneously to see the structural, material, and physical reality of the object and to see in it, at the same time, a metaphor for our own, equally physical, human corporeality. While Stokes called this intimate rapport "a synthesis that the eye alone of the senses can perform," it was, in fact, a myopia in which the known object is absorbed into an image which incorporates all of the physical fantasies of its subjective host. The subject—sexual, physical, and body-bound—and the object—alluring in its "otherness"—were collapsed on the plane of the eye.

The result is an image of the object which is at once its abstraction and its sensuous reconstitution. The abstraction is a result of what is in essence the two-dimensionality of the image, a two-dimensionality implicit in the fact that the image is, for Stokes, the planar interface of subject and object. While Stokes, in the above passage, is aided by the fact that he is not describing the buildings themselves but photographs which have already performed their flattening task, his manner of looking at objects was always one that neutralized the third dimension and its implicit assumptions of visual hierarchy and thereby opened the image up for reinterpretation. In this reinterpretation, the viewer projects his own "inner world"—his unconscious, corporeal fantasies. In the actual writing, then, the effect of this blurred distinction between the architectural and the human body leads to a constantly fluctuating panorama of associations wherein any number of a building's attributes will evoke any number of human characteristics. While Stokes is fond of stating that buildings "symbolize the human process," or that such-and-such building "is a vast and concrete symbol of inner-outer life," they are "symbols" only in the loosest sense of the term, for in his texts, a building doesn't "stand in for" the human body as much as it provides the provocative material upon which the various bodily fantasies of the viewer feed. Buildings are depicted as having human life:

> Yet they live, these buildings, they serve a purpose not modern nor yet an ancient purpose as does the cathedral campanile. Forbidden to grow venerable, they sleep. Not the sleep that breaks with the light. They do not sleep in the dark. Theirs is the light but well-corded slumber of the afternoon. Without recess they are living from the outside, drawing in great breaths of air specked with noise, sound of a cough muffled by a bell,...(II, p. 31)

They also take on the physiognomy of the human body:

> Aperture, empty space, existed first, then the skeleton, then the walls that withstand the water. In these terms, the ribs are still visible in pilaster, pillar and cornice: they are allowed to project as first defence. The wall lies behind them.(II, p. 91)

They become active protagonists in the visual arena:

> At sunset the water reflects the sky. That which the water reflected all day it now clasps and incorporates. Fusion is complete: the sky itself now rocks beneath the grandeur of yet whiter stone. This same rocking sets the more distant churches swaying and swimming, sets their evening bells to roll. The brown prayers of the Redentore are loosed at evening in unmoored sound: and the church slips in upon the sky-and-water, the white embannered Christ upon the dome.(II, p. 92)

And ultimately they take on aspects of other, animal bodies, with which, Stokes suggests, we, too, must also be identified:

> With some days of sirocco Venice is a sea-monster on whose glassy tongue you are scaled. Now this, now that campanile is a sharp decaying tooth, minatory, while the oily sirens of ships are noises in the head of the monster who has caught you, rousing your envy of fish that squirm from between claws to depths of basalt rock. (I, p. 37)

For Stokes, the desire to identify with the buildings he looked at was the necessary means by which to overcome an otherwise crippling sense of self-consciousness. While still in grammar school, absorbed in the reading of Kant's *Critique of Judgement,* Stokes wrote the following passage in one of his personal notebooks:

> ...self-consciousness making sincerity impossible....the real difficulty of life and the cause of most of the contradictions is this: on the one hand [we] must devote all our attention to the work at hand...[and] fulfill our everyday duties; on the other...we can watch our every feeling and imprint, we can hold them up to the light against the unmistakable rock of time... We are slaves to our feelings and cannot be otherwise....Perhaps we are slaves in each glimpse to finally realize the promise of our realization of this consciousness..., like

Kant in our desires.  Consciousness of desires and things outside them but we cannot get outside them or judge them from the outside...[2]

This Kantian dilemma, as Stokes saw it, found a partial solution in the work of F. H. Bradley, the English Hegelian philosopher on whom Stokes wrote his dissertation while at Oxford in 1920-23.  In his *Appearance and Reality* (1893), Bradley proposed that the world was one seamless whole which only language and intellectualization divided into apparent separate entities, or "Appearances."  As part of this monism, Bradley repudiated the British Empiricist notion of the image, which not only assumed the absolute existence of objects, but which assumed as well that our pictorial images were accurate representations of these objects.  Bradley denied the possiblity of isolated, representational images that were divorced from both the sensual and emotional context in which they functioned.  Instead, he insisted, images both subsumed all the other senses and incorporated, at the moment of perception, memories, hopes, anxieties, and interpretations.  Indeed, it was only in this subjective vision, unmediated by the intellect, that "Reality" could be grasped.

On leaving Oxford and beginning a career as a journalist, Stokes repudiated not only Bradley's monist program but all systematic philosophy as well.  In one of his first published essays, "Painting, Giorgione, and Barbaro" (1930), he dismissively asked, "[I]s it credible after all these centuries [that philosophy still debates the problem of knowledge] seeing that there's no subject without the object nor an object without a subject?" (*Criterion IX*, April 1930).  But the nervous breakdown that accompanied this repudiation, as well as Stokes's subsequent psychoanalyzation by Melanie Klein, only served to reinforce the perceptual framework that Bradley had expounded.  Vision, mediator between subject and object, inside and outside, was still the source of sanity; our images were still the source of epistemological apprehension.  They merely became, in the context of Kleinian psychoanalysis, increasingly corporeal.

Klein's work was an elaboration on Freud's topological model of consciousness in which the ego was described as a middle layer sandwiched between those of the preconscious and the unconscious.  As Freud wrote, "it must lie in the borderline between outside and inside; it must be turned towards the external world and must envelope the other psychical systems."[3]  In this model, our perceptual system, "like a hardened rind that withstands the over plus of stimulus," protected us from the onslaught of the external world; but it proposed no such protection from our inner world.  In his later work, Freud elaborated on what this lack of protection implied, describing the manner in which the superego, housing the introjected father figure of the Oedipus complex, produced distorted images of reality. Klein's elaboration on this perceptual model emphasized both its spatial and its corporeal nature. Believing that the superego made its appearance much earlier than the Oedipus complex implied, she depicted a superego that was populated not just by

Freud's father figure but by whole and partial introjected objects belonging to both the mother and the father: penises, breasts, nipples, mouths, tongues, teeth, etc. As described by Klein, it was an "inner world"—one full of guilt and anxiety for its roots in the death instinct—inhabited by "inner objects" that were as real for the child as the external world and its objects onto which the child projected. Stokes describes the process of projection for himself in one of his entries in his personal journal:

> …The new-born baby soon becomes aware that neither his mother nor the surroundinng world is an extension of himself. Henceforth, to his dying day, there remains the huge division between himself and objects, people or things. Throughout life we seek to rival the externality of things. The world of nature is not only a physical habitat and the material of science, not only the material of practical life, but the medium of every mood. Indeed, without this canvas, as it were, on which to apply ourselves, by which we project, transmute and as well satisfy the simple animal needs, we cannot conceive the inner flow of the mind. Mental as well as physical life is a laying outward of shape within, in rivaling, as it were, with the laid-out instantaneous world of space. To project is to distort etc.[4]

At the same time that Stokes turned to Kleinian psychoanalysis for its capacity to explain both the willfulness of our images and their potential for subject/object integration, he turned to art and aesthetic criticism as the means by which one explored, examined, and refined this integrative function. It was a turn inspired by his first trip to Italy when the pure "otherness" of the landscape first made him aware that "things were happening entirely outside me," transforming the external world, for the first time, into a durable "other" capable of both receiving and denying a too-insular and self-conscious ego. It was as if, he wrote, an "attendant oculist has slipped in lenses that clarify" (III, p. 34) and through them he could imagine the synthesis with himself that only an independent "other" would allow.

All of Stokes's works are about this phenomenon of otherness which he felt art alone, and particularly quattrocento art, took as its project. The early works, *The Quattro Cento* (1932) and *The Stones of Rimini* (1935), in which he explored this capacity for a redemptive otherness in physical but not wholly psychoanalytic terms, secured him a not insignificant amount of respect from the aesthetic elite of the time. Ezra Pound not only promoted Stokes's work, but was influential in directing Stokes's attention to the marvels and masterpieces of the Italian quattrocento; T. S. Eliot was the first to publish in his *The Criterion* the essays that eventually were incorporated into *Quattro Cento*; he was asked by Anthony Blunt to replace him as reviewer at *The Spectator*; he was praised and reviewed well by his colleagues Herbert Read and Kenneth Clark. But when the indirect corporeal allusions to the body which characterized the early work were replaced by literal and direct references to psychoanalysis and the sexual body, the praise and admiration dropped away. The sudden change in allegiance, in effect, only served to underscore the fact that Stokes's entire critical project was anathema to the period. In a climate dominated by Clive Bell's and Roger Fry's "Significant Form," Bernard Berenson's historical exactitude, and Eliot's classical objectivism, criticism was expected to be dry, crisp, and detached, without allusion to the subjective phantasies that lurked elsewhere in the aesthetic experience.

Stokes's position on the fringe of mainstream criticism guaranteed that his search for the root of the inside-out capacity of art would be highly personal, and his attachment to architecture above all the arts was an indication of the uniqueness of his path. No early-twentieth-century art critic, British or otherwise, made the connection between our bodies and the arts the single most important criterion of aesthetic value or so unfailingly reminded us that architecture was both the "mother of the arts" and, at the same time, the most potent symbol of "mother" available to us:

[W]e will agree that the work of art is a construction. Inasmuch as man both physically and psychologically is a structure carefully amassed, a coalescence and a pattern, a balance imposed upon opposite drives, building is likely to be not only the most common but the most general symbol of our living and breathing: the house besides is the home and the symbol of the Mother: it is our upright body built cell by cell: a ledge is the foot, the knee, the brow.(III, p. 149)

In his concern for the inside-out connection between self and object, person and building, Stokes avoided literal descriptions of "insides" of buildings. It was, instead, the most tactile and material element of architecture which spoke to him, namely, the wall. It was here that the dual capacity of physicality and symbolism, otherness and subjective fantasy, most clearly functioned. Speaking of the "facade" architecture of quattrocento Italy and the expressive capacity of its surfaces, he wrote:

Colours, textures, smooth and rough planes, apertures, symbolize reciprocity, a thriving in a thorough partnership....[These dichotomies have], of course, many embodiments, a sense of growth and a sense of thrust, for instance, heaviness and lightness, sheerness and recession or projection, rectangularity and rotundity, lit surfaces and shadowed surfaces, a thematic contrast between two principal textures, that is to say, between smooth and rough. I take this last to symbolize all, because it best marks the "bite" of architectural pleasure upon the memory: the dichotomy that permeates our final impression.(II, p. 242)

But beyond the physical attraction to the textures of the surface, Stokes elaborated on the capacity of the wall to conceptually symbolize the human psyche. Over and over, he wishes to direct our attention to the planar, layered capacity of the wall. Whether focusing on the bas-relief of the building's decoration, on the slightly protruding stone of the door jambs, on lichen that added to the stone an extra skin, or on the drying laundry that appeared to be laminated to the exterior facade of a building, we are reminded that these layers recall the Freudian layers of the psyche, or evoke the "active progeny" as the carver/architect reveals the inside lying beyond the exterior surface.

The apertures of the wall also revealed for Stokes the same symbolic capacity. On the one hand, the contrast of the light liston stone window and door frames with the darkness of the apertures themselves are shown to demonstrate in the most abstract—and yet entirely physical—way the fundamental principle of "identity-in-difference," the principle intrinsic to "inside-out" identification, in which opposites are shown to be different aspects of the same unity. On the other hand, the apertures present varied symbols of human life, moments when insides become outsides; they are symbols of birth, of breath, and of consciousness. Indeed, when Stokes deliberately described a window with a human figure inside it, his desire to metaphorically evoke a particularly Kleinian psyche, populated by "inner objects" and "inner figures" is easily recognized.

And again, there is the same emphasis on the symbolic capacity of the wall's material, always and necessarily for Stokes, stone. On the one hand, stone's hardness, durability, and permanence was the epitome of the forceful "other," an "other" which, unlike clay, plaster, or cement, prevented the carver/architect from thoughtlessly imposing his will on the material, forcing him instead to respond to the material's own intrinsic structural demands.[5] On the other hand, stone—especially limestone—symbolized in its own physical makeup the phenomenon of inside-out, subject-object transposition. It did so not only by virtue of the fact that its structural, physical components—the "sea that stands petrified,...[the] compact of salt's bright yet shaggy crystals" as well as the condensed sea animals and shells—were identified with the rain/sea that later wore it down and carved it out; but also by virtue of the fact that it symbolized our subject-object relationships:

> Limestone, for the most part formed of organic deposits, is the link between the organic and inorganic worlds. Limestone exhibits in mummified state the life no longer found of the Silurian and other distant ages, just as the Istrian palaces of Venice present to us in terms of space, the hoard of ancient Venetian enterprise. The very substance of limestone suggests concreted Time....(I, p.196)

Stokes's admiration for the wall and a building's facades was linked to his disparagement of buildings designed according to considerations of plan and volume, considerations that were associated with the denigrated "modeling" attitude in that it gave priority to arbitrary shapes that ignored structural determinants and avoided material demands. Thus his condemnation of Le Corbusier and "modern" architecture:

> With an armature of steel, Le Corbusier can make you a room of any shape you like. He can express speed with a building. Rooms will be fashioned. Their organization will be simple sheer design that has no use for trappings....The creations of Le Corbusier and others show that building will no longer serve as the mother art of stone, no longer as the source at which carving or spatial conception renews strength. Architecture, in that sense of the word, will cease to exist.(I, p.258)

And yet this aspatial attitude was not merely one in which the subtlety of spatial evocation was ignored at the expense of a more obvious material reality. Stokes set aside his concern for the actual interior space of a building to make way for what always was the principle matter of significance: the space of the mind, the realm of his own physical fantasies. To a certain extent, this is achieved through the metaphorical evocations that emerge in the symbolic readings of the facades, in which the buildings, in full personification, appear not only to "spring" from the water or to "suck" us in, but to swim, sway, sing, give birth, etc., describing a world that is not only fully "spatial" but entirely active. But it is also depicted in the context of a most ordinary, but for Stokes most profound, phenomenological space. In Stokes's semiautobiographical *Smooth and Rough* (1951, originally entitled *Outside In*, a followup to his earlier *Inside Out* ), this "space" is precisely and intimately evoked.

> I am sitting in the deep chair of the living-room at Carbis Bay... I hear one gate opened, then shut, and, after a pause, steps begin to scrunch faintly on the drive... These steps will either continue past the house (and my right) and out of the back gate, or else, just before the house they will take a short descending path at right angles to the drive, pass hugely by the window in front of me, and then, having turned left again across the window to that side, will end almost immediately at the front door. Does he come through the front door,

the owner of the steps will have carried inside me something of the journey he has made, not merely the line of his approach, though that be predominant, but a semi-sphere as well as panorama... He comes into the house and with him, as attributes, the surroundings of his passage from the gate. I have a sensation of enrichment and, possibly, of uneasiness. The house contains a new vital element.

The less pre-occupied the stranger, and the more he seems to look about him as it is interpreted by the sound of his gait, the greater the content he will bring with him. If he comes in a hurry he brings little. If he has come to visit me, the impression is cancelled, he is outside me again. Whatever the errand, whatever the directness, we will tend to be like two insects in a dance, each responding to the other's movements by a movement to the side. But those we love we harbour: we take them in with their apparel of things...

[The stranger] contrasts with our son who first appeared in the house without coming into it as a separate being. The stranger brings another aspect, the outside-in.... My son, the inside-out, is also an outside-in: he became identified with the house. It was his trot, his on-coming or receding voice which measured its length.... He listened closely to the Cornish idiom, his father was a farmer; for me this meant a strong tie with the Cornish soil. (II, p. 221-23)

While Stokes increasingly proved himself to be out of step with current aesthetic appreciation, he was looking past his twentieth century colleagues to the Victorians who were the object of the modern critics' scorn. The above passage lands us squarely at the door of Walter Pater, whose "Child in the House" spurred Stokes's investigation of "inside-out"; and places us, as well, firmly in the realm of Ruskin, whose "Two Boyhoods" in *Modern Painters*, matching the childhood of his alter-ego, Turner, with that of Giorgione, is the model for Stokes's *Inside Out*, in which he pairs his childhood with that of Cézanne.

Ruskin, the true Victorian, was obstinately opposed to anything that smacked of that murky realm we now associate with the id. Where Stokes explicitly explores that penetration of the visual plane by the passage to and fro of inner and outer objects, Ruskin describes his perceptual imagination as a mirror, one which allows nature's secrets to reflect *off* him. The true force of the imagination resides in the fact that "in its work, the vanity and individualism of the man himself are crushed, and he becomes a mere instrument or mirror, used by a higher power for the reflection of others of a truth which no effort of his could ever have ascertained."[6]

But behind the theoretical repression that the analogy between the imagination and the mirror implies, the hidden realm of the unconscious surreptitiously appears. In describing the "Imagination Penetrative," Ruskin writes that it is "the penetrating possession taking faculty,"

> ...a peircing pholas-like mind's tongue, that works
> and tastes into the very rock heart; no matter what
> be the subject submitted to it, substance or spirit, all

*is alike divided asunder, joint and marrow, whatever utmost truth, life, principle it has, laid bare, and that which has no truth, life, nor principle, dissipated into its original smoke at a touch.*[7]

While in describing his own "faculty," he says:

*There is this strong instinct in me which I cannot analyse to draw and describe the things I love—not for reputation, not for the good of others, nor for my own advantage, but a sort of instinct like that for eating and drinking. I should like to draw all St. Mark's, all this Verona stone by stone, to eat it all up into my mind, touch by touch.*[8]

Indeed, a passage from Ruskin's *St. Mark's Rest*, worth quoting in full, explicitly brings to mind the Kleinian notion of inner objects and infantile introjection:

*Those were the kind of images and shadows they lived on: ...these thin dry bones of art were nourishing meat to the Venetian race: that they grew and throve on that diet, every day spiritually fatter for it, and more comfortably sound in human soul: —no illustrated papers to be had, no Academy Exhibition to be seen. If their eyes were to be entertained at all, such must be their lugubrious delectation; pleasure difficult enough to imagine, but real and pure, I doubt not; even passionate. In as quite singularly incomprehensible fidelity of sentiment, my cousin's least baby has fallen in love with a wooden spoon.... The two are inseparable all about the house, vainly the unimaginative by-standers endeavouring to perceive, for their part, any amiableness in the spoon. But baby thrives on its pacific attachment, —nay, is under the most perfect moral control, pliant as a reed, under the slightest threat of being parted from his spoon. And I am assured that the crescent Venetian imagination did indeed find pleasantness in these figures...*[9]

This sensuality invades, then, his appreciation of architecture, which, like Stokes's after him, sprung from his very close, almost tactile rapport with the texture and material of the building. In *The Seven Lamps of Architecture*, he writes:

*I do not believe that ever any building was truly great, unless it had mighty masses, vigorous and deep, of shadow mingled with its surface. And among the first habits that an architect should learn, is that of thinking in shadow, not looking at a design in its miserable liny skeleton; but conceiving it as it will be when the dawn lights it, and the dusk leaves it; when its stones will be hot and its crannies cool.... His paper lines and proportions have no value: all that he has to do must be done by spaces of lightness and darkness....*[10]

It was Pater, however, who brought the murky subconscious out of the closet and gleefully suggested that Ruskin's "innocence of the eye" should rightfully be the "lust of the eye." His criticism—and the type of image it attempted to describe—drew on the entire spectrum of sensations and thus not only made his writing an invaluable source for Freud[11] but indicated that the object of the critical text need not be the artwork itself but the physical response we have to it. In this, he drew heavily on the epistemological work of Hippolyte Taine, who believed that the ego, acting as mediator between the external world and the body, located an "adjunction" of the visual and tactile perceptions in various parts of the body; and who suggested, as well, that the visual image, made up of sensations whose link to the external world relied only on a delicate correspondence of "spatial rhythms," was structurally no different from hallucinations.[12]

In criticism, then, that was as sensual and subjective as his generation of readers would allow, Pater consistently drew the reader/viewer's attention to the latent sexuality of the work of art. In describing Leonardo's *La Gioconda*, he writes:

> *The presence that thus rose so strangely beside the waters, is expressive of what in the ways of a thousand years men had come to desire. Hers is the head upon which all 'the ends of the world had come,' and the eyelids are a little weary. It is a beauty wrought out from within upon the flesh, the deposit, little cell by little cell, of strange thoughts and fantastic reveries and exquisite passions....She is older than the rocks among which she sits; like the vampire, she has been dead many times, and learned the secrets of the grave; and has been a diver in deep seas, and keeps their fallen day about her....*[13]

But the most profound affinity between Stokes and Pater is in the above-mentioned autobiographical short story, "Child in the House." While it prefigures Stokes's own "inside-out" experiences depicted in *Smooth and Rough* only loosely, it is in this text that the notion of a phenomenological inside-out is clearly laid out. Describing the child, Florian, who was "under the necessity...(of) associating all thoughts to touch and sight, as a sympathetic link between himself and actual, feeling, living objects," Pater writes:

> *In that half-spiritualised house, he could watch the better, over again, the gradual expansion of the soul which had come to be there—of which indeed, through the law which makes the material objects about them so large an element in the children's lives, it had actually become a part; inward and outward being woven through and through each other into one inextricable texture—half, tint and trace and accident of homely colour and form, from the wood and the bricks; half, mere soul-stuff, floated thither from who knows how far.*

The house, objectively, is ordinary, but the child can see its specialness:

*For it is false to suppose that a child's sense of beauty is dependent on choiceness or special fineness, in the objects which present themselves to it, though this indeed comes to be the rule with most of us in later life; earlier, in some degree, we see inwardly; and the child finds for itself, and with unstinted delight, a difference for the sense, in those whites and reds through the smoke on every homely building....*

Florian associates this house with his own personality:

*[T]he early habitation becomes a sort of material shrine or sanctuary of sentiment; a system of visible symbolism interweaves itself through all our thoughts and passions; and irresistibly, little shapes, voices, accidents—the angle at which the sun in the morning fell on the pillow—become part of the great chain wherewith we are bound.*[14]

English criticism in Stokes's time flirted with two themes of traditional aesthetics, namely that of synaesthetics and empathy; but in general, it did so only to confirm, in the dominant British fashion, the empirical and objective side of the issues. Stokes, as Ruskin and Pater before him, was drawn in the opposite, Continental direction. While he never referred directly to the nineteenth century German aestheticians that he was most certainly able to draw on,[15] Stokes nevertheless demonstrated a remarkable affinity to both the neo-Kantian and Hegelian Germans who ushered in "modern" aesthetic theories.

With regard to synaesthetics, Stokes's emphasis on vision and its sensual and epistemological capacity put him at variance with perhaps the most influential and fashionable aesthetic opinions of his day. Bernard Berenson, in his *The Florentine Painters of the Renaissance* (1909), revived the eighteenth-century Empiricist view that vision was flat, relying on tactile memory to "construct" the third dimension:

*Now, painting is an art which aims at giving an abiding impression of artistic reality with only two dimensions. The painter must, therefore, do consciously what we all do unconsciously—construct his third dimension. And he can accomplish his task only as we accomplish ours, by giving tactile values to retinal impressions. His first business then is to rouse the tactile sense, for I must have the illusion of being able to touch a figure...before I shall take it for granted as real, and let it affect me lastingly.*[16]

Stokes, as we have seen, agreed with the idea that vision was flat, but unlike Berenson, who thus deduced vision's weakness and dependence, Stokes saw in the flatness vision's claim to superiority, its capacity to grasp the object instantly, without intellectual mediation. Drawing here on Bradley's similar view of undivided and unmediated visual apprehension, the moment of visual perception for Stokes unveiled the object in all of its otherness. In describing the unique appeal of stone's "mass-effect," Stokes writes of this visual capacity:

[Mass-effect] is in part an appeal to the sense of touch though the object be a building and not a piece of sculpture. But solids afford an effect of mass only when they also allow the immediate, the instantaneous synthesis that the eye alone can perform.... I would isolate and stress this far more pregnant quality of mass, its appeal to the quickness of the eye, its power to captivate in one second or less. Exploring sense of touch, I admit, introduces a succession, and therefore entails an element of time though it be turned into an instantaneous impression by the quickness of the perceiving eye. (I, p. 134-35)

At the same time, again drawing on Bradley's monism, the visual interpretation of the world did not exclude but subsumed the other sensations. As the quote above indicates, Stokes never completely denied the tactile response that was implicit in visual apprehension, and in this he alludes to Berenson. But unlike the American, Stokes was anxious to emphasize that these other sensations were implicit in vision; they formed the context of its meaning. If it was through vision that we apprehended, it was through the other sensations that we responded.

Stokes's understanding of vision as both first among the senses and superior in apprehension to intellectual rationalization recalls the neo-Kantian aesthetics of Conrad Fiedler and "pure visibility." Fiedler, in his *On Judging Works of Visual Art* (1876) and his unfinished *Three Fragments* (1895), based his work on the notion that vision and visual knowledge were distinct from but in no way inferior to intellectual/verbal understanding. In attempting to define the unique status of the artist in exploring and exposing vision's unique capabilities, he stressed the fact that while most people allow their visual images to be immediately absorbed into perceptual conventions—particularly those imposed from the outside by language—artistic vision, isolating the activities of the eye, allowed the image to have its own life, one that confirmed rather than denied its nonobjective nature.[17] It was an understanding of apprehension which, in the manner of Stokes after him, invited the same subject/object, inside/outside identification:

> *The recognition that everything outside us is, in the last analysis, within us...destroys the illusion that there is an external world which we need quite simply to take in with our bodily organs and mental faculties in order to possess it....*
>
> *Existence only has a reasonable sense for us in so far as something of a specific kind appears in consciousness.... We have become aware that all reality exists only and exclusively in the processes operating in and through us.*
>
> *Nothing, it appears, can be more sensory, more physical, than the stuff of the world which surrounds us, with which we are aquainted and to which we ourselves belong with our physical bodies. Nothing can be more spiritual, so to speak, unsubstantial, than the concepts through which we dominate the spiritual world.*[18]

Fiedler's colleague, the sculptor Adolf Hildebrand, in his *The Problem of Form* (1893), carried "pure visibility" farther into the realm of sculpture and viewer/object dynamics. Hildebrand distinguished between two kinds of vision, distant and near.  Distant vision, the proper realm of the artist, was that which grasped the object frontally and directly, without resorting to successive movement close to and around it.  Near vision was the fragmented, sequential one that required intellectual reconstruction.  In an attitude that supported relief sculpture, it was the subtle gradations of the planes parallel to that of the observer, as well as the planar angles of recession and the layered play of light and shade, that conveyed the aesthetic emotion.

But Stokes's overriding empathy with and personification of the architectural object, enhanced by the fact that Stokes's visual rapport was merely an entrée into a more total sensual identification, also aligned him with those Hegelian aestheticians who combatted what they felt was the too narrowly confined formalist program of the aforementioned neo-Kantians.  The concept of empathy was first identified and studied by Robert Vischer in 1873 with the publication of his *Das Optische Formgefuhl*.  It was subsequently made popular by Theodor Lipps and then picked up by Wölfflin and Worringer in Germany, and Vernon Lee and Geoffery Scott in England.  Exploring the aesthetic response described by Lipps as "*Sich in etwas einfuehlen*," "to feel oneself into something," empathy implied that the "Soul" is not innate in the object, as Hegel had maintained, but a projection of the individual observer.  Originally, empathy was used to explain our general ability both to understand the third dimension (maintaining once again that we only do so with recourse to tactile memory) and to respond to spatial forms by way of their source in the mass and dimensions of the human body.  As Vischer asked, "What mean Space and Time to me, what are Projection, Dimension, Rest and Movement, what all Forms, if in them does not stream the red blood of life?"[19]

Later, as the psychological aspects of subject/object identification were explored in a more systematic way, empathy, with varying degrees of explicitness, was utilized as a concept to explain issues of both space and mass.  Schmarsow, Riegl, and Frankl, emphasizing the movement and activity of the body as the referent against which space and spatial concepts are interpreted, examined a relatively abstract, but highly influential, notion of architectural empathy.  Wölfflin, on the other hand, was more intent on explaining, in the manner of Vitruvius, our identification with the corporeal mass of a building, its capacity to be read as human form.  While Stokes utilized the first, spatial notion of empathy in examining the importance of approach to and around buildings, it is this second, more radical identification with the building's mass that marks Stokes's criticism and aligns him with Wölfflin.  In a passage from his Renaissance and Baroque  that could be found as easily in one of Stokes's texts, Wölfflin writes:

> We judge every body by analogy with our own bodies.  The object—even if completely
> dissimilar to ourselves—will not only transform itself immediately into a creature, with head
> and foot, back and front; and not only are we convinced that this creature must feel ill at ease
> if it does not stand upright and seems about to fall over, but we go so far as to experience,
> to highly sensitive degree, the spiritual condition and contentment or discontent expressed
> by any configuration, however different from ourselves.[20]

The affinity that Stokes had with both Fiedler's "pure visibility" and Wölfflin's corporeal empathy rested not only on the similarity of his views with regard to visual apprehension and bodily projection respectively, but on the fact that both theories represented the first generation of a type of aesthetic criticism that he himself so persistently pursued, one that did not see aesthetics as an extension of either moral demands or issues of object-bound criteria of beauty; aesthetics, in their hands, became a function of epistemology and psychological apprehension.  This underlying philosophic premise spoke directly to Stokes's own psychological needs.  Interestingly, this also coincided with an emphasis on architecture as a paradigmatic art.  But it should also be clear that Stokes, in his criticism, employed these ideas in a radically different manner.  Fiedler and Wölfflin still functioned in the positivist realm of epistemology, and their work pursued the cause/effect relationship of perception, understanding, and appreciation. Stokes, on the other hand, was not anxious to pinpoint these phenomena as much as he hoped to evoke their power and depict their meaning. In this metaphorical application of "pure visibility" and empathy, at once less real and more powerful than the Germanic theories which were their source, interpretation dominates over analysis, hermeneutics over explanation. Stokes's descriptions of buildings functioned, therefore, with an evocative power unfathomed by the German aestheticians.

We partake of an inexhaustible feeding mother (a fine building announces), though we have bitten, torn, dirtied and pinched her, though we thought to have lost her utterly, to have destroyed her utterly in fantasy and act. We are grateful to stone buildings for their stubborn material, hacked and hewed but put together carefully, restored in better shape than those pieces that the infant imagined he had chewed or scattered, for which he searched. Much crude rock stands rearranged; now in the form of apertures, of suffusion at the sides of the apertures, the bites, the tears, the pinches are miraculously identified with the recipient passages of the body, with sense organs, with features; as well as with the good mother which we would eat more mercifully for preservation and safety within, and for our own. (II, p. 241)

It is in the realm of hermeneutics, then, that Stokes's contribution to twentieth-century criticism as a whole can be evaluated. Writing, as we have seen, at the time when Bell and Fry's "Significant Form" and with it a broader context of formalist criticism were in ascendency, Stokes, perhaps more than he was willing to admit, absorbed the effects of this trend and produced a criticism that explored issues of form directly derived from these Bloomsbury critics. But as early as 1930, Stokes saw that if formalism was to have substantial critical value, it must dispense with the idea, implicit in "Significant Form," of form's "privileged autonomy." Indeed, in his criticism, Stokes's discussion of form—the degree of shadow, the connection from ground to wall, the play of shapes and rhythms—was so intimately bound to the building and the entirety of its effect that he never escaped the hermeneutic circle joining him and the object. His work, therefore, was not opposed to the formal criticism that surrounded him as much as it critiqued it from within. Stokes was willing to respond to the power of form as it was manifest in the buildings he loved—the canal buildings of Venice, Sigismondo's Tempio at Rimini, Luciano's courtyard at Urbino—but not to grant this power Platonic status. In this, one is reminded again of Ruskin who was criticized by his contemporaries for theoretical and "formal" inconsistency, but who was later vindicated on this very account by one of his most astute disciples, Marcel Proust. Here, in a passage from Pastiches et Mélanges in which Proust could be describing Stokes as easily as Ruskin, he both locates the essence of the value of the Ruskin/Stokes form of evocative criticism and depicts a type of criticism that only now, with the advent of deconstructive criticism, is understood to challenge more accepted modes of formalist criticism.

> [T]he thought of Ruskin is not like the thought of Emerson, for example, which is contained in its entirety in one book, that is to say something abstract, a pure sign of itself. The object to which a type of thought like Ruskin's applies, and from which it is inseparable, is not immaterial, it is distributed here and there over the surface of the earth. One must go and look for it where it is found, at Pisa, Florence, Venice, in the National Gallery, at Rouen, Amiens and in the mountains of Switzerland. Such a type of thought which has another object besides itself, which has been realized in space, which is no longer infinite and free thought, but limited and subjected thought, which has incarnated itself in bodies of sculpted marble, snowy mountains, painted faces, is perhaps less divine than pure thought. But it greatly embellishes the universe for us, or at least some individual parts of it, some named parts, because it has touched them, and initiating us into them by obliging us, if we wish to understand them, to love them.[21]

1. Adrian Stokes, *The Critical Writings of Adrain Stokes*, ed. Lawrence Gowing, London: Thames and Hudson, 1978, vol. II, pp. 98-9. All subsequent references to this work, in the volumes, are made in the text.

2. Stokes, personal notebook, "Oxford Days." I wish to thank Ann Angus, Stokes's widow, for giving me access to Stokes's personal notebooks.

3. Sigmund Freud, *The Complete Psychological Works of Sigmund Freud*; Standard Edition, ed. and trans. by James Strachey, New York: W. W. Norton, 1976, vol. 18, p. 24.

4. *PN Review 15*, vol. 7, no. 1, pp. 41-2.

5. Stokes's first three books were largely elaborations of this carving/ modeling distinction. While it began as a fairly literal distinction in sculptural technique, it increasingly became a conceptual distinction regarding the mental attitude the artist had towards his work. In *Colour and Form*, it was applied to the use of color in painting. The distinction was later absorbed into the Kleinian depressive/schizophrenic one.

6. John Ruskin, *Modern Painters IV* in *The Works of John Ruskin*, Library Edition, ed. Cook and Wedderburn, London: George Allen, 1903-12, vol. 6, par. 21.

7. Ruskin, *Modern Painters II*, in *Works*, vol. 4, par. 4.

8. Ruskin, Letter to father from Verona, *Works*, vol. 10, par. xxvi.

9. Ruskin, *St. Marks Rest* in *Works*, vol. 24, chap. 8, par. 110.

10. Ruskin, *The Seven Lamps of Architecture* in *Works*, vol. 8, chap. 3, par. 13.

11. Freud drew on Pater in his discussion of Leonardo and the artistic personality. Indeed, Freud's depiction of sight and the implicit role it might play in aesthetics reminds one of Pater's as he describes both the Mona Lisa and Leonardo: "an activity that is ultimately derived from touching...the progressive concealment of the body which goes along with civilization keeps sexual curiosity awake. This curiosity seeks to complete the sexual object by revealing its hidden parts. It can, however, be diverted in the direction of art, if its interest can be shifted away from the genitals onto the shape of the body as a whole." Freud, *The Complete Psychological Works*, vol. 6, p. 56.

12. I am indebted to Richard Read for pointing out, in his dissertation for Reading University, England, on Hazlitt, Ruskin, Pater, and Stokes the influence of Taine on Pater. Taine is extremely sensuous in his description of the artistic sensibility, describing it as one where "the whole body speaks." The influence of Taine on Pater is also witnessed in Pater's conclusion to *The Renaissance* and his essay on "Style," in which Pater depicts the self as a constantly changing flux of molecules.

13. Walter Pater, *The Renaissance*, ed. Donald Hill, Berkeley: University of California Press,1980, p. 99.

14. Walter Pater, *Selected Writings of Walter Pater*, ed. Harold Bloom, New York: Columbia University Press,1980, pp. 2-4.

15. Stokes was rather cagey about his sources and rarely admitted to being influenced by anyone other than Melanie Klein, and even here he made it clear that he had developed his own carving/modeling ideas before he discovered the applicability of her psychoanalytic theories. In a letter to Richard Wollheim, he specifically denies being interested in Wolfflin, although he refers to him in a footnote in his 1937 *Colour and Form*.

16. Bernard Berenson, *The Florentine Painters of the Renaissance*, Oxford: Clarendon Press, 1909, 3rd ed., pp. 3-5.

17. For Fiedler on vision, see "Three Fragments," *A Documentary History of Art, III*, ed. Holt, Garden City, New york: Doubleday and Co., Inc., 1966, p. 451.

18. Quoted in Michael Podro, *The Manifold in Perception*, Oxford: Clarendon Press, 1972, p. 111.

19. See Cornelis van de Ven, "Ideas of Space in German Architectural Theory," *Architectural Association Quarterly*, vol. 9, no. 2-3, 1977, p. 30.

20. Heinrich Wölfflin, *Renaissance and Baroque*, trans. Kathrin Simon, Ithica, New York: Cornell University Press, 1967, p. 77.

21. Quoted from Stephen Bann, "The Case for Stokes (and Pater)," in *PN Review 9*, vol 6, no. 1, p. 8.

Each *cho-nai* also constructs a *hariban*, a neighborhood altar, which is built in a space facing the street which on ordinary days, *ke-no-hi*, might be a parking garage or some other utilitarian space. The *hariban* is the equivalent of *otabisho*, the field shrine of the Shinto shrine for agrarian communities. The *hariban* is the place where the *Kami* is brought by the festival wagons, *hiki-yama*, of each *cho-nai*. The *hariban*

thereby becomes the temporary resting place for *Kami* during *matsuri*, after which the *Kami* is believed to return to the natural metaphysical space or *oku*, the inner space of the natural mountains.

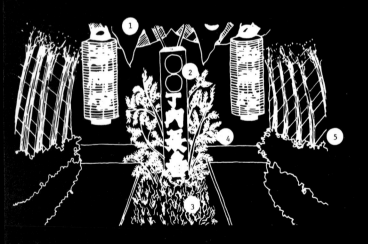

LOOKING OUT FROM A *HARIBAN*:

1 *KOKKI*      NATIONAL FLAG.
2 *CHONAI*     LOCAL NEIGHBORHOOD.
3 *SUSUKI*     JAPANESE PAMPAS GRASS.
4 *MATSU*      JAPANESE PINE.
5 *YARAI*      FENCE OF SPLIT BAMBOO.

LOOKING INTO A *HARIBAN*:

| | | |
|---|---|---|
| 1 | *SURUME* | DRIED CUTTLEFISH (SYMBOL OF WEALTH FROM THE OCEAN). |
| 2 | *MOCHI* | RICE CAKE WHICH SYMBOLIZES A "SPECIAL" OCCASION, USUALLY FESTIVE OCCASIONS. |
| 3 | *SANBO* | AN UNPAINTED WOODEN CONTAINER FOR ALL SORTS OF FORMAL OCCASIONS. |
| 4 | *HATSUHO* | THE FIRST RICE OF THE HARVEST, SYMBOLIZING THE WEALTH OF THE LAND. |
| 5 | *HIBACHI* | A HAND WARMER. |
| 6 | *KISETSU NO KUDAMONO* | FRUITS OF THE SEASON, SYMBOLIZING THE WEALTH OF THE LAND. |
| 7 | *KISETSU NO YASAI* | VEGETABLES OF THE SEASON, SYMBOLIZING THE WEALTH OF THE LAND. |
| 8 | *MATSU* | PINE TREE, SYMBOLIZING LONG LIFE. |
| 9 | *OMIKI ZAKE* | RICE WINE DEDICATED TO THE GODS. |

INSTRUCTIONS FOR DECORATING A *HARIBAN*

*Hariban* decorations vary from one *chonai* (local neighborhood) to another. The foods dedicated to the gods seem alike everywhere. As the *Amaterasu Omikami* (the Sun Goddess) is worshipped, any *Hariban* could carry considerable authority.

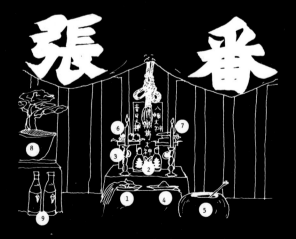

*Figures and Notes*[1]

# At the End of the Architectural

**Lars Lerup**

# Promenade

## 1.1 The Absentminded Examiners

Figure 1[2]

We are in Walter Benjamin's Berlin of the teens, standing on the sidewalk of a grand boulevard (it may be Unter den Linden) watching a parade. A group of men look intently at us as they march by. Though they are civilians they appear to be military men just out of their uniforms. Most probably, they are the fathers of the new Germany that was to be known as the Third Reich. Shoulder to shoulder, united and strong, they march with purpose into their future—our all–too–painful past.

Their gazes brush past our faces without focus. What is important is the gaze itself: the beam that bridges the depths of their eyes and our blank faces. It is hope, direction, and determination coupled with a certain absentmindedness, even self-indulgence, because the gaze doesn't see—it dosen't need to see since it has already seen what it needs to see: the marcher's version of the future.

Through the benefit of hindsight we know that from our point of view the errand of these men was foolish, even murderous, since thirty years later they indirectly caused Walter Benjamin to take his life at Port Bou. Yet he warned about these "absentminded examiners," when he wrote in the classic "The Work of Art in the Age of Mechanical Reproduction:"

"The mass is a matrix from which all traditional behavior toward works of art issues today in a new form. Quantity has been transmuted into quality. The greatly increased mass of participants has produced a change in the mode of participation." He continues, writing about the analysis of film: *Distraction and concentration form polar opposites which may be stated as follows: A man who concentrates before a work of art is absorbed by it. He enters into the work the way legend tells of the Chinese painter when he viewed his finished painting. In contrast, the distracted mass absorbs the work of art. This is most obvious with regards to buildings. Architecture has always represented the prototypes of a work of art the reception of which is consummated by a collectivity in a state of distraction. The laws of its reception are most instructive.*

*Buildings have been man's companions since primeval times. Many art forms have developed and perished....But the human need for shelter is lasting. Architecture has never been idle. Its history is more ancient than that of any art, and its claim to being a living force has significance in every attempt to comprehend the relationship of the masses to art. Buildings are appropriated in a twofold manner: by use and perception—or rather, by touch and sight. Such appropriation cannot be understood in terms of the attentive concentration of a tourist before a famous building. On the tactile side there is no counterpart to contemplation on the optical side. Tactile appropriation is accomplished not so much by attention as by habit. As regards architecture, habit determines to a large extent even optical reception. The latter, too, occurs much less through rapt attention than by noticing the object in incidental fashion....The public is an examiner, but an absentminded one.*[3]

Back on the boulevard, in the spectacle of the city, they march as the actors and we watch as the audience. As rapt bystanders we are part of the architecture, the backdrop for the events of history, only stepping stones in a narrative that is eagerly trying to get to the end—to a future that they thought would be better than their present.

## 1.2 Their Plans

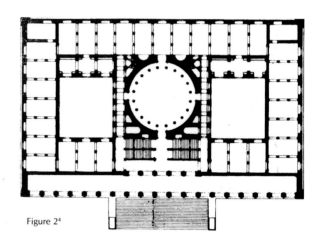

Figure 2[4]

## 2.1 The Boxer

## 2.2 His Body

Figure 3[5]

The symbolic footprint of this narrative can be seen in the plan of a building not far from the boulevard: Karl Friedrich Schinkel's Altes Museum of 1823–30, with its unbroken row of Ionic columns, Pantheon-like rotunda, and relentless matrix of exhibition rooms. Here room upon room marches in an endless enfilade, mirroring the scene on the boulevard—the immobile bystanders are the walls, the space they enclose become the marching men, and the door leading from one room to the other, the inscription of one of the men: the man in the city suit, top hat, and white beard. It is this vigorous, determined character that I have picked out as the straw man. He will appear, fully modernized, at the bottom of the ramp in Le Corbusier's Villa Savoye—the beginning of the architectural promenade.

The intention is to seek the implications of architectural movement and the dichotomy of absorption/distraction for us, the inheritors of this legacy, in the relations between the parade, Benjamin, the Altes Museum, and below, Le Corbusier and his utopian enthusiasm.

Corbusian man appears full-fledged in Project Wanner of 1928–29. Here, in the application of the concept of the Immeubles-villas of 1923 and 1925, he is shown in a drawing of an interior dressed in trunks and tank top vigorously pounding a punching bag in one of *les jardins suspendu* while a woman stands watching on a balcony as a mother would watch a child. It could be his wife, or *la bonne* for that matter—her hands are resting on a railing on which a blanket hangs—as much a symbol for her as the punching bag is for him.

The drawing shows the distinctive double height space that became the insignia of Corbusian space of this vintage despite the constraints of what Colin Rowe has called the "paralysed section" of the floors as tables, one on top of the other, that first appeared in the Dom-ino System of 1914. Aside from the open book on the table and the immobile female bystander, the suspended garden is vibrant with architectural movement: the oblong column, the curving wall, and a rope suspended from the ceiling taken directly from a jungle gym. This is the first trace of the architectural promenade and its technologies.

In Le Corbusier's transformation, our straw man in the demonstration on Unter den Linden has become the consummate modern athlete, whose politics have receded in favor of the care of the body. "Culture of the body," says Le Corbusier, "is to care with wisdom for one's bodily frame—the human body, the most perfect machine in the world, the physical prop of our whole existence. The body can thrive or wither, be resplendent or decay in sickness or deformity. For this, adequate sites and environments must be chosen. It is for architecture and urbanism to create the means."[6]

## 2.3 His Section

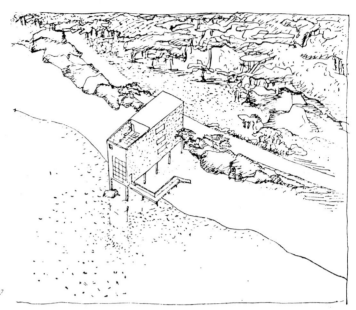

Figure 4[7]

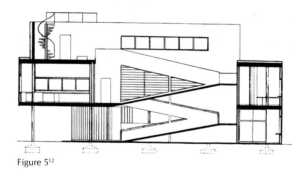

Figure 5[12]

## 2.4 The Moving Subject

Figure 6[11]

Our man arrives by automobile at Villa Savoye and Le Corbusier describes the arrival: "The auto enters under the pilotis, turns around the common services, arrives at the center, at the door of entry, enters in the garage where it may await its pursuit of the return: this is the fundamental idea." [8] He marches no longer in the company of others; our man is alone in his car. The footprint is no longer the enfilade of rooms or the plan, but the entire array of road and, as we shall see, its extension—the ramp and its associated technologies. The house itself is a mere stop on a much longer journey than the "circular ruin" the Altes museum implied—"...this is the fundamental idea", Le Corbusier continues: "The open house poses in the middle of the open as an object, without displacing anything."[9] Once inside the vestibule, our man steps out of his city clothes and dons shorts and a tank top. Half running, his fingertips run absentmindedly along the handrail of the ramp that takes him to the floor of the house proper. "But we'll continue the promenade. After the garden on this floor, we climb via the ramp to the roof of the house where the solarium is."[10] The domain of our straw man is no longer the plan but the section, and here at its cusp, we have reached the end of the promenade, but before we contemplate this event, Le Corbusier has more to tell: *Arab architecture gives us a precious piece of information. It is appreciated while walking, with the feet; it is walking, while moving that one sees the development of the architectural order. It is a principle contrary to the one used by baroque architecture that is conceived on paper from a fixed theoretical point. I prefer the insights of Arab architecture. This particular house acts as a real architectural promenade, offering constantly varying aspects, unexpected and occasionlly astonishing.*[11]

Succinctly, elegantly, Le Corbusier offers us the entire agenda of a filmic or scenographic view of architecture. It appears at first as an illustration of Benjamin's previous argument. However, our man, having shed his former garb, is, according to Le Corbusier, all attention and completely aware of "*un schema de poteaux et de poutres*" (a matrix of beams and columns) as well as the site, the suspended garden, and the free plan, and we realize that he is talking about a superman who can do two things at the same time: pursue his everyday narrative while simultaneously appreciating architecture. Assuming that Benjamin is right in principle, an actual boxer sees the architecture only from the corner of his eye, while the everyday narrative dominates his vision.

The enfilade of rooms in the Altes Museum marches endlessly in its own footsteps, one story layed on top of another. The doors as erect rectangles hint at the physiognomy of the pedestrian. This circularity must have appeared completely ridiculous to Le Corbusier, who saw the great errand into the modern world as a stair, corridor, rope, and ramp reaching up and away from the constraints of the past.

The *Oeuvre Complet* of the period between 1910 and 1940 was replete with sectional technologies, all promising speed, efficiency, and fortunes beyond. This message was, as we all know, all too optimistic and thereby cast a critical light on the invisible seam between architecture and utopia.

## 2.5 The End: Alternative I

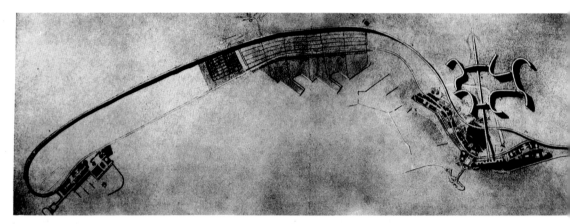

Figure 7[17]

## 2.6 The Murder of the Future

## 3.1 The End: Alternative II

Figure 8[18]

The "pure topological field" brilliantly recognized by Manfredo Tafuri in his interpretation of Le Corbusier's Obus Plan for Algiers of 1931, was created by the serpentine strip-city that the latter was planned to overlay on the city and its environs: "Absorb that multiplicity, reconcile the improbable through the certainty of the plan, offset organic and disorganic qualities by accentuating their interrelationship, demonstrate that the maximum level of programming of productivity coincides with the maximum level of the productivity of the spirit: these are the objectives delineated by Le Corbusier with a lucidity that has no comparison in progressive European culture."[14] Consequently, the entire region is turned into a *plan libre* and the strip becomes the ultimate architectural promenade. It no longer just suggests the optimal path through the "field" but is, by containing within it a continuous presence of an entire population of "boxers." The architecture is absolutely synomorphic with behavior. The promenade as a pedantic and didactic instrument for a privileged view of architecture has at Algiers become the only way to see. Futhermore, the locus of hope—*le jardin suspendu*—at the end of the promenade has rather anticlimactically become the on and off ramps to the linear city. On the other hand, since the Obus Plan is utopia, we no longer need the promise since, as Tafuri writes,"The technological universe is impervious to the here and there."[15]

The image of the half-running boxer on his way up along the ramp strongly suggests the basis of the neurosis of our time. Manfredo Tafuri said in a recent interview: *One of the greatest problems of our times is dealing with the uncontrollable acceleration of time, a process that began with nineteenth century industrializations; it keeps continually disposing of things in expectation of the future, of the next thing. All avant-garde movements were in fact based on the continual destruction of preceeding works in order to go on to something new. Implicit in this is the murder of the future. The program of the modern artist was always to anticipate the next thing. It's just like when you see a coming attraction ad for a film, essentially you have already consumed the film and the event of going to see the film is predictably disappointing and makes you anxious for something new.*[16]

John Hejduk's Silent Witnesses of 1984, shown in the New National Gallery in connection with the IBA exhibition in Berlin, reminds us of Le Corbusier's garden stair at Garches but *sans* villa. They serve, seen in light of Tafuri's remarks, as the tombstone of *la promenade architecturale*. Leading nowhere and therefore pointing only at themselves, the mad rush towards the future has come to an abrupt halt; does this mean the end of innovation, utopia, and theory, leaving us with skill only (of the type that Richard Meier flaunts)? Tafuri seems to think so.

## 4.1 Swedish Parenthesis: An Alternative Beginning of the Promenade

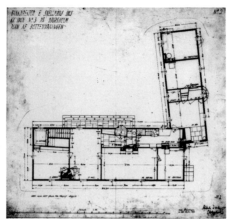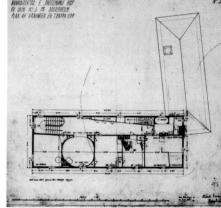

Figure 9[19]

## 5.1 The End: Alternative III or the Murder of the Architectural Promenade

Figure 10[21]

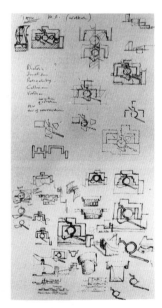

Figure 11[22]

Just as several ends may be envisioned, other beginnings are also possible.  One such beginning can be found by stepping back ten years from Villa Savoye to Erik Gunnar Asplund's Villa Snellman of 1917–18.  Hypothetically there are only two kinds of plans, those with rooms in enfilade and those with rooms served by a corridor.  And in Villa Snellman the corridor contains some telling architectonic marks that pertain to the beginning of the privileged form of "communication" between a moving subject and a movement within architecture itself that Le Corbusier called the architectural promenade.  Asplund writes: "The building is an attempt to accommodate a modern home in a structure one-and-a-half rooms wide.  The one-room width, formerly used in the 'paired cottage,' and its descendants is not really equal to modern requirements as regards ancillary spaces, heating and communication."[20]

The halfroom, or "the gallery" as he also calls it, is the space of communication, desirable for the modern house.  (The enfilade of the rooms from the "paired cottage" is still retained next to the corridor for more ancient rituals.)  The promenade begins downstairs at the entry, in the corridor, that is flared such that the straw man stands in a focal point of a built perspective, with its picture plane just behind the stair at the end of the corridor.  The flair is achieved by a poché in the exterior wall (hiding closets, a bathroom, and a service stair).  The same perspectival corridor is repeated on the second floor.  Although there are some practical aspects behind the form of the corridor, its seductive qualities, leading on the pedestrian, are undeniable.  Combined with the mad swarming of windows on the facades of the villa, the flared corridor provides us with an alternative "origin" of the Modernist movement *architecturale*.

The relationship between Schinkel's Altes Museum and James Stirling's addition to the 1985 Staatsgallerie, Stuttgart, is well known.  A large U-shaped fragment of the old enfilade of rooms from the museum in Berlin is almost reconstructed in the addition; but simultaneously a public pedestrian link is laid across the galleries, in the shape of a giant ramp much like the ramp in the Carpenter Center of 1963.  With postmodernist bravura and informality Stirling combines the world of the enfilade with that of the architectural promenade, closing the circle, possibly suggesting that one is just the extension of the other.  More potently, Stirling has manifested Benjamin's dichotomy of distraction and concentration by giving the strolling public their own path across the museum, only lightly brushing by its demanding displays of art, and also by giving the good old enfilade back to the art aficionado who in the backwater of the swift river of the city can concentrate on the displays undisturbed.  Like Alexander, Stirling has severed the Gordian knot with one swift chop.

We have again come to the end of the promenade, but unlike our encounter with the end at the solarium on the roof of the Villa Savoye, this is the conceptual end (although Stirling's promenade actually connects with the entire street system of the city).  The promenade is finite, a mere prosthetic device that meets needs of a particular kind, presented on equal terms with the enfilade.  It holds no false promises about the future.  Unfortunately, this also makes Stirling's compromise no solution to our hope of delaying Tafuri's "murder of the future."  Stripped of its utopia and Corbusian pathos, the promenade has become just another technology left in the graveyard of modernism—another place to hurry through.

## 6.1 The Flâneur and His Turtle

## 6.2 Flânade I: Delays

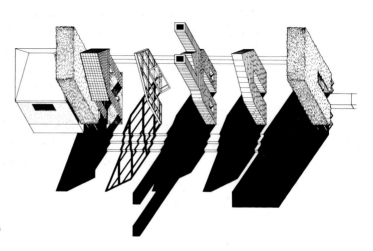

Figure 12[24]

1. Soft wall
2. Dry wall
3. Hot wall
4. Hard wall
5. Wet wall
6. Soft wall
7. Bedroom

7

6   5   4   3   2   1

Figure 13[25]

Walter Benjamin writes: "Around 1840 it was briefly fashionable to take turtles for a walk in the arcades. The *flâneurs* liked to have the turtles set the pace for them. If they had had their way, progress would have been obliged to accommodate itself to this pace. But this attitude did not prevail; Taylor (American and father of Scientific Management, a method that led Ford to revolutionize car production), who popularized the watchword 'Down with dawdling!,' carried the day."[23] The *flâneur*, or dandy—possibly the inventor of the concept of leisure—attempted to slow down the pace of the rushing crowd that went about its everyday life to the beat of scientific management, much like cogs in a machine. The turtle served as a delay of the everyday narrative and its inevitable end. And, as Benjamin realized, the aesthetic strategy to end the mad rush of time was miserably defeated. Therefore, to use it again, as I shall do below, frees it from all utopian aspiration, placing it in the realm of stubbornness or in less flattering domains.

In 1977 I designed a house for a client that was never built, but it has served as a key to my work and in a sense as the beginning of my tangles with both enfilade and promenade. My aspiration in Villa Prima Facie (A House at First Appearance) was to create a place for Benjamin's *flâneur*—to create a *flânade*, if you excuse my abuse of the French language. I prefer this term to the proper French term *flânerie* since it refers entirely to the activity, while the *flânade*, just as the architectural promenade, refers both to the activity and the physical setting.

According to the client, the new house should remind him as little as possible of the master bedrooms and living rooms of his past. Therefore, the stereotypical plan was erased and a tabula rasa in the modernist spirit was created, on which a series of walls was placed in an enfilade. Each wall was an independent element rather than a part of a room. These soft, dry, hot, hard, and wet walls were finally sheltered by a greenhouse.

Activities associated with the separate walls, such as the regular clipping of the topiary soft wall, or the reading by the dry wall while the rain pattered on the greenhouse, or the daily shower under the wet wall, were all delays that slowed down the end of the enfilade—an end that was inevitable, since, unlike the Altes Museum, the enfilade was not "circular," but linear—the promenade hovered surreptitiously in the openings cut in each of the walls, thereby suggesting the future beyond. However, the end in the Villa Prima Facie was a bedroom, in which the murder of the future was exchanged for a mock death: a night of good sleep.

## 6.3 Flânade II: Traps

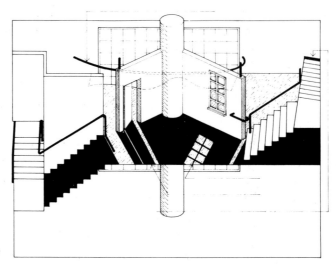

Figure 14[27]

## 6.4 Flânade III: A Plan Degree Zero

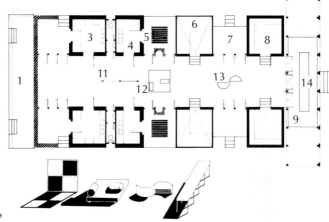

1. Front porch
2. Entry court
3. Kitchen
4. Bath
5. Court with plunge
6. Bed (pyramid)
7. Bed court
8. Bed (cube)
9. Arcade
10. The hall
11. Which-way-mirror
12. Sofa/bed
13. Which-way-chair
14. First work table / last supper table

Figure 15[28]

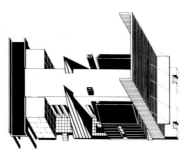

Figure 16[29]

The Nofamily House of 1978-81 was designed for an imaginary and stereotypical family whose everyday narrative was juxtaposed on a house filled with traps set to delay or completely stop it. A Liberated Handrail stopped at one point to serve its dull assignment, in order to simply revel in its form. This was done by having the rail cut loose from its proper place—by breaking the syntax of the stepping stones in the family narrative. Likewise, a Useless Door stared accusingly at its frustrated user, while the Fresh Window allowed a new point of view on family life. Finally, the Stair That Leads Nowhere stops the architectural promenade just at the ceiling, prohibiting a Corbusian conclusion at a potential solarium.

The inspiration here was Duchamp's coat hanger nailed to the floor, causing everyone to trip, and the atmosphere of frustration and endless delay described by Jorge Luis Borges in "The Immortal" of 1956:

A labyrinth is a structure compounded to confuse men; its architecture, rich in symmetries, is subordinated to that end. In the palace the architecture lacked any such finality. It abounded in deadened corridors, high unattainable windows, portentous doors which led to a cell or pit, incredible inverted stairways whose steps and balustrades hung downwards. Other stairways, clinging airily to the side of a monumental wall, would die without leading anywhere, after making two or three turns in the lofty darkness of the cupolas.[26]

Recently, I designed a house for four imaginary clients: two women with their young sons. The house was to be set in the Garden District in New Orleans. The project is called the New Zero because it is the offspring of another house called the Texas Zero. The principle here is to create a neutral plane—a plan degree zero—that, unlike the Corbusian plan libre, does not promise freedom but establishes a status quo: a genteel version of Borges' palace.

This neutrality was achieved by using a common rhetorical device called reversion, exemplified in the statement:

"he has, has he?"

The statement is formally symmetrical across the comma but the meaning is not; "has he?" puts the first assertion in question and therefore turns the sentence in upon itself, creating a neutrality or status quo. The plan of the New Zero is replete with components of these figures: two leaning fireplaces (one in compression, the other in tension), The Which-Way-Mirror, The Sofa/Bed, The Which-Way-Chair, The First Worktable/Last Supper Table, and the Almost Symmetrical Kitchen-Toilet-Bathroom Houses. Assembled in "sentences," the components form reversions and in other cases palindromes ("sentences" that read the same forwards and backwards).

# 7.1 For Ambiguity

# 7.2 The Clasp and the Bridge

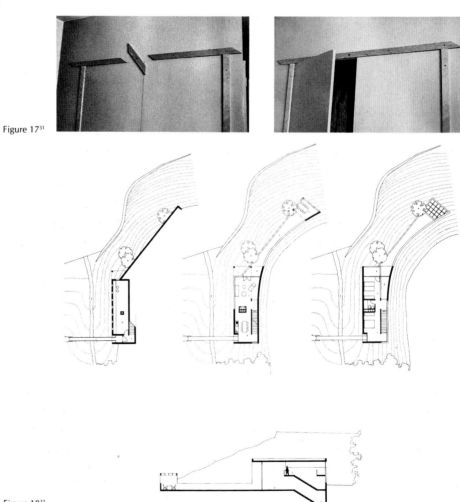

Figure 17[31]

Figure 18[32]

There was a distinct distance between the body and the marching rooms of the enfilade. Here the walls lived separated from the pedestrian whose only reflection was the outline of the doors. This clarity of distinction between the human and the artificial was completely abandoned in the architectural promenade that served as a prosthetic device for the new man—surreptitiously we slipped from the realm of flesh and blood to the world of artifice. No wonder that we have begun to confuse ourselves with it, and call out for more anthropomorphic semblance. Yet this is truly a fool's errand. There are shades of both schizophrenia and megalomania in this confusion of self and world. The confusion is most apparent in the insistence that architecture is representative of man, when by now, after so many years of internal formation, architecture must be seen as a separate and parallel enterprise, whose relationship with us is at best ambiguous.

Two examples of built objects will illustrate this desirable ambiguity, and simultaneously cater to the well being of our straw man.


As Umberto Eco has pointed out in his *Theory of Semiotics*, the Russian formalists were fond of using the so-called "device of making it strange," *priem ostrannenja*, in an attempt to increase the "difficulty and the duration of the perception, of the art object itself—"…the text becomes self-focusing: it directs the attention of the addressee primarily to its own shape.[30] This is thus an attempt to overcome the chasm between Benjamin's "distraction and concentration," and bring subject and object closer together, because there is a distinct distance between subject and object in their common habitual relation.

Recently, historicism has led many architects to return to columns, porticos and alas, broken pediments. These devices attempt to create ambiguity by putting the structure of the building into (some) question. The closet clasp that I made in my own house profits from the lesson of the broken pediment but instead of producing superficial ambiguity (after all, the building still must stand despite its breaks), here actual ambiguity is present, because when the closet is closed, the "pediment" is broken and thus works as a closing mechanism, but when the door is open, the pediment is momentarily mended, yet it no longer works as a clasp.

Luigi Snozzi's work has eluded acclaim by a wider audience, yet his work will prove important in the long run, particularly in a Corbusian geography. Snozzi, like Le Corbusier, has his obsessions, one of which is relevant to this discussion. In his Casa Kalman of 1974–76, in Brione, Ticino, a long narrow path or terrace connects the main house with an outdoor room and its pergola. This "bridge" appears also in Casa Bianchetti of 1975–77, and in Casa Heschl of 1983–84, but in each case with a somewhat different purpose. Its relationship to Le Corbusier's sectional technologies—the various stairs, the rope, and the ramp—is obvious when we include the corridor in the genealogy of these devices. However, here in the hands of Snozzi, the ramp has been ironed out, flattened, and its sectional characteristics—the source of its utopian aspiration, taking the boxer up and away, have been exchanged for a more grounded motion; here the "bridge" conforms with the landscape. Consequently any thought about motion is internalized, adding tension within rather than aspirations beyond. We are left with a device that literally stretches the boundaries of the house to claim a maximum of territory. The footprint of the house becomes long and narrow like a Giacometti figure that now precariously, almost pathetically, reaches out to the point of its own demise (by snapping off at the waist). Yes, there is a great view, and indeed the "bridge" goes along the slope retracing the landscape, but ultimately it leads nowhere but back to itself. By stretching and flexing the architectural body, our boxer can rest his own, and let his mind wander.

## 8.1 The End:
## An Alternative

Figure 19[34]

**Notes on Notes**

1.  This text is one version of work done over the last ten years. I have attempted to tell the story in several ways; my book: *Planned Assualts: Nofamily House, Love?House, Texas Zero*, Canadian Centre for Architecture and M.I.T. Press, Montreal and Cambridge,1987, is the most complete. Despite its compactness the text at hand attempts to cover the entire terrain. I want to thank my friend and colleague Richard Ingersoll for his ability to see the text a bit before I did.

2.  Fig. 1. The Parade, Berlin, early 1900s. The photograph is by Waldemar Titzenthaler, taken sometime around the turn of the century. It is published in Berlin in *Photographien des 19.Jahrhunderts*; Friedrich Terveen, Waldemar Titzenthaler, Berlin: Rembrandt Verlag, 1986, p. 69. I have shown it to illustrate Benjamin's text.

3.  Walter Benjamin, *Illuminations*, ed. Hannah Arendt, New York: Schocken Book, 1969, pp. 239-241.

4.  Fig. 2. Ground plan of the Altes Museum, K. F. Schinkel. The illustration is reproduced from *Neue Statsgalerie Und Kammertheater Stuttgart*, Stuttgart: Finnanzministerium Baden-Wurtenberg, 1984, p. 16. The intimate conection between the Beaux Arts dual concept of enfilade/marche and architectural promenade is most interesting. Based on David Van Zanten's comments in "Architectural Composition at the Ecole Des Beaux-Arts: From Charles Percier to Charles Garnier," in *The Architecture of the Ecole Des Beaux-Arts*, ed. A. Drexler, New York: The Museum of Modern Art, M.I.T. Press, 1977, there seems to be a direct link between enfilade and architecture and between marche and promenade—further investigation is called for.

5.  Fig. 3. Le Jardin Suspendu d'un Appartement, Le Corbusier, 1928-29. The illustration of the boxer is taken from *Oeuvre Complet de 1910-1929*; Le

Corbusier and Pierre Jeanneret, Zurich: Editions Dr. H. Girsberger, 1937, p. 182.

6.  "Man of the Month: Le Corbusier," *Scope Magazine*, London: Creative Journals Limited, August, 1951, pp. 67-68.

7.  Fig. 4. Ramp and Solarium: A Villa Next to the Sea, Le Corbusier, 1928. Taken from *Oeuvre Complet de 1910-1929*; Le Corbusier and Pierre Jeanneret, Zurich: Editions Dr. H. Girsberger, 1937, p. 47.

8.  *Ibid.*, p. 24. The French text reads:

    L'Auto s'engage sous les pilotis, tourne autour des services communs, arrive au milieu, à la porte du vestibule, entre dans le garage ou pouruit sa route pour le retour: telle est la donnée fondamentale.

9.  *Ibid.*, The French text reads:

    La maison se posera au milieu de l'herbe comme un objet, sans rien déranger.

10.  *Ibid.*, The French text reads:

    Mais on continue la promenade. Depuis le jardin à l'étage, on monte par la rampe sur le toit de la maison où est le solarium.

11.  *Ibid.*, The French text reads:

    L'architecture arabe nous donne un enseignement précieux. Elle s'apprécie à la marche, ave le pied; c'est en marchant, an se déplacant que l'on voit se développer les ordonnances de l'architecture. C'est un principe contraire à l'architecture baroque qui est concue sur le papier, autour d'un point fixe théorique. Je préfère l'enseignement de l'architecture arabe.

    Dans cette maison-ci, il s'agit d'une véritable promenade architecturale, offrant des aspects constamment variés, inattendus, parfois étonnants.

The end is imminent, and as in all privileged readings, the circular ruins of the enfilade, the hopes of the athletic promenade and its various termini, may appear to have been set aside for the neutral plane or, as in the latter case, the imminent bridge. Yet this is not the point. This was not meant to be a exercise in dogma.

Returning briefly to the hypothesis that there are only two kinds of plans, the enfilade and the corridor-generated, I would like to propose a new hypothesis: there are three kinds of plans, thereby adding the plan *libre* and in particular its postmodern version that I have called the neutral plane and the associated *flânade* with its various technologies of delay and ambiguity. This adds new dimensions to the communication between the subject, its mind and body, and architecture.

Utopia, or more simply, hope, cannot be severed from architecture, even if at this time they must be found inside architecture: there is a fork at the end of the promenade. Borges writes, reflecting on a statement by one of his fictional characters, Ts'ui Pen: "I leave the various futures (not to all) my garden of forking paths." In all fictional works, each time a man is confronted with several alternatives, he chooses one and eliminates the others; in the fiction of Ts'ui Pen, he chooses—simultaneously—all of them. He creates, in this way, diverse futures, diverse times which themselves also proliferate and fork.[33]

12. Fig. 5. Cross Section of Villa Savoye, Le Corbusier, 1929-30. "By the pilotis one ascends surreptitiously via a ramp, a sensation totally different from one of a stair formed by steps. A stair separates one story from another: a ramp connects." The illustration is taken from *Ihr Gesamtes Werk Von 1929-1934*; Le Corbusier and Pierre Jeanneret, Zurich: Verlag Dr. H. Girsberger, 1941, p. 25.

13. Fig. 6. Sectional Technologies: After Le Corbusier. L. L.,1986. The illustrations of stairs and ramps are taken from *Oeuvre Complet De 1910-1929*; Le Corbusier and Pierre Jeanneret, Zurich: Editions Dr. H. Girsberger, 1937, p. 28, 31, 53, 54, 59, 127, 157, 185.

14. Manfredo Tafuri, *Architecture and Utopia: Design and Capitalist Development*, Cambridge: M.I.T. Press, 1976, p. 125.

15. *Ibid.*, p. 128.

16. Manfredo Tafuri, "There Is No Criticism, Only History," in *Design Book Review* (Spring 1986), p. 10.

17. Fig. 7. Plan *Obus*. The illustration is taken form Le Corbusier 1910-65, Zurich: Les Editions d'Architecture, 1967, p. 327.

18. Fig. 8. Victims: Studio for a Musician, John Hejduk. The illustration is from *John Hejduk, Mask of Medusa*, New York: Rizzoli, 1986, p. 463. There is most certainly a conection between Hejduk's mechanical cranes and Malaparte's villa-as-stair—further investigation is necessary.

19. Fig. 9. Ground and second floor plans, Villa Snellman, E. G. Asplund, 1917. The illustration is from *Asplund*; Caldenby and Hultin, Stockholm: Arkitektur Forlag in association with Gingko Press, 1985, p. 55.

20. *Ibid.*, p. 54.

21. Fig. 10. Extension of the State Gallery and the New Chamber Theater, Stuttgart, James Stirling, 1979-84. The illustration is from *Neue Staatsgalerie Und Kammertheater Stuttgart*, Stuttgart: Finanzminiterium Baden-Wurtenberg, 1984, p. 59.

22. Fig. 11. The Cemetery of Modernism? Sketches by Stirling. *Ibid.*, p. 65.

23. Benjamin, *Illuminations*, p. 197.

24. Fig. 12. Villa Prima Facie, Lars Lerup, 1984. Drawn by Patrick Winters.

25. Fig. 13. Villa Prima Facie, axonometric, Lars Lerup, 1985. Drawn by Brett Bennett.

26. Jorge Luis Borges, *Labyrinths: Selected Stories & Other Writings*, ed. Yates and Irby, New York: New Directions, 1964, pp. 110-111.

27. Fig. 14. Traps: The Liberated Handrail, the Useless Door, the Fresh Window, the Stair That Leads Nowhere, Lars Lerup, 1986. Drawn by Hassan Afrookhteh.

28. Fig. 15. Plan of New Zero + Fixed Furniture, Lars Lerup, 1986. Drawn by Hassan Afrookhteh.

29. Fig. 16. Projection of New Zero, Lars Lerup, 1986.

30. Umberto Eco, *A Theory of Semiotics*, Bloomington: Indiana University Press, 1979, p. 264.

31. Fig. 17. 1234 House: Clasp, Lars Lerup, 1986. Constructed by L. L. and David Hanawalt. Photographs by Antonio Lao.

32. Fig. 18. Plans and section of Villa Kalmann, Luigi Snozzi, 1974-76. Illustrations from *Luigi Snozzi: Progetti e architetture 1957-1984*, Milano: Electa Editrice, 1984, p. 45.

33. Borges, *Labyrinths*, p. 26.

34. Fig. 19. Three Plans: Enfilade, Corridor, and Free and a Postmodern Coda: The Plan Degree Zero, Lars Lerup. Illustration by L.L.

7 SEPT...DAWN
...IN THE MORNING WE GATHERED AT THE
SHINMEI-SHA SHRINE TO WITNESS THE WEL-
COMING OF THE GODS TO THE FESTIVAL...

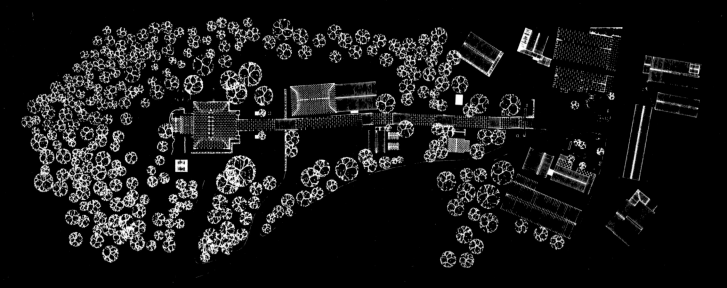

The festival begins at dawn when an area to the left of the *Shinmei-sha* is swept and delineated by four bamboo poles connected by a plaited rope. It is believed that the *Kami* descends into this sacred area, where the priest and parishioners wait, after being awakened and summoned from its inner mountain habitat by fireworks. The priest sprays the congregation with a wet *sakaki* tree branch, both as a process of

purification and a spreading of the *Kami* energy. The *Kami* is also summoned by the dance of the priestess. In dance, space is bound by movement and sound: opposing circular movements reflect two spirits, *aratama*, the rough wild spirit, and *nigitama*, the benevolent spirit. The priestess's stamping serves to exorcise the evil spirits.

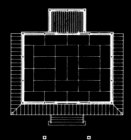

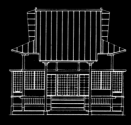

...WE PULLED OUR WAGON THROUGH THE STREETS TO THE SHINMEI-SHA SHRINE TO RE-CEIVE THE GODS.   OUR WAGON BECAME ALIVE...

7 SEPT.

The progress of the wagons is very slow due to their weight.  The rigid alignment of the four wheels also means that in order to change the wagon's direction to ease its way through the narrow streets, the front of the wagon has to be lifted and moved sideways on the shoulders of ten or more young people.  This happens, on the average, every three or four meters along a street.

The *hiki-yama* are completed by the addition of the driver and *hayashi*, musicians and dancers. The dancers perform, standing in front of the *kabuki ningyoo*. Sitting below the sacred *yama* are the musicians hidden from view, inspiring the *yama* with the music of ritual ecstasy; hence the name of the festival, *Oyana Bayashi*, "mountain music." In *Noh* theater, it is believed there is a hidden song that sleeps in all things.

# Intimations of

## *Sentimental Topography*

Dimitri Pikionis

Kenneth Frampton

Excerpts from a Fragmentary Polemic

# Tactility:

*Man's history will progressively become a vast explanation in which each civilization will work out its perception of the world by confronting all others. But this process has hardly begun. It is probably the great task of the generations to come. No one can say what will become of our civilization when it has really met different civilizations by means other than the shock of conquest and domination. But we have to admit that this encounter has not yet taken place at the level of an authentic dialogue. That is why we are in a kind of lull or interrugnum in which we can no longer practice the dogmatism of a single truth, and in which we are not yet capable of conquering the skepticism into which we have stepped.*

Paul Ricoeur[1]

**1. Perspective.** Andre Bazin, aware that perspective was a limitation as well as a triumph, delivered himself of the aphorism that "Perspective was the original sin of Western painting."[2] According to its etymological roots, perspective means 'clear seeing', thereby presupposing emotional distance as a condition for rational vision; within the rules of per-

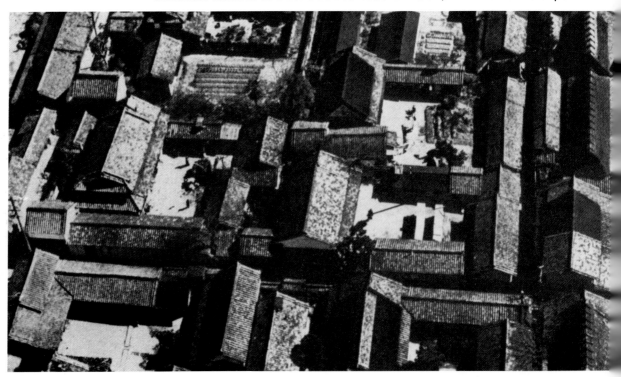

Typical Japanese Village,
Yamato Basin.

As we walk upon the earth, our hearts experience anew that overwhelming joy we felt as children when we first discovered our ability to move in space—the alternating disruption and restoration of balance which is walking.[1] We rejoice in the progress of our body across the uneven surface of the earth. Our spirit delights in the endless interplay of the three dimensions that we encounter at every step, shifting and changing with the mere passage of a cloud.

We walk past a rock, a tree trunk, or a tree's tasseled foliage. Our body rises and falls following the undulating surface of the earth, its elevated hills and mountains, its deep valleys. We rejoice in the wide flat expanse of the plains; we measure the earth by the toil of our bodies.

spective, the relative size of the objects represented on the picture surface is rigorously determined by their displacement in illusory space, and not according to their relative value within the culture. Brunelleschi was the first in a long line of Renaissance architects to order the architectural construct in such a way as to facilitate a decoding of the experience according to perspective.

**2. Instrumentality.** With J.N.L. Durand, perspectival space decomposes into instrumentality. Orthogonal coordinates now function less as registers for the guidance of foreshortened sight than as modular components in an economic and universal system of assembly. Architecture begins to divide at this juncture into polar aspects—into pure technique and pure ideology, the abacus and the mask. His *Precis des leçons d'architecture donnees a l'ecole polytechnique*, 1802-9, posits a variable connection between orthogonal logic and physiognomy. The "heads, bodies and legs" of reduced historical styles are pressed into the service of the absolutist state. The customs house, the prison, the museum, each takes its fitting but still arbitrary mask from Durand's catalogue. The volume itself is left as open-ended as possible; the Crystal Palace (1851) testifies, in a disturbing way, to the empty lucidity of Durand's vision. It was to fill its technical void with *objets d'art* or machine tools all reduced to the two categories of either commodity or productive means.

**3. Gesamtkunstwerk.** "Digression on *art nouveau* ." The shattering of the interior took place around the turn of the century in *art nouveau.* And yet the latter appeared, according to its ideology, to bring with it the

Jan Vredeman de Vries,
from *Perspective*, 1604-05. Plate 28 of Part 1.

We meditate upon the spirit which emanates from each particular land or place.[2] Here the land is hard, rocky, precipitous, and the soil is brittle and dry. There the ground is level, with water surging up from mossy patches; the breeze, the altitude, and the configuration of the ground announce the presence of the sea. Farther on, vegetation runs riot, and the surface of the earth's plastic form adapts itself to the change of seasons with new clothing.

The natural forces, the geometry of the earth, the quality of the light and air single out this land as a birthplace of civilization. Mysterious exhalations seem to rise from the ground and a precipice fills one's soul with awe. A nearby cave is the dwelling place of mysterious spirits and supernatural powers. Faced with this primeval image of the earth, the soul is shot through with a mystical tremor, as the water finder experiences when his divining rod comes upon the invisible presence of a subterranean stream.

perfecting of the interior. The transfiguration of the lone soul was its apparent aim. Individualism was its theory. With Van de Velde there appeared the house as expression of the personality. Ornament was to such a house what the signature is to a painting. The real significance of the *art nouveau* was not expressed in this ideology. It represented the last attempt at a sortie on the part of Art imprisoned by technical advance within her ivory tower. It mobilized all the reserve forces of interiority. They found their expression in the mediumistic language of line, in the flower as symbol of the naked, vegetable Nature that confronted the technologically armed ornament. The new elements of construction in iron—girder-forms—obsessed art nouveau. Through ornament, it strove to win back these forms for Art. Concrete offered it new possibilities for the creation of plastic forms in architecture. Around this time the real centre of gravity of the sphere of existence was displaced to the office. The de-realized centre of gravity created its abode in the private home. Ibsen's *Masterbuilder* summed up *art nouveau*: the attempt of the individual, on the basis of his interiority, to vie with technical progress leads to his down-

Dimitri Pikionis,
Lycabettus Primary School.
Athens, 1933.

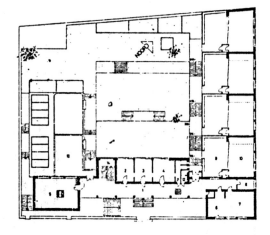

Light created the world. Light preserves it and makes it fruitful. It is Light that reveals the world to our corporeal eyes, in order that the light of our spirit may in turn illuminate the world. Above the fixed, motionless[3] geometry of the earth stretches the perpetually moving dominion of Light and Air.[4] Light, the infinite world of Form and Color, delights the soul. It meditates upon the principles of Time, upon the angle of the sun's rays, the length of shadows, the temperament of rain and drought, heat and cold,[5] the conformation of the clouds.

The Star of Life revolves, comes and goes, producing day and night. As it approaches the earth and then moves away, it creates heat and cold, showers or drought, bright

fall."[3] As a way of compensating for the progressive alienation of commutation and Taylorized production and for what Simone Weil was later to recognize as *L'Enracinement*[4], the home gives itself over to the scenographic, to dream imagery. But this hallucinatory decor—literally hermetic in the case of Ludwig of Bavaria's *Träumeschlossen*—only facilitates the triumph of "distanced" vision. Wagnerian indulgence in the creation of a compensatory *Gesamtkunstwerk* has the effect of bestowing greater freedom on instrumentality. Meanwhile the continuous curve of surveillance and control quietly extends it efficacy and breadth from Bentham's "one-way mirror" in his Panopticon (1796) to the equally ubiquitous cathode-ray tube in today's suburbs. As Robert Venturi so sensibly put it some 15 years ago in *Complexity and Contradiction in Architecture*: "The piazza, in fact, is 'un-American'. Americans feel uncomfortable sitting in a square: they should be working at the office or at home with the family looking at television."

**4. Privatization.** The automobile and the television combine to enforce the "privatization" of the suburb; that is, the elimination of the sidewalk and the usurpation of the "space of public appearance" in the home. For the rest, the average subdivision is reduced to the instrumentality of balloon-frame assembly. The required stacks of pre-cut scantlings are set down at regular intervals, while for optimum economy the site is bulldozed flat. Apparently, the cheapest of masks is considered sufficient to sustain an illusion of rootedness—a pitched roof here, a dormer there. These structural features may be accorded additional "iconicity" through the

or dark skies, clouds, rain or wind. The human soul rejoices in this mobile geometry of Light and Air which constitutes the seasons.

But on this particular day I enjoy observing the spectacle of the ground bathing in the calm, wintry light. There are petrified formations fashioned by divine forces, fractured boulders, stones; the dust born of the fertile soil, as infinite in number as the stars.

I stoop and pick up a stone. I caress it with my eyes, with my fingers: it is a piece of gray limestone. Fire molded its divine shape, water sculpted it and endowed it with this fine integument of clay that has alternating bands of white and ferruginous reddish yellow. I turn it around in my hands. I study the harmony of its contours. I delight in the way indentations and protuberances, light and shadow balance each other on its surface. I rejoice in the way the universal laws are embodied and fulfilled in this stone—the laws which would have remained unknown to us if, as Goethe said, an innate sense of beauty had not revealed them to the poet and the artist.

application of a plywood pediment or plastic flute.

**5. Convergence.** We live in a period of repetition and convergence. The apparent "avant-garde" reasserts itself in all its rhetoric, but only the agitation is radical, for the content is reactionary. *N'épatez pas le bourgeois!* Drawn at random from the emporium of the past, styles are now being pressed upon us in the form of "simulacra". The aim, we are assured, is to save us from the nihilism of an impoverished age; to redeem us from the precipice of materialist abstraction. But there is now an unfortunate convergence of purveyors of kitsch and a conciliatory avant-garde, both of which groups seem to be equally determined by the voracious demands of the media. And the major question becomes: how is one to distinguish today between a responsiveness towards history and a regurgitation of meaningless references, or, more specifically, between Barthes' concept of *répétition différente* and mere empty repetition?

**6. History.** The brutalization of the environment and that strange alienation that eerily insinuates itself into much modern building—that hallu-

Photos: William Garnett,
Subdivision under construction near Los Angeles.

Dimitri Pikionis,
Lycabettus Primary School.
Athens, 1933.

In truth, it occurs to me, O Stone, that ever since the incandescent mass of this planet was torn away from the sun and set spinning around it like a ring of fire, eventually condensing into our earth, the place you happened to occupy within its vast expanse was in no way accidental: the harmony of the Whole, which determined the inclination of our planet's axis, also apportioned this particular place to you as your home, as the generator of your supremely spiritual form in an atmosphere and light that are spiritually attuned to you.[6]

The dance of your atoms, governed by Number, shapes your constituent parts according to the Law of your Individuality. You thus enact the twofold law of Universal and

cinatory *éclat* in which vast and complex public structures uncannily reduce themselves to the status of commodities—finds its compensatory but pathetic parallel in the current proliferation of information about the lost architecture of even the relatively recent past, or the unbuilt and often unbuildable architecture of the future. Before this prospect one is reminded of Ernst Junger's lament in his elegiac novel *On the Marble Cliffs*, where he wrote: "There are periods of decline when the pattern fades to which our inmost life must conform. When we enter upon them we sway and lose our balance. From hollow joy we sink to leaden sorrow, and past and future acquire a new charm from our sense of loss. So we wander aimlessly in the irretrievable past or in distant utopias, but the fleeting moment we cannot grasp."[5]

**7. Kitsch.** "The environment grows, sprawls, dissipates itself and leaves behind it a trail of refuse, all as a concomitant of our activities. Its relationship with us becomes ever more imperious as it virtually imposes upon us the laws of a second nature whose characteristics, whether on an urban or a domestic scale, whether in the house, in the city or in the country, stem in the great majority of cases from the conception of kitsch as a midcult....Yet we may still ask how much of midcult was already inherent in the same idealistic principles of modern culture, or to what extent the concern for humanity, the focus on the housing problem and the family unit and that same preoccupation with the potential broadening of the benefits of art are also embodied in the principles of kitsch....Kitsch is at work as much in the physical exuberance of certain buildings as in the extravagant

Individual Harmony. I feel you growing, expanding in my imagination. Your lateral surfaces turn into hill slopes, ridges, and noble precipices. Your hollows become caverns where water silently trickles from the cracks in the rose-colored rock.

Stone, you compose the lineaments of the landscape. You are the landscape. You are the temple that is to crown the precipitous rocks of your own Acropolis. In truth, does not the Temple enact the same twofold Law which you serve? Above all, is not the Temple an explanation of "architecture as a whole"?[7] Is not the equipoise that holds it together similar to that of the mountains, vegetation, and of all living creatures?

All the forces of nature converge and work together to produce this particular conformation: the refined air, the bright light, the color of the sky, the clouds perched high above the mountain peaks, the stones scattered about the temple's stylobate, and the bits of grass

futility of various gadgets....This is the true projection of that spiteful lust for power which midcult evinces and technics express: the two combine to produce an architecture built purely for effect and devoid not only of meaning but lacking even in practical use....Kitsch augments the variety of forms present in the world very considerably, and at the same time substantially reduces their significance, but kitsch is not to be numbered among the things which rational thought has shown to be recoverable....Kitsch is, on the contrary, one of the invalid sociological and aesthetic techniques concerned with the production and enjoyment of things. These techniques are themselves based on...an inherent lack of clarity. ...[Kitsch] does not accept the nature of things in the light of their critical or revelatory attributes, but to the extent which they cover and protect, relieve, and console.[6]

**8. Simulacra.** The present project to reduce architectural practice to the proliferation of supposedly reassuring, historical simulacra has as its ultimate aim the optimization of instrumentality. As Jean Baudrillard has argued in his book *Le Miroir de la Production* (1973), the practice of culture

Dimitri Pikioinis,
Lycabettus Primary School.
Athens, 1933.

growing in the cracks. O earth, you reduce everything to yourself as the measure of all things. You are truly the modulus which penetrates all things. You gave shape to cities and to governments. You gave shape to the sounds that make up language and determined the art of words and forms.

Perhaps, because of the congruence—that the same laws apply to both nature and art—we are able to see the metamorphosis of forms of life and nature into forms of art, and vice versa. Or the transformation of one art form into another. Is it not apparent that this congruency is the fundamental force that governs the most diverse realizations of creation and that it is the element which has the power to reveal and explain them?

today is frequently reduced to simulacra, to the signs of signs. In this connection it is relevant to note that the creation of a poetic architectural image does not depend upon the visual consideration alone. In fact it could be claimed that the dominance of the visual is detrimental to architecture. This seems to have been understood by Adalberto Libera when he designed Curzio Malaparte's house in Capri (1940). This house rises from the cliff face as an acropolis of vertigo and terror, as a reinterpretation of the 18th century esthetic of the *genre terrible.*

**9. Reproduction.** Abraham Moles once wrote that the monuments of Europe are being worn out by Kodaks. The veil that photolithography draws over architecture is not neutral. High speed photographic and reproductive processes are surely not only the agents of the political economy of the sign but also provide an insidious filter through which our tactile environment tends to lose its concrete responsiveness. When much of modern building is experienced in actuality, its photogenic, sculptural qualtity is denied by the poverty and brutality of its detailing. Time and again an expensive and ostentationus display of either structure or form results in the impoverishment of intimacy—in that which Heidegger has recognized as the loss of nearness.

**10. Tactility.** The tactile returns us literally to detail, to handrails and other anthropomorphic elements with which he have intimate contact; to the hypersensitivity of Alvar Aalto, to the coldness of metal and the warmth of wood; to a comparable sensibility in the work of Carlo Scarpa who was capable of articulating a building in such a way that its surface implied a range of sensuous experience. In Scarpa's later work, the built-

As I walked this land, across this kingdom of limestone and clay, I saw the limestone changing into a lintel, and the red clay coloring the walls of an imaginary shrine. The gravel of the Claddeus River appeared to be the heads of heroes, the statues on the pediment as mountains. Zeus's long hair became a sheer precipice, and this mountain of a thousand shapes, whose harmonious contours recomposed themselves in my mind as I walked around it, took on the form of a Greek statue.

O Limestone, you fashioned the stern brow of Aeschylus. Musical notes emanate from the stylobate. The molded echinus evokes an ancient manuscript. The same austere structure is to be found in language and statuary.

The pleats and folds on the costume of a peasant woman flutter around her ankles, leaving traces of mountain shapes on the ground. The woven ornamentation around the hem of her skirt stands out as vividly as a frieze. The dance unfolds like a moving colonnade

form is inlaid with binary stimuli and associations: smooth versus rough, polished versus pitted, distended versus recessed, labial versus phallic.

**11. Boundary.** Heidegger's critique of the Renaissance begins with his recognition of the difference between *spatium in extensio* (space) and *raum* (place). One may extend Heidegger's thesis to argue that the former accords primacy to the visual—to the rational distance of perspective—while the latter is disposed towards the tactile. The architectural significance of Heidegger's "Building, Dwelling, Thinking" (first published in 1954) surely resides in these distinctions. Thus we find him writing: "What the word for space, *Raum*, *Rum*, designates is said by its ancient meaning. *Raum* means a place cleared or freed for settlement and lodging. A space is…something that is cleared and free, namely within a boundary, Greek *peras*. A boundary is not that at which something stops but, as the Greeks recognized, the boundary is that from which something *begins its presencing*."[7]

**12. Ritual.** Two interdependent channels of resistance proffer themselves against the ubiquity of the Megalopolis and the exclusivity of sight.

Adalberto Libera,
Villa Malaparte,
Capri, 1940.

Dimitri Pikionis, Drawing from the Attica Series, 1940-50.

and the sound of the flute, interwoven with the dancer's song, makes the mountaintops sway and the rivers flow. The rhythm of the gait, the rippling garments that are draped across the body, the design of the brow or forearm, the waves and curls of hair; all explain the landscape.

O almighty Number, what are the secret bonds that you have established between the geometry of creation and the crystalline air which allows the essence of divine light to filter through to us?

Why have the tufted clouds drawn apart high up in the pale blue sky, while gentle, transparent veils float across the mountaintops? What have the innumerable blades of grass to tell

They presuppose a mediation of the mind/body split in Western thought. They may be regarded as archaic agents with which to counter the potential universality of rootless civilization. The first of these is the tactile resilience of the place-form; the second is the sensorium of the body. These two are posited here as interdependent, because each is contingent on the other. The place-form is inaccessible to sight alone just as simulacra exclude the tactile capacity of the body. The configuration of the *peras* must be felt as much as seen. Thus one encounters in pre-Renaissance agrarian culture the "beating of the bounds", a ritual for the experiential and legal establishment of territory. Similar rites that are enacted cyclically and seasonally, and that serve not only to reify the *peras*, but also to reaffirm the body politic in relation to a specific place, spring to mind. The bull festivals of Spain or the binding rituals in Japan are but two examples. They are alluded to here not as an archaic precondition for a tactile architecture, but rather as evidence that there have existed cultures in which the visual considerations played a less exclusive role.

**13. Sensuality.** It is symptomatic of the dominance of the visual that it should be necessary to remind the reader that the tactile dimension belongs legitimately to the poetics of built form. One has in mind not only a typical Islamic court, where the ambulatroy experience of the place-form is inseparable from the sound of water with which it invariably resonates, but also a whole range of composite sensory perceptions, the sum experience of which is affected by the movement of air or by relative humidity, or by the intensity of light or darkness, heat

Carlo Scarpa,
Querini Stampalia,
Venice, 1961-63.

as they break through the dark moist soil? Are they voices from the past, or spirits rising from the kingdom of Hades? And what of these rough boulders—white, blue-gray, pink—and the shards of pottery scattered about the grass?[8]

The voices of children at play and the crowing of a rooster echo mysteriously through the fine rarefied air. Dried-up wells gape like the dark open mouths of tragic masks, adding depth to the landscape. The skin expands under the warm rays of the sun, and then contracts under the cool touch of the shade. The gentle breeze plays sweetly with the blades of grass and the asphodels, both nourished by the earth's bitter green sap.[9]

A profound mystery connects the light at this hour to the golden hide of the wild animals, to the convoluted horns and thick fleece of grazing sheep, yellow as weathered marble or black as the shadow of a dark rock. Through the agency of this hour, the mystery of

and cold, or by the aroma of material, or by the most palpable presence of enclosure or by the body's own momentum, gait and weight as it passes in and out of the domain. Examples abound where such various and diverse phenomena are an intrinsic part of the architecture itself. One thinks of staircases where the state of our psychophysical being, our rhythm and poise, are determined by the "going" itself, or conversely, one may recall a sudden confrontation with an open body of water, where scent, sound and air movement are part of the poetic experience.

**14. Posture**. While filming *The Damned*, Luchino Visconti insisted that the set for the mansion in the film be paved with real parquet. It was his opinion that without a solid wooden floor underfoot the actors would be incapable of assuming an appropriate gait. Likewise, in Alvar Aalto's Säynätsalo Town Hall (1950-52), the architectural promenade leading to the second floor council chamber is orchestrated in tactile terms. Not only is the staircase lined in raked brickwork, but the treads and risers are paved in brick. The kinetic impetus of climbing is thus checked by the friction of the steps. After

 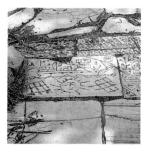 

Dimitri Pikionis,
Landscaping and steps of the
approach to the Acropolis,
Athens, 1951-57.

Time becomes one with the mystery of Space. What irreconcilable elements have merged here? Wherever one turns, one sees the two-headed hermae of antithesis. Faced with a mystery as abstruse as this, the soul no longer searches for reason; for in nature's deepening mystery, the soul suffers, and at the depths of this pathos lies understanding.

At this moment, O Doric column, your mystery is revealed to me. Now I understand: the tension that governs your lines is not only meant to serve the laws of statics, but also to heighten our sensitivity toward nature by introducing Art.[10] The grooves of your fluted body are meant not only to distribute light equally across your surface, allowing light to penetrate shade

this "resistance" the polished timber floor of the council chamber announces its honorific status through sound, smell and texture and above all through its slipperyness and its springy deflection under the weight of the body.

**15. Landscape.** The gardener Roberto Burle Marx conceived his post-Cubist landscape with regard not only to color, form and texture, but also to its acoustic capacity. Apart from the movement of water, the aural experience of his garden depended on the acoustic resonance of certain plants, which rustled when agitated by the wind or resonated with their resident animal and insect life. Aside from Burle Marx the capacity of tactile landscape to affect the entire sensorium has never been more intensely realized than in Katsura Palace, where changes in route rhythm not only represent metaphysical shifts in an instantaneous but progressive apprehension of the cosmos but also induce, in pursuit of the garden "narrative," corresponding changes in the state of the body, contingent upon revetment, fragmentation, continuity, registered in terms of paving texture, ground cover, etc.

**16. Earth.** The tactile gravitates towards the earth, towards the horizontal, towards a technology of building that is timeless and archaic, towards pisé, abobe, ashlar and even rock itself. The work of Jørn Utzon exemplifies an architecture of the earth, set invariably against the "canopy of the aerial." It is an architecture of section predicated upon a decisive configuration in the ground, regardless of whether this profile is manmade or natural. The preferred natural forms are the mountain, the declivity, the escarpment and the cave; their artificial equivalents are the platform, the atrium, the terrace and the cistern. These forms are occasions in which the tactile

Dimitri Pikionis,
Reconstruction and addition,
Church at Philopoppou,
Athens, 1951-57.

Roberto Burle Marx,
Garden of the Alberto Kronsforth residence,
Terezopolis, Brazil, 1955.

and shade to penetrate light, but also to blend the tones of your stone shaft with the tones of the sky above you and the rock beneath you.

You do not appear to be merely an animate being striving for union as you revolve about your axis; your grooves like eyes try to retain, within their revolving motion, what has come to pass and to contemplate what is to happen. Above all, this hour reveals to me that if you do achieve this longed-for union, it is in order that you become the extension and manifestation of an art form homologous to nature at the culminating point of nature's dramatic mystery.

Indeed, an inexplicable relationship links the harmony of your form to the stones, this bitter grass, the green shadows, these voices that pierce the air, the southern breeze, the torn plumes of the clouds; all these dramatic mysteries that appear to be incongruous. Is your form not made of irreconcilable elements held together in perfect harmony? And the coldness of marble, the austerity of your vertical

emerges into its own, for the articulation of form resides in the texture of the ground. This is an esthetic which has to be decoded by the body. In Utzon's work one invariably rises onto an acropolis, enters into an atrium, descends an escarpment or penetrates a cave. Utzon's exemplary types may be readily listed: the Sydney Opera House, the Fredensborg Housing, the Elviria Complex, and the Silkeborg Museum. Archaic parallels can be drawn, and in some instances are cited by the architect: the Athenian Acropolis, the ziggurats at Uxmal and Chichen-Itza and the court of the Friday Mosque in Isfahan. For the paradigm of the cave evident in the unbuilt Silkeborg Museum, Utzon was to return to his experience of the Buddhist shrine at Tatung, China, of which he wrote: "The inspiration for the design of the museum emerges from a number of different experiences—among these, my visit to the caves in Tatung, west of Peking, where hundreds of Buddha sculptures and other figures have been carved in a number of rock caves at the river bed. These sculptures have all kinds of shapes—in contrast to, or in harmony with, the surrounding space. All the caves are of different sizes and shapes and have different sources of light.

Katsura, Kyoto, ca. 1590;
the stepping stones at the junction of various passages in the moss of the entrance court.

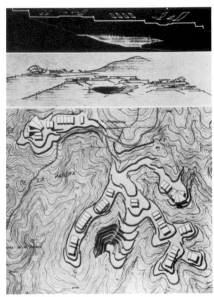

Jørn Utzon, Elviria Complex, Denmark, 1960.

shaft, your parallel lines—have they not merged with the warmth of the sun and with the unsurpassable sensitivity of the Spirit?

It was surely at an hour such as this that the artist conceived you. And your mystery is reborn in the perpetual recurrence of this hour. It is illuminated each time Number establishes the ineffable harmony between the hour and your form.

This is how I apprehended you: on an early April day, I perceived you in the slanting rays of the afternoon sun and behind the golden dust rising from passing chariots. Or was it on a summer evening when darkness spread across the mountains in the west enveloping the

The old chinese sculptors have been experimenting with all these possibilities, and the most fantastic result is one cave which is almost completely filled up by a Buddha figure with a face more than 20 feet high. Three narrow platforms connected with ladders give the visitor an opportunity to walk around and get close to the gigantic figure."[8]

**17. Water.** "My earliest childhood memories are related to a ranch my family owned near the village of Mazamitla. It was a pueblo with hills, formed by houses with tile roofs and immense eaves to shield passersby from the heavy rains which fall in that area. Even the earth's color was interesting because it was red earth. In this village, the water distribution system consisted of great gutted logs, in the form of troughs, which ran on a support structure of tree forks, five meters high, above the roofs. The acqueduct crossed over the town, reaching the patios, where there were great stone fountains to receive the water. The patios housed the stables, with cows and chickens, all together. Outside, in the street, there were iron rings to tie the horses. The channeled logs, covered with moss, dripped water all over town, of course. It gave this village the ambience of a fairy tale."

"No, there are no photographs. I have only its memory."[9]

**18. Air.** The archaic tradition of inscribing memory in the earth (cf. Heizer, Smithson) is to be complemented by the paradoxical monumentality of the aerial, as in the canopies of Utzon or even more astringently in the trellises, banners, kites and fireworks (cf. Christo, Piene) that are to be commonly found in Oriental culture;

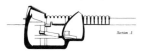  

Jørn Utzon, Silkebourg Museum, Denmark, 1963.

Dimitri Pikionis, Church at Philopoppou, Athens, 1951-57. Caretakers house.

Jørn Utzon, Sydney Opera House, Australia, 1956.

 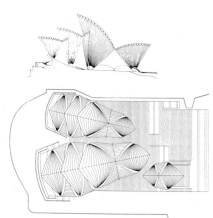

whole land, while rose-colored bands streaked the sky in the east?

But in this wintry hour I am thinking of you, O Doric column, as you poise the stern music of your form high up on the acropolis, high above the sheer rocks and the clay soil of the olive groves. I reflect upon the winter light that falls on your harmonious curves, the cool shadows that nestle there and that constitute your darkness. It is profound that your austerity,[11] sharpness, and sensitively modeled profile are all composed by the harmony of your mathematical form.

I can visualize the men who wrought you. I can see how their robes draped across the beautiful limbs of their symmetrical bodies. They have serene yet stern brows, furrowed by absolute prudence. There is an austerity about their eyes, temples, and beards.

But how is one to bring to mind all these spirits? The spirits of the hours, the years, and of every single day? The days of summer

the talisman rather than the tragic ruin, the eternal return rather than the myth of progress, the dynamic, impermanent rather than the static, permanent. A profound untapped expressiveness resides in this opposition between the earth and the aerial; a potential that cuts across history and culture to oppose the archaic gravity of the fixed to the volatile tectonic of light. This much already lies latent as a dormant poetic in Le Corbusier's *Pavillion des Temps Nouveaux* (1937).

**19. Body.** "Anything which tends to alter the expression of weight, whatever end it serves, weakens bodily expression. The first principle for what Appia henceforth calls 'living art', perhaps the sole one from which all the others are automatically derived, is this: all forms other than bodily forms tend to be in opposition to the latter and never become one with them. It is the opposition offered to the body by space which makes it possible for the space to share in the life of the body, and, reciprocally, it is the body's opposition which animates spatial form. Let us imagine a square, vertical pillar with its sharply defined right angles. This pillar without base rests on horizontal

The Temple of the Warriors, 11th Century AD, Chichen-Itza, Mexico.

Dimitri Pikionis, Church at Philopoppou, Athens, 1951-57.

and spring, the halcyon days of winter and autumn? The days when the wind blows from the north or the south, the east or the west? For these are the spirits that will enable us to witness the passion and the transformation of Form and Space within the principles of Time.

This sentimental journal is by no means complete. Does it matter? Is it not enough if the perusal thus far helps to make manifest the principle which I believe Nature wishes to teach us: that nothing exists independently of the Universal Harmony? All things interpenetrate, affect, and change one another. In order to apprehend one thing we must conceive of it through the intermediary of all others.

blocks which form the floor.  It creates an impression of stabiltiy, of power to resist.  A body approaches the pillar; from the contrast created between the movement of this body and the tranquil immobility of the pillar a sensation of expressive life is born, which neither the body without the pillar, nor the pillar without the body, would have been able to evoke.  Moreover, the sinuous and rounded lines of the body differ essentially from the plane surfaces and angles of the pillar and this contrast is itself expressive.  Now the body touches the pillar; at once the opposition becomes more evident.  Finally the body leans against the pillar, whose immobility offers it solid support; the pillar resists, it is active.  Opposition has thus created life in inanimate form.  Space has become living!"[10]

Adolphe Appia in his *L'Oeuvre d'Art Vivant* (1929) has this to say of the body in relation to architecture:  "Music imposes its successive intervals on the movement of the body; this body transports them to the proportions of the space; the inanimate forms oppose the body with their rigidity and this closes the circle; beyond that there is nothing."[11]

**20. Membrane**.  In the Megalopolis *avant la lettre* Frank Lloyd Wright already recognized the crisis of the visual, and the perceptual instability of the facade.  He also saw that this would have greater consequences for the public rather than the private realm.  Hence his reduction of the public exterior to a silent, if not opaque, membrane; his renderings of the monument as an obdurate shell against the instrumental triumph of *spatium in extensio*.  Thus, from the Larkin Building in Buffalo (1904) to the Guggenheim Museum (1956-59), Wright

The flying team, kite association members and a shinto priest (far left) pose for a formal photograph before the annual flying of the Hoshubana Showa ò-dako.

1.    After having studied the human act of walking, Rodin concludes with the admiration that "Man is a walking cathedral." ("*Les Cathedrales de France.*")

2.    The geometry of a place is a product of its composition.  By composition, I mean the nature of the materials that go into its making, and the nature of the diverse forces that have acted and continue to act upon it.  The nature of matter has to do with chemistry, which, like all things, is ruled by Number.  Although the work of the external forces (such as fire, water, earthquakes) may appear uncontrolled, blind, and incidental, it is, in essence, as strictly calculated by Nature as the proliferation of the most minute creatures in the universe.

3.    "Fixed" in a relative sense only, since the geometry of the earth is also subject to and affected by changes in the light and air that encompass it.

assured the bounded "nearness" of his public monuments, by rendering them as introverted, top-lit atria enclosed on all sides by the tactility of penetrable and ultimately avisual "facades".

**21. Polemic.** Some 40 years have elapsed since the 20th-century avant-garde first adopted an anti-Enlightenment stance. One may still imagine the general outrage caused among the aficionados of modern architecture when Le Corbusier first committed the *brut* sacrilege of combining, into a convincing synthesis, traditional rubble stone cross-walling, reinforced concrete Catalonian vaults, grass sod roofing, bent plywood, glass lenses, plate glass, exposed brickwork, and steel-framed fenestration, in his infamous Week-end House, built in the suburbs of Paris in 1935. The shock, one presumes, was hardly less when it became evident that his *Pavilion des Temps Nouveaux* had poetically inverted the nomadic tented diaphragm of the Hebraic temple in the wilderness. Once again one was confronted with a facadeless, avisual structure.

The elevation of the tactile and the impermanent to the same level

Adolphe Appia, set for King Lear, 1926.

Dimitri Pikionis,
Church at Philopoppou, Athens, 1951-57. Caretakers house.

4.    Climate, in other words, the mobile geometry of the atmosphere of a place, is a derivative of its relative position on this planet. The position of that place determines its distance from the sun, which changes with the seasons. The light is differentiated by its intensity and quality, by the angle of the sun's rays, and by the quality of the atmosphere. A sentient nature often ascribes that quality of atmosphere to light.

5.    Our sentient nature cannot conceive of "matter" as independent from temperature (the constitution of the atmosphere), or as independent from the intensity and quality of light. I will cite some examples that refer to our "natural" way of perceiving. As grasped by

as the visual and the permanent begins to undermine the hold of perspective over the perceptive faculties of the mind. With this shift the camera stands to lose its monopoly over the representation of architectural form, and it is surely no accident that the more powerful examples of tactile work being realized today—that is, the buildings of Utzon, Barragan and Alvaro Siza—subtly evade all efforts on the part of the photolithographic media to reduce their complex substance to mere images.

Throughout the foregoing, I have patently sought to stress the *nearness* of tactility as distinct from the *distance* of sight, although obviously these relative "proximities" are by no means mutually exclusive. However, to revalidate the tactile by articulating the difference between the two is to renounce the prospect of Utopia as it has mesmerized the Western mind since the Renaissance. The tactile favors the concrete experience and is antithetical to simulation and postponement. It may still embody metaphor or represent "absent" metaphysical or ideological entities, but is an intractable experimental agent, with which to rationalize the present in terms of the future. With the demise of the myth of progress, today's "arrière-avant-gardism" tends to become an irrelevant posture, a superfluity pertinent neither to culture nor civilization.

This polemic is both fragmentary and dialectical. Thus while it moves to resist the forces of reaction, this by no means assures immunity against absorption or against those aspects, lying latent within, that would tend to gravitate towards the reactionary in their turn. Nonetheless, it seeks to return architecture, or for that matter, all

Le Corbusier,
Le Pavillion des Temps Nouveaux, 1937.
Large conference hall.

Dimitri Pikionis,
Church at Philopoppou, Athens,
1951-57. Caretakers house.

sensation, a space appears smaller when it is hot and larger when it is cold, the weight of matter greater with heat, shape sharper with cold.

6. The profound sense of wonder aroused in man at the sight of the absolute accord between the light and air of a land and the geometry of its soil compels him to accept the existence of a harmonious unity that links these three elements together. How else is one to explain the incomparable harmony between the pure, spiritual, perfectly modeled shape of the mountains of Attica, and the fine mellow air and brilliant light in which they stand?

Indeed, I do not think it would be an arbitrary assumption—on the contrary, it would be fully in accord with our innate sense of Universal Harmony—to acknowledge that this harmony is not incidental, but a rigorous consequence of the inherent harmony of Creation. We may therefore accept as axiomatic that the geometry of a land and its light and air are entirely consonant elements.

plastic art, to a more concrete and tactile poetic. It looks towards the enactment of a mythic condition that is lived as well as imagined. In this regard, the current vulgar opposition betweeen the figurative and the abstract, the decorative and the spatial, and above all between the historicist and the modernist, seems irrelevant to its concerns, for as Lissitzky wrote in 1923, beyond the constraints of perspective and the pathos of a false vernacular: "We reject space as a painted coffin for our living bodies."[12]

Le Corbusier, Une maison de week-end, Paris, 1935.

Frank Lloyd Wright, Imperial Hotel, Tokyo, 1922.

7.    To recall the words of Heraclitus: "Yet although the Logos is common to all, most men live as if each of them had a private intelligence of his own". In response, Sextus Empiricus comments: "And this is nothing other that an explanation of the way in which the entirety of things is arranged. Therefore, insofar as we share in the memory of this we say what is true, but when we depend on private experience we say what is false."(*Heraclitus*, translated by Philip Wheelwright, Atheneum, New York: 1964).

8.    An inexplicable relationship between their contrasting evolution and shared descent links green vegetation and the red soil to the two colors that adorn ancient Greek vases:

1. Paul Ricoeur, "Universal Civilization and National Cultures," in *History and Truth*, Evanston, Ill.: Northwestern University Press, 1965.

2. André Bazin, "The Ontology of the Photographic Image," in *What is Cinema?* trans. by Hugh Gray, Berkeley and Los Angeles: University of California Press, 1967, p.12.

3. Walter Benjamin, "Paris, Capital of the Nineteenth Century," trans. from *New Left Review*, in *Perspecta 12: The Yale Architectural Journal*, 1969, p.169; originally published in *Illuminationen*, Frankfort Am Main: Suhrkamp Verlag, 1955.

4. Simone Weil, *L'Enracinement: Prelude à une déclaration des devoirs envers l'etre humain*, Paris: Gallimard, 1959.

5. Ernst Jünger, *On the Marble Cliffs*, New York: Penguin Books, 1970, p.33.

6. Vittorio Gregotti, "Kitsch and Architecture," in Gillo Dorfles, in *Kitsch: The World of Bad Taste*, New York: Universe Books, 1969, pp.259-76 passim.

7. Martin Heidegger, "Building Dwelling Thinking," in *Poetry, Language, and Thought*, trans. by Albert Hofstadter, New York: Harper and Row, 1971, p.154.

8. Jørn Utzon, "Silkeborg Museum," *Zodiac* 14 (1965), Milan, Italy, p.89.

9. Luis Barragán, quoted in Emilio Ambasz, *The Architecture of Luis Barragan*, New York: The Museum of Modern Art, 1976, p.9.

10. Walter Renee Furst, *Twentieth Century Stage Decorations*, New York: Dover Press, 1967, p. 27.

11. Furst, p.28.

12. El Lissitzky, "PROUN SPACE, The Great Berlin Art Exhibition of 1923," in *Russia: An Art For World Revolution*, trans. by Eric Dluhosch, Cambridge, Mass: The MIT Press, 1970, p. 140.

Dimitri Pikionis,
Landscaping and steps of the approach to the Acropolis, Athens, 1951-57.

black and red.

9. At this hour, form and motion take on a strange stillness, become static. One can imagine that the vertical, the horizontal, and inclined planes take on the configuration of a square.

10. Our sensitivity toward nature merges with the perception of art through the sensitivity of our spirit. What appears to be the rectilinear geometry of architecture is in reality a geometry of curves and their translation into matter can only be achieved by the finest artistic sensibility.

11. The austerity of the Greek column is of a different nature from the theocratic austerity of the Egyptian column. The latter is subject to divine attributes, whereas the former emerges as the product of a spirit that is austere, but is also human and free.

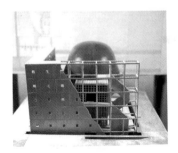

Giuliano Fiorenzoli

# Drawings
# and Work

Drawings are the open inquisitive eyes, searching and imagining places of the mind.

I would like to affirm the idea that Architecture, as an abstraction and moral ideal, exists and has a place, consciously or unconsciously, in everyone's mind. The idea of "space" exists within us as an abstract experience which anticipates and directs the act of physically erecting a structure. There is contained in this abstract process a realm of thinking which acts upon what one sees or remembers. In so doing one encounters continuity, that inner force that links old cities to new ones.

In a world of imagined and realized magnificent structures we find harmony in all those forces that, in nature, once gave us birth. Gravity, earth, water, sky, movement, light, our bodies, if given a purpose, are all rediscovered in an act of synthesis through physical form.

In spite of these considerations, we seem to be experiencing the unfortunate consequences of predominant attitudes that have reduced architecture to a commodity. The architect is thought to be mainly a choreographer of embellished pieces of hardware and flimsily preceived historical vignetes. Such structures are often felt as external to us, referred to and literally promoted by the same logical parameters used by the packaging industry or by the overwhelmingly simplistic imagery of the world's public media

These effects are quite disturbing. Ironically, in a world that permissively portrays the rightness of a free association of forms, formal choices are effectively reduced to a very few. The notion of

Casa Aperta, 1978.
*This sequence of drawings and model were part of an exhibition entitled "The Home." The theme is the presence of the human body. The 'head' in the model touches the wall structure which surround it at points of the senses thereby inspiring the individual drawings.*

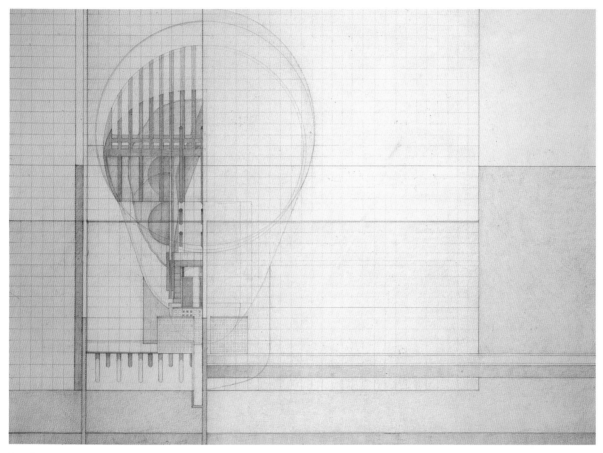

Casa Rossa, 1978

architectural "style" is therefore introduced with the unconscious effect of limiting a deeper investigation. Thus, the possibilities for architecture are stifled while paradoxically claiming a renewed interest in it.

A sort of "expanded" realism of vast proportions has dramatically entered into the many grids of our cities. This has created an emotional vacuum in which people are assaulted and diminished by their own creations. Beyond any form of cultural control, there is some sort of inversion of roles where buildings tell us of our identity. We are surrounded more and more by generic artifacts, built objects of various shape, size, texture, and use. The most simple physical laws of gravity are violated even before these are understood. The same gravitational laws control our corporeal world, allowing us to stand and move in balance with our own body's structure. We are physical entities in a universe of physical forces.

The apparent disappearance of meaning in what we build represents a tragic price to be paid in view of our increased need for human interiority. A loss of innocence toward what we don't yet know prevents the architect from adventuring in the promising and yet rigorous territories of fantasy and discovery. The commitment to a search for an "otherness" in architecture substantiates the need for an expressed poetry in our lives, as John Hejduk rightly affirms.

Man measures the spaces he occupies. This occurs through the architectural archetypes of the most significant institutions such as the workplace, school, home,

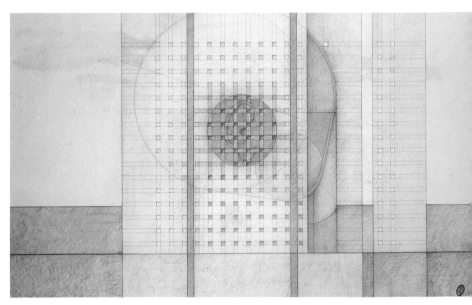

Lo Spazio del Suono I, 1978

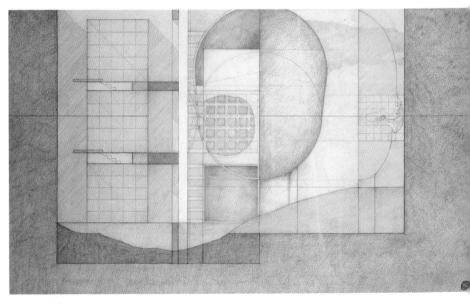

Lo Spazio del Suono II, 1978

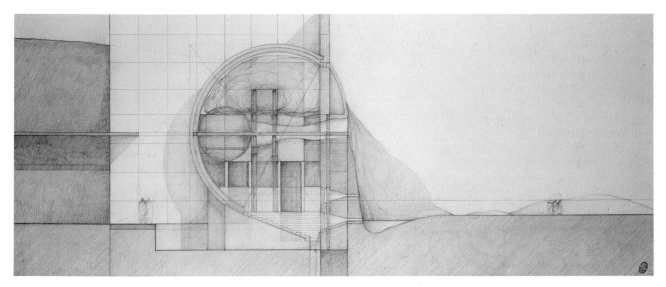

Spazio Interno, 1980

*The drawings are not architecture. They are an attempt to make physical, as much as possible, a way of thinking which anticipates something further which, if applied to architecture, may become a building. In the beginning, instead of progressing toward a building, these drawings suggests a way of thinking which goes in the opposite direction. They don't want to give answers…instead, their purpose is to sustain a certain interest in associations between architecture and our presence in space: how our presence coincides with the drawing, how the drawing coincides with a building and finally, how the building comes back to our presence.*

church, museum. In this way there is a conscious participatory act being reaffirmed in the continuous process of building the "city." In a world which is increasingly more processed, the struggle to define a "physical place" becomes more essential. It is the search for the "place," the investigation of archetypes, that can be found in my work. Through this personal investigation, using drawings as tools, one rediscovers humanity, the idea that man is not alone. It is within these archetypes that the connection between spirit, body, and built form emerges.

Drawing offers to the mind new territories in which to investigate possibilities rarely present in the everyday practice of architecture. Drawing refer to ideas of what can be. This process retraces an experience, in my opinion, present in most of the significant buildings conceived throughout the world. They not only take into account local circumstances but intentionally transcend them in an act of synthesis where an order of a higher degree proceeds from the architecture and back to us.

Drawing help us to defend a territory where the geometries of circles, squares, and triangles of various size and dimension are incorporated into a greater scheme affecting the quality of our lives. This intent is essential. The drawings and projects presented here have one common aspiration: they are investigations of the human psyche. They all belong to the "inner" world of feelings. There is a specific history for each instance in the drawings; details, textures, colors, and forms. Unexplained sites suggest possible landscapes

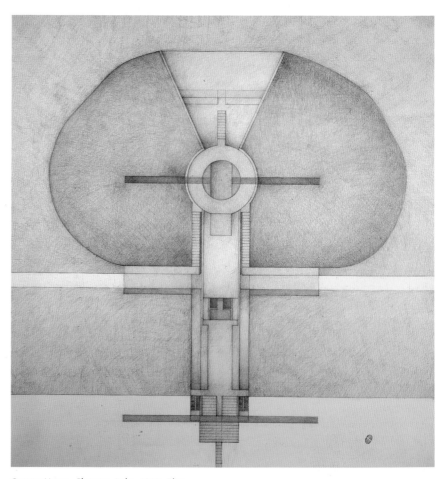

Country House , Florence, Italy. 1975. Plan

Country House , Florence, Italy.  1975

and morphologies that refer to forms of the body. The subject of these compositions is found in the source, the human senses. This personal experience seeks expression and is manifested through the act of drawing. Memory is the fluid and the conveyor. It is impossible to draw architecture without the remembrance of having been there if even for a moment. In this sense my drawings want to be myself. The architecture of my presence in them is a moment suspended in an expanded time.

Metaphors are invented to allow this process to take place. There is a vocabulary of forms and light, colors and suggested structures that don't necessarily refer to habitable shelters, but yet a "presence" is felt, not an obvious one, which is diffused throughout the composition of the proposed images. At moments, secret inhabitants can be perceived in the expressed sensuality of specific, chosen architectural forms. Such forms exist in geometry. They are "places of the mind" where architecture can affirm the right to exist as a magnificent human intent before being abused or quantified.

In this work the question is not representation. It is a projection of a world where conflicts have been suspended and a sense of serenity is gained. This state of mind requires attention and speaks of a world with greater humanistic values. Are these drawings architecture? I think so, in the same way Le Corbusier's cubist paintings are architecture because they contribute to giving form to an architectural vocabulary. Architecture has to redefine its purpose, and any research that can further that end is greatly needed.

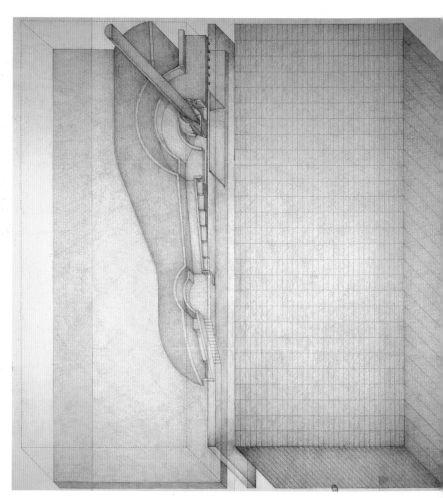

Rainbow Plaza Center, Niagara Falls, NY. 1974. Axonometric Project with Raimund Abraham and A.W. Geller.

The site was excavated into a rectangle with some soil left to create a form. This form was used as an overimposed image to organize the site. Two bridges were built to connect the two sides of the excavation. A projection theater, which projects 360° images of Niagara Falls, is located within this form, below the circular fountain. The fountain is a source of water—the water runs down the hill, disappearing and reappearing several times before reaching the bottom. The sunken rectangle is a plaza in the summer and a skating rink in the winter.

Where are the new public monuments, the new symbols and the buildings of which to be proud? Where is the searching for the "rooms" of man? Where is the silence that gives dimension to our peace of mind? Where are the spaces where one can be momentarily lost in visual pleasure, where we are ennobled rather than excluded? Where is the sense of having your footsteps fall in the places of those who have traveled before or will come after we are no longer, that reassurance of continuity? Where is the music of forms in light that we can consider ours? Where are the symbols of a greater and more passionate humanity? Are we too late? Why is the future so close to the present as to almost not exist any longer? Are we to be the new ground to build upon? Perhaps yes, but we must begin to know ourselves better. In architecture, drawings are the investigations of our existence.

Competition for a Cultural and Performance Center, Melbourne, Australia.

*As an initial step, an attempt is made to transfer the formal character of the Ayers Rock into the city of Melbourne, the given site, as a way to generate a program for a building. In so doing to suggest a recognizable symbol for the city of Melbourne which reflects a connection to the natural history of the country. The proposed project consists of a bridge supporting a highly visible mound constructed of the natural red sandstone found in the Ayers Rock many miles away.*

...NOW OUR WAGONS WERE ALIVE AS WE ROAMED THE STREETS SPREADING THE LIFE ENERGY OF THE GODS...THEN WE MET AN-OTHER WAGON IN A HEAD-ON COLLISION...
9 SEPT.

At one time crashes were rare. Wagons would skillfully navigate the streets in order to avoid conflict. When such maneuvering led to negotiations which became hostile, crashes were inevitable. The crashing does not happen accidentally. When two wagons meet on a street, they go into a negotiation, *Kosho*, for the right of way under a set of rules traditionally handed down by word of mouth. Each wagon usually has about one hundred young men, *wakamono*, whose job it is to bring the wagons into position. Two negotiators for each wagon come forward to a space midway between the two opposing wagons and over the din of the crowd and the cheers of the *wakamono* they negotiate for a crash. The negotiation often takes several hours and throughout the negotiation the *Kagura Bayashi* music is continuously performed to stir excitement and thirst for the crashing. As the negotiation is prolonged, the thirst for the crashing swells and fills the space.

Interior view of the Yoshijima brewery and household.
Takayama, Gifu Prefecture, Japan.

Built in 1907 by the master carpenter Nishida Isaburo, the Yoshijima
house and brewery exemplifies the traditional townhouse architecture of
this area. Since the construction of this house, members of the Yoshijima
household have, to this day, polished the lacquered surfaces of these
beams and pillars periodically with dry cloth. This accounts for the
sumptuous tones and smooth, silken texture which unfolds in endless
variations over the course of time. As Teiji Itoh remarks, "It is as though
the completion of the house, for the members of the Yoshijima family at
least, was simply a starting point; that only with use was its beauty brought
into full being."

Tadao Ando

# SHINTAI AND SPACE

Worker, sake brewery
Takayama, Gifu Prefecture, Japan, 1985

The breweries, as well as farmhouses, of this mountainous region of
Japan are characterized by cool, dark, wooden spaces intermittently
punctured by strong shafts of natural light descending from above.

Architecture is the art of articulating the world through geometry. However, the world is not to be articulated as isotropic, homogeneous spaces. It is to be articulated not abstractly, but as concrete places (*topi*) that are each related to a totality of history, culture, climate, topography, and urbanity. A "place" is not the absolute space of Newtonian physics, that is, a universal space, but a space with meaningful directionality and a heterogeneous density that is born of a relationship to what I choose to call *shintai*. (*Shintai* is ordinarily translated as "body," but in my use of the word I do not intend to make a clear distinction between mind and body; by *shintai*, I mean a union of spirit and the flesh. It takes cognizance of the world and at same time takes cognizance of the self).

Man articulates the world through his body. Man is not a dualistic being in whom spirit and the flesh are essentially distinct, but a living, corporeal being active in the world. The "here and now" in which this distinct body is placed is what is first taken as granted, and subsequently a "there" appears. Through a perception of that distance, or rather the living of that distance, the

surrounding space becomes manifest as a thing endowed with various meanings and values. Since man has an asymmetrical physical structure with a top and a bottom, a left and a right, and a front and a back, the articulated world, in turn, naturally becomes a heterogeneous space. The world that appears to man's senses and the state of man's body become in this way interdependent. The world articulated by the body is a vivid, lived-in space.

The body articulates the world. At the same time, the body is articulated by the world. When "I" perceive the concrete to be something cold and hard, "I" recognize the body as something warm and soft. In this way the body in its dynamic relationship with the world becomes the *shintai*. It is only the *shintai* in this sense that builds or understands architecture. The *shintai* is a sentient being that responds to the world. When one stands on a site which is still empty, one can sometimes hear the land voice a need for a building. The old anthropomorphic idea of the *genius loci* was a recognition of this phenomenon. What this voice is saying is actually "understandable" only to the *shintai*. (By understandable I obviously do not mean comprehensible only

Cleaning of the Isutzu House. Osaka, Japan, 1982.

We arrived at this house, located in a dense, rather wearisome, section of Osaka, only to find a crew of workers from Ando's office diligently scrubbing every surface of exposed concrete, metal, wood and glass. This rather remarkable affirmation of traditional Japanese custom underscores Ando's longstanding policy of maintaining life-long relationships between himself and the clients for whom he designs houses.

through reasoning). Architecture must also be understood through the senses of the *shintai*.

In order to perceive an object in all its diversity, the distance between the self and the object must be changed in some way. This change is brought about by the movement of the *shintai*. Spatiality is the result not of a single, absolute vision, but of a multiplicity of directions of vision from a multiplicity of viewpoints made possible by the movement of the *shintai*. Not only the movement of the *shintai* but natural movement such as that of light, wind, or rain can change the phenomenal (as opposed to physical) distance between the self and the object. By introducing nature and human movement into simple geometrical forms, I have been trying to create complex spaces. What had been self-sufficient and still is transformed, by the addition of natural or human movement, into what is motion, and diverse views are thus superimposed in the eyes of the peripatetic observer. Order is reconstructed within the *shintai* through the recognition of differences between the total image inscribed on the *shintai* by that superimposition, and what is immediately and visually apprehended. What I care about is precisely the way in which each person relates to architecture.

The problem with modern architecture lies in the abstract and homogeneous character of its spaces. Such spaces and the *shintai* simply do not blend. Architecture is given order through abstract geometry and thereby assumes an autonomous existence. However, that order is something essentially different from everyday order. Architecture, though a material presence, is a medium that can take into account factors without palpable form such as climate and history; this is what gives architectural forms their "order."

Today, the functionalistic approach is being questioned in the architectural world, and various contending approaches to architectural expression are making the situation complex. Postmodernism, which is prominent among these approaches, chooses to interpret modernism, the greatest architectural heritage of the twentieth century, in a one-dimensional fashion and capriciously rejects it. There is nothing to be gained by simply introducing ornament solely because modernism rejects it. If modernism has an inhuman aspect, then the problem lies in its basic ideas about architecture and not its architectural forms. The problem is to be corrected by the expressive character of architecture and the individual who is the expresser, while at the same time satisfying the need for rationality and functionality. The distinctive national character and sensibility of each individual are being rejected while our world becomes more and more homogenous. Cultural factors which make architecture possible, such as history and tradition, and even natural conditions, are being turned into abstractions; and the uniformity and mediocrity that are the by-products of a pursuit of economic rationality are dominant qualities of our era. I care not for interesting forms, but for the spatiality of forms. Through the medium of simple geometrical forms, I seek to introduce a diversity of intentions and emotions and to take into account intangible factors.

Eight-legged robot descending a set of steps at "The Pavilion of Man."
Expo '85, Tsukuba City, Japan.

Four legs are used to lift the entire mechanism up while the other four
enable it to step forward and down.

Mechanical musician at "The Pavilion of Man."
Expo '85, Tsukubu City, Japan.

A crowd of Japanese observe a technician repairing a malfunctioning
robot.  Musical notes are read from the screen and transmitted into
physical commands which enable the robot to perform a symphony by
Mozart.

Stairs leading to the Takase Canal.
Time's Building, Kyoto, Japan.

With the singular exception of Ando's TIME'S building, every structure
lining the vibrant Takase Canal, which weaves through the heart of
Kyoto, remains absolutely indifferent to the particular qualities that the
passage of water affords the city.  This building, by directly connecting
the public street above to the water below and by opening up its
internal spaces to the canal, bridges cultural and geographical terrain
within the urban environment.  This gesture becomes both matter and
knowledge; matter insofar as it physically provides a tray on which
bodies can gather and occupy space previously denied the city;
knowledge inasmuch as the occupation of these once ignored spaces
opens up new desires—"The water looks so clear and cool that one is
tempted to dip one's hand in it.  I began with the image of people
going down to the stream.  I wanted to make people aware of forgotten
ties to the environment."*

*Tadao Ando

My ultimate objective is not expression, but instead simply the creation of symbolic spaces founded on substantiality.

It is as someone whose sensibility has been shaped by a distinctive culture and history that I have in the past concerned myself with architecture, and it is as such a person that I hope to continue to concern myself with architecture in the future. I hope to continue to resist the homogenization of the world. In this the *shintai* will no doubt provide a key.

Tadao Ando
Osaka    1986

Bombardment of Osaka by B-29's.
March, 1945.

Within a period of just several weeks in March, beginning with the March 9th bombardment of Tokyo, American troops carried out the most intensive episode of urban devastation in the history of civilized societies. This unprecendented assault, focused primarily on Japan's major urban centers, was specifically a strategy of place annihilation as one-third of Japan's urban land was laid waste by artillery fire.*

*see Kenneth Hewitt's "The Meaning and the Loss of Place in War" in *FUDO*, eds. A.V. Liman and Fred Thompson, Univ. of Waterloo Press, 1984.

Koshino House.
Ashiya , Japan.

"The cheap sprawl and crowded conditions of the modern Japanese city reduce to a mere dream the liberation of space by modern architectural means and the resulting close connections between interior and exterior. Today, the major task is building walls that cut the interior off entirely from the exterior...I am implying that walls can be used to help break the unrelieved monotony and random irrelativity of walls used in the modern urban environment. In other words, I think walls can be used to control walls."* The twofold nature of Ando's walls becomes all the more evident as one enters this house. Aggressive and exclusionary on the outside—Recuperative and nourishing from within.

*Tadao Ando, in "The Wall as Territorial Delineation" in *Japan Architect*, no. 254, June, 1978.

All captions by the editors.

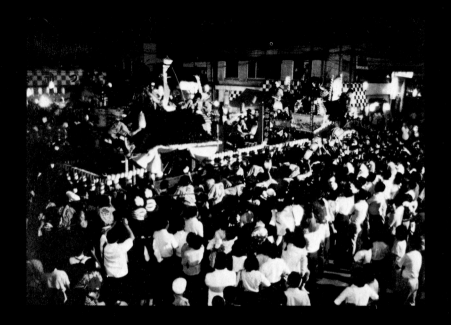

From midnight until dawn, the fifteen wagons crash with each other in the middle of the streets all over the town. When the six-ton wagons pulled by fifty to one hundred people crash against each other, there is an enormous outbreak of energy. The wagons crash against each other again and again until everyone is completely exhausted.

| | |
|---|---|
| 1 | THIS IS WHERE WE BUILT OUR WAGON |
| 2 | THIS IS WHERE WE WAITED FOR THE |
| | KATSURAKU-CHO WAGON |
| 3 | THIS IS WHERE THE IWASE WAGON |
| | WAITED |
| 4 | THIS IS WHERE WE RESTED |
| 5 | THIS IS WHERE SATAKE GREETED US |
| 6 | THIS IS WHERE THE TEKIYA SET UP SHOP |
| 7 | THIS IS WHERE THE KABUKI DOLLS WERE |

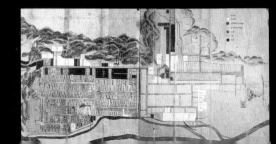

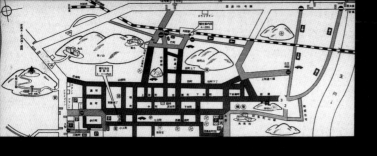

In order to get back home by the shortest route, Yamane turned its wagon around before it went as far as the Iwase *hariban* and came face to face with the wagon of Kamishinmachi. Since Yamane challenged Kamishinmachi after that wagon had passed the Shinmeisha Shrine, both wagons met under the same conditions (they were both "alive" and they were both descending from a temporary altar), and neither had the right of way. Yamane was able to negotiate the right to go past the Kamishinmachi wagon since neither side wanted a battle before they had been to the Yakushido Shrine and to the house of Satake. The *nemban-gumi* at the Iwase *hariban* could have acted as mediators if it had been necessary.

## THE APPROXIMATE LOCATION OF VARIOUS WAGONS BY 10 P.M. ON THE FINAL NIGHT OF THE FESTIVAL

Usually many wagons gathered on this street. However, because of the unusual behavior of Yamane, the wagons were spread out over the town.

13        YAMANE
14        IWASE
15        YOKOMACHI

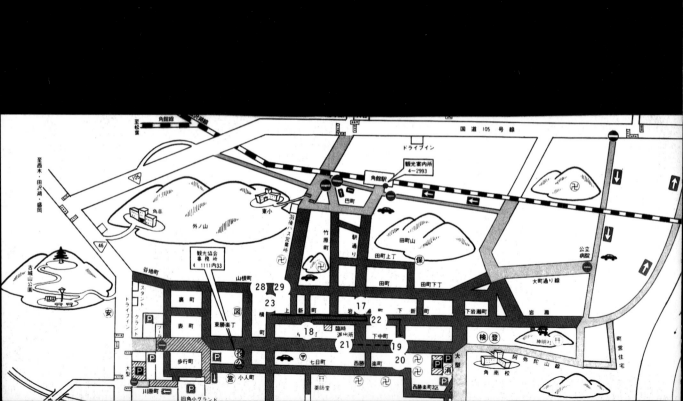

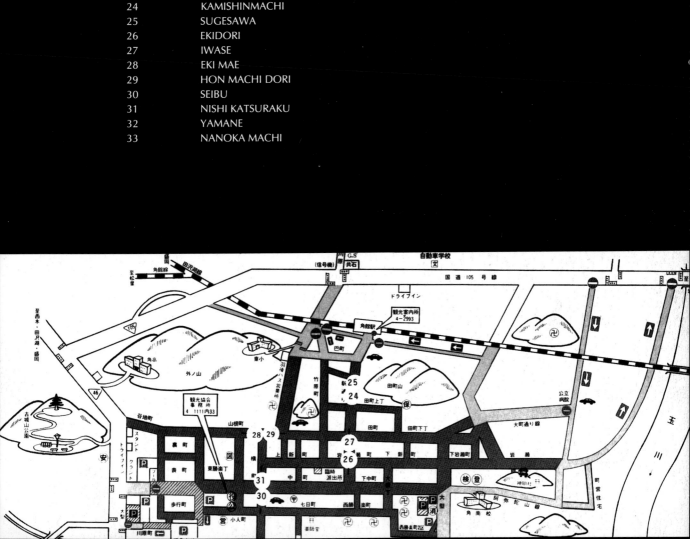

...I WAS REMINDED OF THE GAME OF *GO* WITH ITS BLACK AND WHITE STONES WHEN I THOUGHT OF THE DAY OF *HARE*, THE SUNNY DAY DAY, AND THE DAY OF *KE*, THE DAY OF WORK AND INCREASING POLLUTION.

The rules of the game of wagon crashing are similar to those of the Japanese game of *go*, which are learned through experience. The game of *go* is also peculiar in that like the battles between *hiki-yama* the moves occur at the intersection rather than in the middle of a block. This can be compared to the Western game of chess in which the pieces are moved from the containment of one square to the containment of another. Chess has been likened to conventional warfare, and *go* to guerrilla warfare: in chess the rules are clear and the hierarchy is established, while in go the game is won through a possession of territory rather than by means of hierarchical strength.

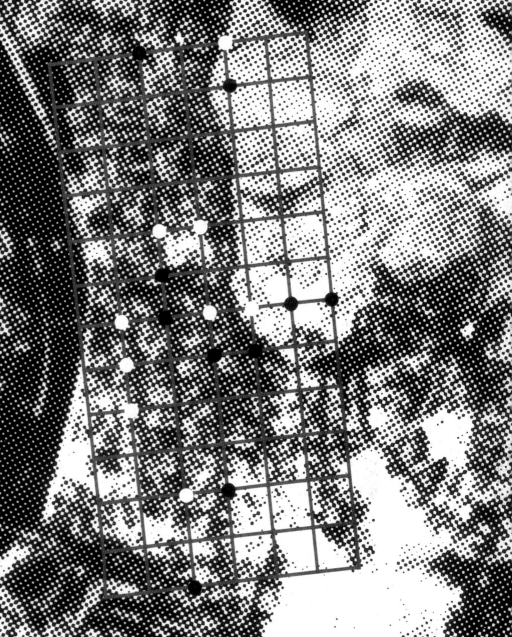

1.  I have presented this project in various places,

Alvaro Siza

# PORTO

always amid laughter,

...but not without appreciation. The manner of presentation may have been interpreted as ironic, or may have appeared demagogic.

It was not.

The project results—very directly in this case—from the analysis of that which conditions it; to such an extent that now I am unable to imagine it otherwise. I recognize that it could have assumed a thousand other forms—less strange, possibly less controlled.

What makes it different is alien to the time of design. What makes it comprehensible has to do with centuries of elaboration, of which each of us knows only an infinitesimal part.

2. I am impressed by the frenetic search for originality; so anxious that it achieves nothing other than the banal; a monotonous accumulation of varieties.

I am amazed by the "lack of imagination" complex. As if imagination were something outside and beyond reason to be introduced into the project as an autonomous process; or as if it were one more instrument to be used, in this or that moment, in response to methods or intuitions; or as if it were a rare aptitude. Yet that which fluctuates, subconciously, is not illness or "other." Let us say that the boundary between the conscious and the unconscious depends upon the paths of reason, and upon its energy and demands. Living in liberty—learning to live—always involves breaking this boundary.

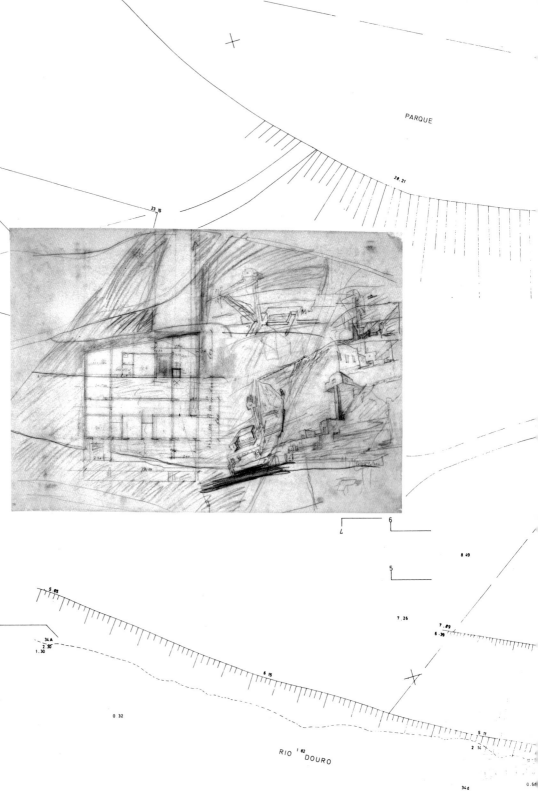

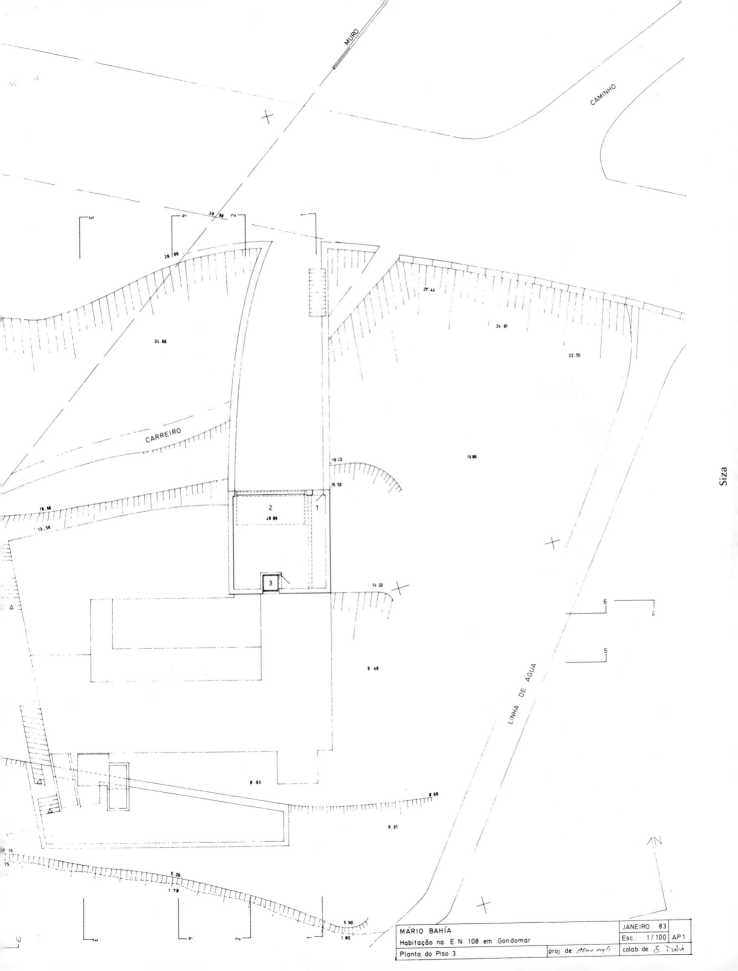

MURO

CAMINHO

Siza

CARREIRO

LINHA DE ÁGUA

MÁRIO BAHÍA

Habitação na E.N. 108 em Gondomar

Planta do Piso 3

proj. de Almeida

colab. de S. Dias

JANEIRO 83

Esc. 1/100  AP 1

### 3. A brief description of the project.

a) A house is to be built on the right bank of the Douro River near the city of Porto, on a narrow site between the river road and the water. The steep slope of the land is controlled by retaining walls of dry laid stone that form the terraces of the vineyards, which run from east to west and construct the landscape of the Douro Valley.

b) The profile of the river road, elevated 28.88 meters above the river, does not allow for parking automobiles outside the boundaries of the site; local construction regulations impose a setback of 15 meters from the edge of the road; the slope and terrain of the site allows only one platform of sufficient size (which has a median elevation of 9.50 meters) in which to situate the house. These circumstances render the thought of an access ramp directly to the house unfeasible. As a result the solution to the parking problem results in the construction of a garage at street level, accessible only by means of a bridge.

c) The difference in elevation between the garage and the location of the platform imposes a serious constraint on the comfort of the dwelling if one does not have the alternative of access by elevator, and the connection necessary for the elevator to join the two determines a close visual relationship between the volumes of the house and the garage.

This relationship is further accentuated by the necessary complement of a stairway—a diagonal which allows for consistency of structure and image.

d) The stair and elevator lead to an atrium.

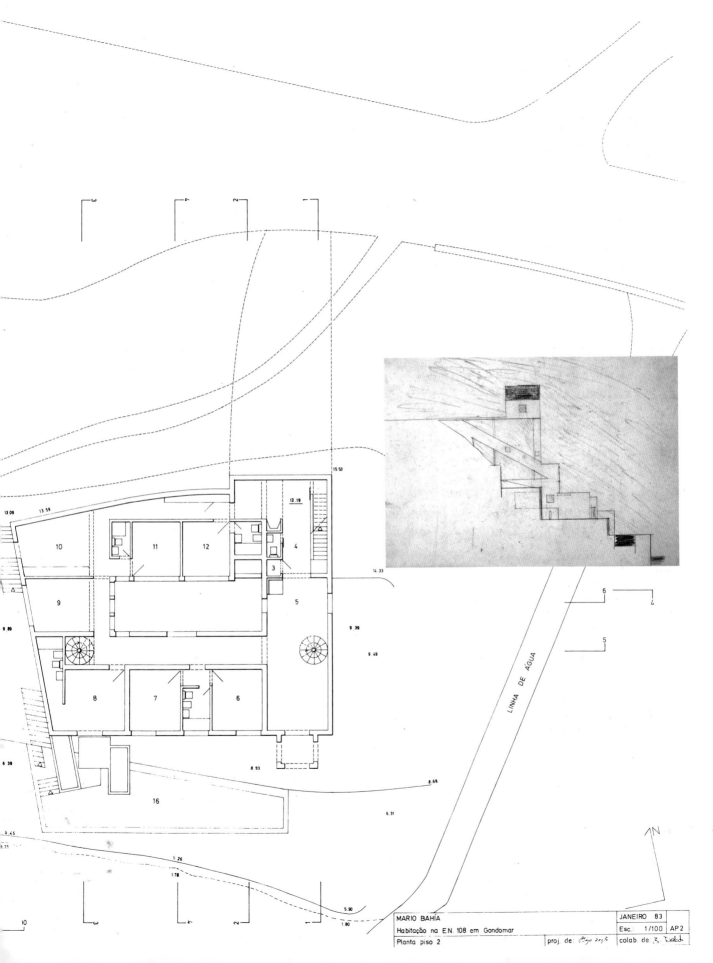

Siza

| MARIO BAHÍA | JANEIRO 83 | |
| --- | --- | --- |
| Habitação na E.N. 108 em Gondomar | Esc.: 1/100 | AP2 |
| Planta piso 2 | proj. de: *Álvaro Siza* | colab de: *B. Dekok* |

The various spaces of the house develop around a courtyard, elevated above the land. As a result of this elevation the patio opens to the landscape, without diminishing its interiorization and spatial clarity. This interiorization is indispensable, when confronted with the constant presence of a landscape of great beauty.

e) There is no caprice.

4. That which "pure reason" produces tends toward the monstrous. Architecture—"cosa mentale"—endures by means of a control which transcends subjectivity; codes which become universalized, (a consensus concerning good proportions,) tested by an experience for which the I— who designs—is not enough, and to which the various experiences must refer, allow the project clear definition.

A system of control, a secure code (and therefore universal) of the organization of space and form, was always the "responsible" objective: the Orders. The distance from the navel to the ground corresponded to the height of a classical base. By means of the Orders, man (and that which he constructed) situated himself such that he would not be a body foreign to nature out of which he emerged. But how many today accept the Orders, even if desperately or joyfully exhumed?

When a code enters crisis; when already too few carry its references; when reading it no longer yields meaning; what remains is to transform it, from the interior of doubts, by means of renewed attention to direct sources in nature: landscapes, passing clouds, clearings, bodies, movement, stability.

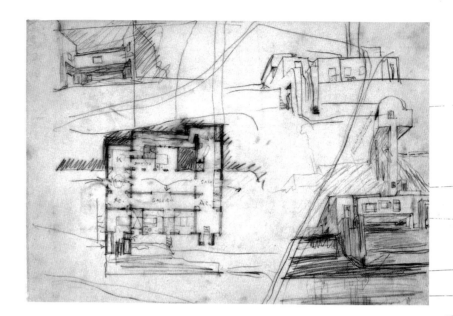

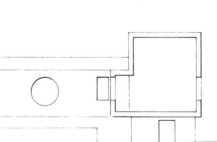

alçado norte

alçado sul

corte 7.7

planta piso 1

13. Serviços 14. Sala comum 15. Chuveiro 16. Piscina

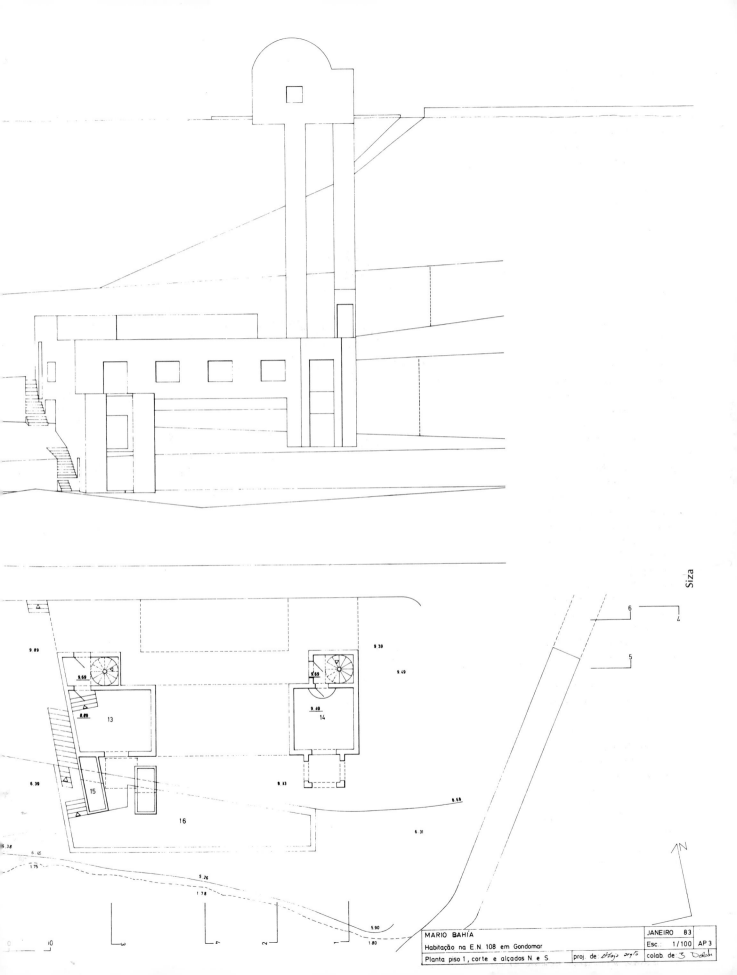

Siza

MARIO BAHÍA

Habitação na E.N. 108 em Gondomar

Planta piso 1, corte e alçados N e S

proj. de *Álvaro Siza*

colab. de *J. Delati*

JANEIRO 83

Esc.: 1/100 AP 3

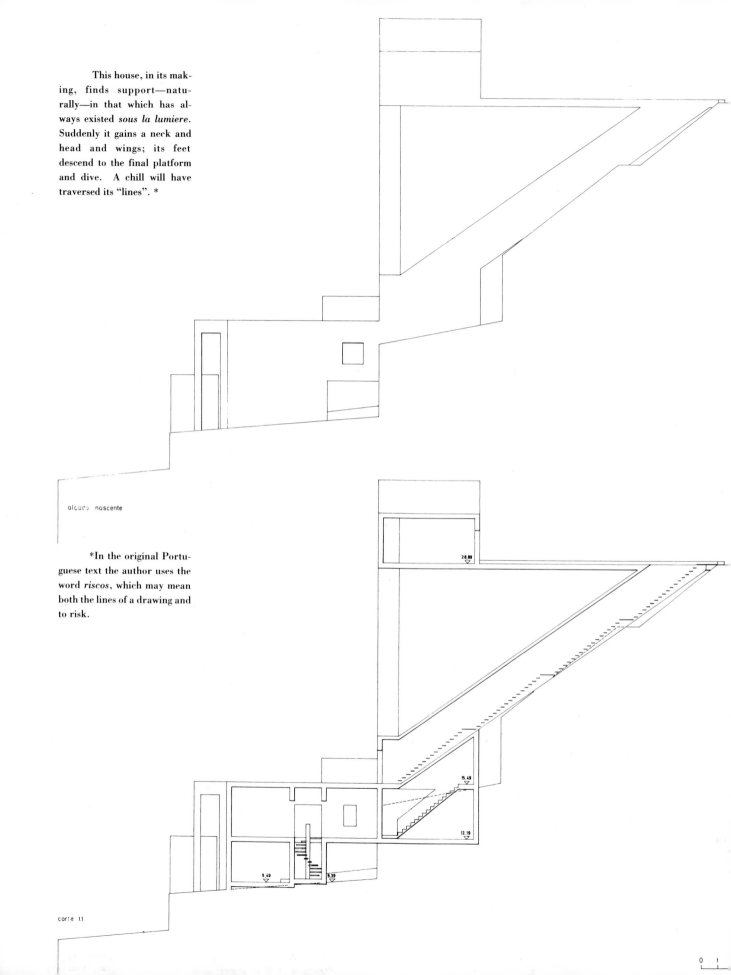

This house, in its making, finds support—naturally—in that which has always existed *sous la lumiere*. Suddenly it gains a neck and head and wings; its feet descend to the final platform and dive. A chill will have traversed its "lines". *

alçado nascente

*In the original Portuguese text the author uses the word *riscos*, which may mean both the lines of a drawing and to risk.

28.89

15.49

12.19

9.49

5.39

corte 11

0   1

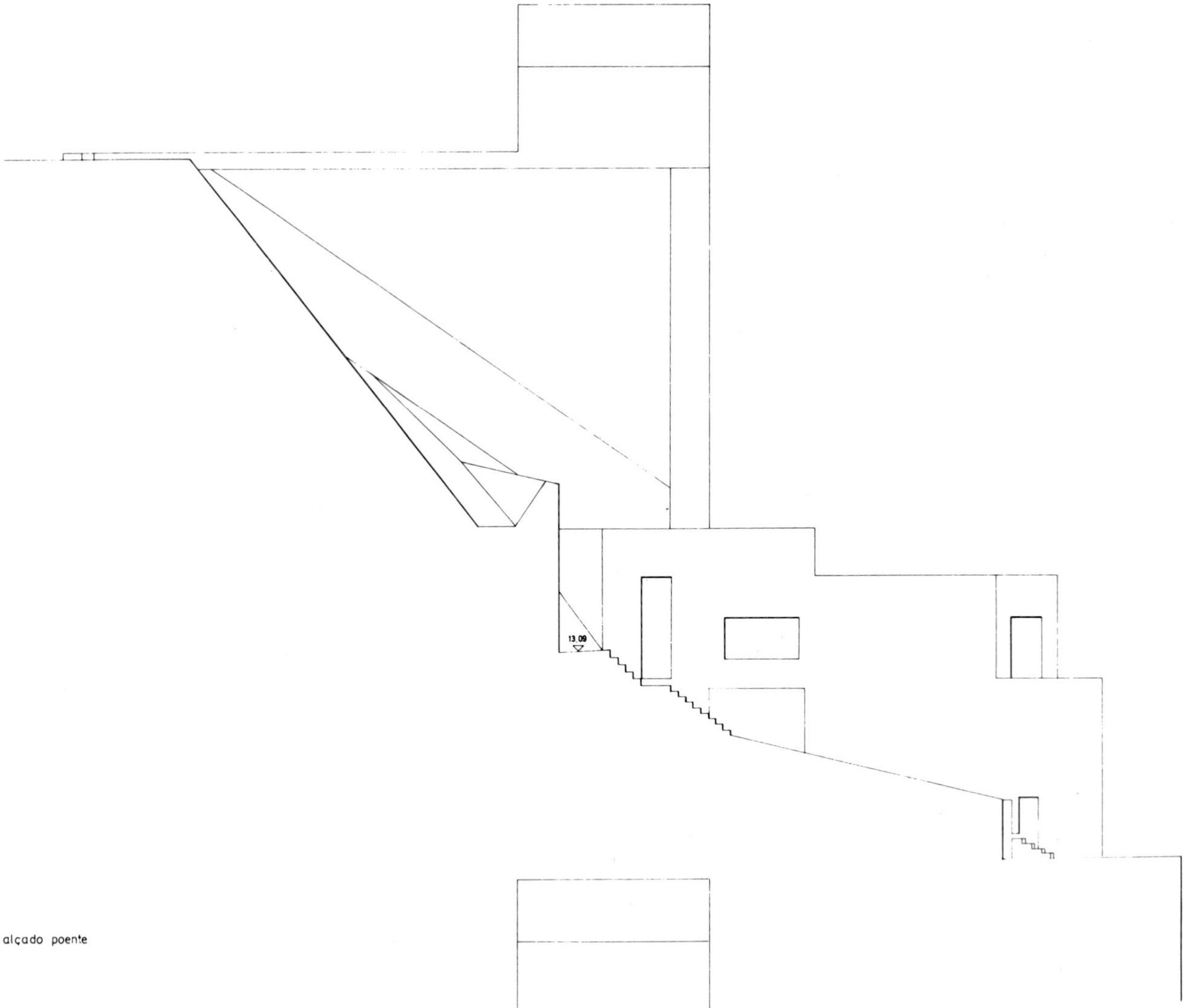

alçado poente

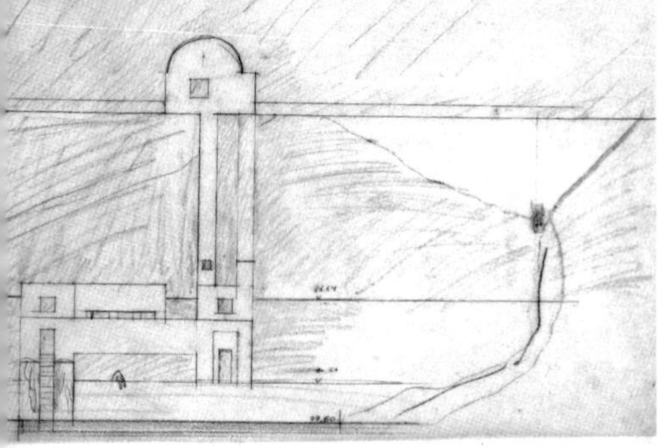

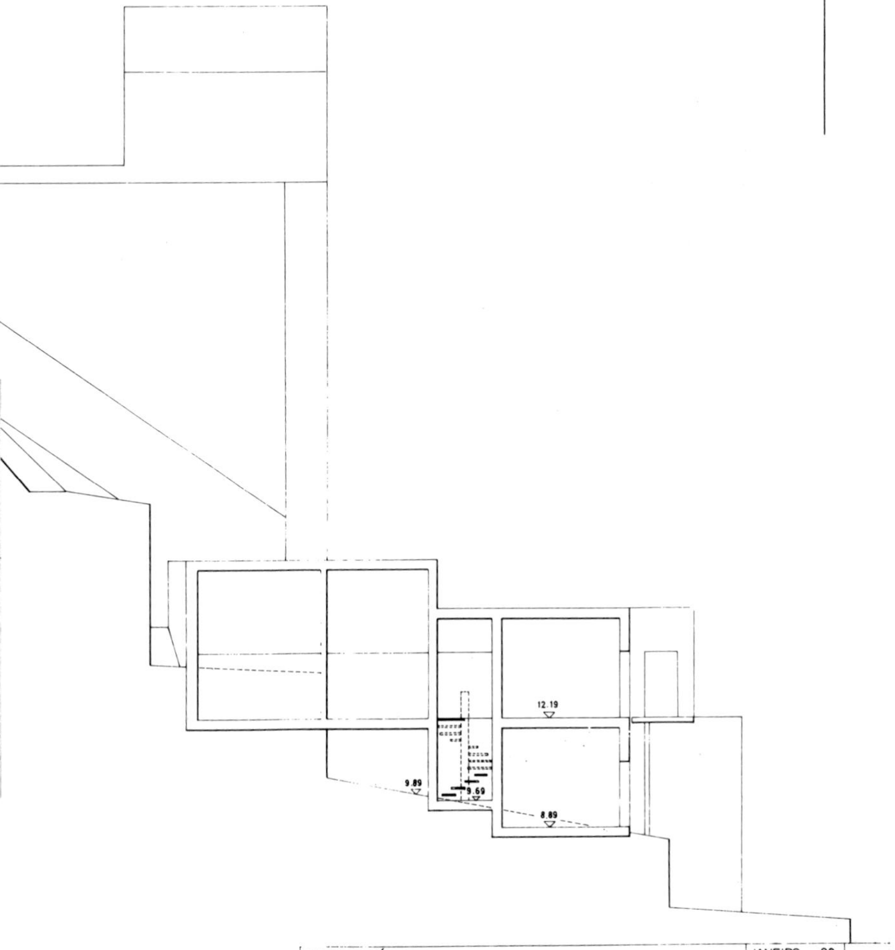

Siza

corte 33

MARIO BAHÍA

Habitação na E.N. 108 em Gondomar

JANEIRO 83

Esc. 1/100 | AP 4

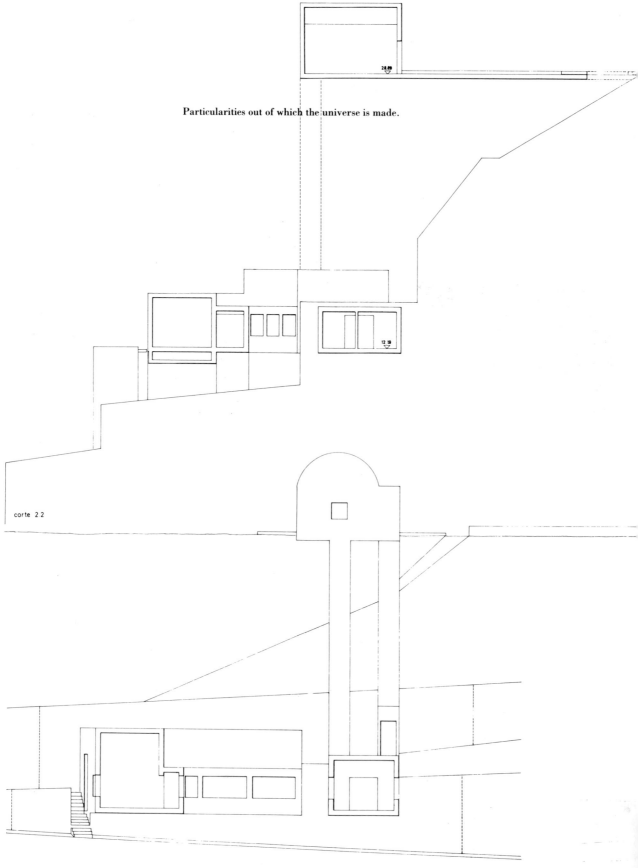

Particularities out of which the universe is made.

corte 2.2

corte 6.6

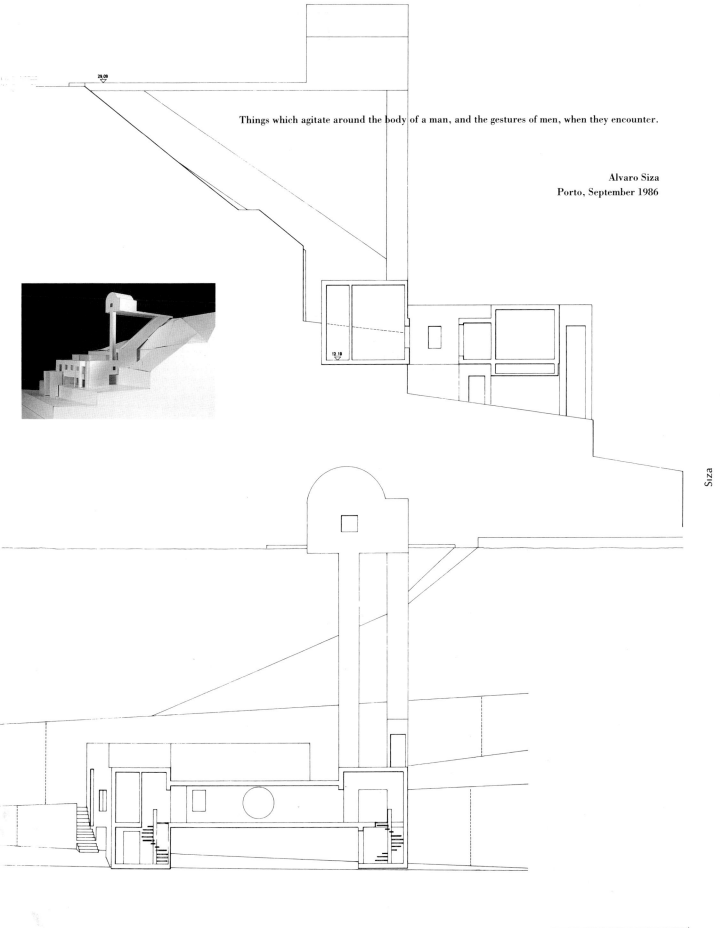

Things which agitate around the body of a man, and the gestures of men, when they encounter.

Alvaro Siza
Porto, September 1986

Siza

**Photo Credits:**

**Introduction**

Aldo van Eyck, Speelplaats, Amsterdam, Holland; from *FORUM voor architectuur*.

Mothers of the Plaza de Mayo, Buenos Aires, Argentina, 1987; photograph by D. Goldberg / SYGMA.

**Table of Contents**

All photographs courtesy of the authors except:

Walter Pichler; from *Walter Pichler SKULPTUREN GEBÄUDE PROJEKTE*, Residenz Verlag, Salzburg und Wien.

Rogelio Salmona; from *Summa*, No. 235, p. 29.

Kunio Kudo; photograph by Erica Lansner.

**Festival at Kakunodate**

all illustrations courtesy of the author except:

Wagon crashing scene; photograph by Chiba.

*1er Mai*

all photographs by the author.

**Architecture and Laughter**

The Body—*Der Holzkern mit Strohurmmantelung*; from *Walter Pichler SKULPTUREN GEBÄUDE PROJEKTE*, Residenz Verlag, Salzburg und Wien.

Simulation—Tsukuba Expo '85; photograph by Marwan Al-Sayed.

Architecture and the Body—Økern Housing for the Elderly; from *Sverre Fehn: The Thought of Construction*, Rizzoli International Publications, Inc.

Still, the Body—Tenayuca; from *Living Architecture:*

*Ancient Mexican*, Grosset & Dunlap, New York.

Finally, The Laughter of the Gods— Foro Romano Roma; from *Sankai Juku*, Sinyasosho Limited.

Affirmation—Kabuki dollmaker's sketches; courtesy of Fred Thompson.

Critical Affirmation as the Discipline of Design—Banco Borges & Irmão III; from *Alvaro Siza Poetic Profession*, Edizioni Electa.

First Series of Affirmations Retracings and Repetitions—Kojima Housing Project; courtesy of Tadao Ando.

Aerial view of Kojima Housing Project; from *Tadao Ando-Building*, *Projects*, *Writings*, Rizzoli International Publications, Inc.

**Letter to a Client**

all illustrations courtesy of the author.

**Reflections upon Latin American Architecture**

all photographs and illustrations courtesy of the author.

**Sensorial Architecture and Contextuality**

all photographs courtesy of the author except:

Barrio Las Colinas, Trujillo Bogotá, Las Torres del Parque, Casa rural-Tabio, Casa de Huéspedes de Colombia, and Castillo San Felipe de Barajas; all from *La Architectura en Columbia*, Universidad National de Columbia-Universidad de Los Andes-Escala.

*Jyo, Kyo, and Iyu: Purity, Insanity, and Playfulness*

Edinburgh, Parque Güell Barcelona, Northern Japan, and T.V.Location for Young European, Venice; all from *Sankai Juku*, Sinyasosho Limited.

Fireworks, Japan; photograph by Susumu Morimura courtesy of Akio Arakawa, Manager, Nikon House, N.Y., N.Y.

Salk Institute; photograph by Rick Gooding.

Wall at Ryoan-ji, Eels and Taxi Driver; photographs by Marwan Al-Sayed.

Japanese calligraphy by Takefuma Aida.

### St. Martin

all photograghs from *Walter Pichler SKULPTUREN GEBÄUDE PROJEKTE*, and *Walter Pichler BILDER*, Residenz Verlag, Salzburg und Wien.

all drawings courtesy of Walter Pichler.

### Adolf Loos: *das andere*

Photographs from *Kunst* or *Das Andere* as noted in captions.

Goldman and Salatsch tailoring studio from Benedeto Gravagnuolo, *Adolf Loos*, Rizzoli International Publications, Inc.

Freud's mirror from *Berggase 19: Sigmund Freud's Home and Offices, Vienna, 1939*, Basic Books, New York.

Moller House and Müller House photographs from *The Architecture of Adolf Loos, Catalogue of an Arts Council Exhibition*, Arts Council of Great Britain.

House of Josephine Baker from *Der Architekt Adolf Loos*.

Diagram by Descartes from A. Ozenfant, *Fundamentals of Modern Art*.

### Four Stories

all photographs courtesy of the author or from; *Sverre Fehn, The Thought of Construction*, Rizzoli International Publications Inc.

### Inside/Out: Adrian Stokes and Corporeal Criticism

Photograph of Adrian Stokes; from *Barbara Hepworth, a memoir by Margaret Gardiner*, The Salamander Press, Edinburgh.

### At The End of the Architectural Promenade: Figures and Notes

See footnotes at end of article.

### Intimations of Tactility; Excerpts from a Fragmentary Polemic

all photographs from *Artforum*

### Sentimental Topography

photographs and illustrations courtesy of Alexandra Papageorgiu and David Smiley.

### Drawings and Work

all photographs and illustrations courtesy of the author except: *Interior Space*; courtesy of Metro Media Corp.

### *Shintai* and Space

Yoshijima brewery, Isutzu house, Tsukuba Expo '86, and Time's Building; photographs by Marwan Al-Sayed.

Bombardment of Osaka by B-29's; from *A Century of Japanese Photography*, Pantheon Books, N. Y. Random House, Inc.

Koshino House; courtesy of the author.

### Porto

all photographs and drawings courtesy of the author.

### Following page

Chambre A Coucher De Mme Loos; from *Adolf Loos*, Les Editions G. Cres, Paris.

363002

Contributions:
Anderson Schwartz Architects, C. Clark
Construction Corp., Herbert Construction,
David and Phyliss Koch, Peggy Koch, Lauren
Kogod, Robert and Arlene Kogod, The
Learning Circle, Inc., Shirley Marble,
Michael and Mary O'Rourke, Dr. Stanley
Preiser and Barbara A. Melnick, Harold and
Victoria Reiss, Morton Smiley, Anonymous